MOSAIC; definition

A picture on a wall or floor, consisting of small, colorful pieces.

A connected composition, whose motif can't be captured at close range
but shows itself from a certain distance only.

Something composed of many fragments.

Realizations about Our Life, Consciousness, and Existence

THE MOSAIC

Markus Obrock

1. Edition: Nov 2020

Author: Markus Obrock
Editing: Gitta Wolf
Cover Design: Zlatko Vickovic
Book Design: Markus Obrock

KDP ISBN: 979-8-5688-7829-2
Independently published

Contents

Our Life

Each day of our life is the expansion of a unique story. Many chapters are exciting and make us eager to continue reading, while stressful, tedious, or sad pages make us want to fast-forward through them. But in the end, what matters is that WE remain the author of our story and hopefully tell it well until the book is closed at night and all the lights go out. Nobody likes endless repetitions, intentions never realized, and questions unsolved. What's the meaning of life? How was the universe created? Does God exist? What happens after death? And is answering these questions truly impossible?

This is a book about life, consciousness, and existence. It aims to fulfill the desire to understand what's happening both within and outside of us. We won't search for explanations in the past but rather question the here and now, with an unending curiosity that Einstein called his only talent.[a] And like Einstein, we'll find something new: Answers that will change us, allow no turning back, and grant wisdom rather than knowledge. Knowledge allows us to name the flowers in the garden. But wisdom lets us pause and enjoy their beauty.

The catch is that our mind follows no consistent, reliable, or independent logic and thus isn't easily guided. *Misconceptions* were not only awarded their own term but also made psychology a necessity and moneymaking more meaningful than the cosmos. Additionally, today's general knowledge doesn't provide a stable foundation of learning as it's merely an intermediate result and may even require unlearning because of newer discoveries.

Knowing this, we must not favor any specific way of viewing life. Materialistic, idealistic, and dualistic voices must all have their opportunity to explain why the world should arise only from matter, only from spirit, or indeed from the interplay of both – and then to explain together, why the same world offers so much scope for speculation. Also,

---

[a] Albert Einstein in a letter to Carl Seelig from 1952.

in the religious domain, the atheistic, theistic, and Far Eastern traditions will be given equal significance, so that we succeed in dealing with their wisdom, contradictions, or gaps of knowledge without generalizing their perspectives.

My intention is to make you more aware of the real world behind all the different worldviews. Yet every success is entirely yours because these words turn into meaningful experiences through your presence only, just like the sunrise.

The big picture – the sunrise, the flowers in a garden, or the truth about existence – will reveal itself to you without the need of attaching to every little detail. Simply pay attention to the inner resonance with a higher, entirely possible truth. The answers are there. You'll soon realize with awe that these answers lie beyond your mind, beyond your usual thought patterns, and accepted logic. Therefore, you will reach your limits: the outermost boundaries of your self-understanding and beyond.

That's not a problem. We are more than just a story told every day. Something allows us, at any time, to embark on paths unknown and unexpected.

1 Human

Human striving. The automatic and conditioned mind. The difference between deciding and choosing. The origin of wishes. The paradox of our worries. The selective perception of the bad. Our desires as guideposts. The highest goal.

We all have specific ideas of how the world is and how it should be. The sun rises in the east – this is now assumed to be known by everyone. And the days are more beautiful when the sun is shining, without dense clouds concealing it – probably everyone can relate to this view.

This is how the things we've learned and no longer think about condense in front of reality and then cover it up, just like clouds concealing the sun, so that our perception is constricted. It's no longer possible to see the horizon, at least for as long as our ideas don't break open. Also, the *unknown* beyond the horizon, which contains all things that belong neither to our knowledge nor our beliefs, remains hidden to us. Our attention is stuck in the current worldview, loses the possibility of wandering freely, and rarely allows us to discover anything new. We increasingly experience this life as narrow, hard, and fast, and eventually notice that something is wrong.

As humankind, at home on a beautiful planet, we are much less happy than the benign situation we start out with, our unique opportunity, and our responsibility would suggest. Even as an individual human being, we often feel no different – which means that here is where it all begins. Our ideas about the world have indeed become limitations that we must put aside now, so that we can see reality.

Striving

The whole world simply exists, but human beings strive for *more*. We are rarely satisfied for long, and even less often are happy, without ever questioning the root cause of this. At all times, we must "make and do" things, and even resting or doing nothing is exhausting, because we first need to deserve it. And so, life spins in a circle of agitation and idleness that hardly anyone can miss, but hardly anyone ever leaves. We are lived, one could say, and are helplessly at life's mercy.

Human striving may be forceful or feeble at times, but mostly it is present. We wouldn't be human without this driving force because being human means to dream and to create. Many great moments arise from our steadfast striving: Times in which we surpass ourselves and discover unimagined abilities. But our dark sides also originate here: Our darkest moments, when we suffer greatly and have become strangers to ourselves. So why aren't we just utilizing the bright side of striving? Why aren't we using its creative power to do the right thing – or to find out what the right thing would be?

The problem is our mind. Unconsciously, it wavers back and forth, first doubting and then regretting every decision. If we decide upon one action (A), our mind will believe a short time later that it has turned against everything else (B to Z) and its alleged advantages. We're basically like a "sick centaur" who is unsure whether to see a doctor or a veterinarian – and therefore dies.[a2]

Your joy of life can die too, if you postpone important decisions for too long. "Left or right?" "Yes or no?" "Heads or tails?" If you'd already know the result, there wouldn't be anything to decide; you could simply make a *choice* then and choose the foreseeably better option. Robbing a bank, for example, would be a bad choice as its negative consequences are foreseeable. But your path of life isn't foreseeable. You can't predict what's going to happen. Only the next seconds, hours, or years will enlighten you and thus never set you back, because "tails" (when the coin lands on "heads") doesn't prove you wrong retrospectively (in the past). In the moment you took the decision, there was no certainty: You had to evaluate the situation, you took a step into the unknown, and so avoided grinding to a halt in your life.

---

[a] Jorge Bucay (Let Me Tell You a Story)

Sometimes, we feel that making decisions is stressful, exhausting, and might even be a cause for later regrets. This feeling explains why we are reluctant to change our life. But our life is only rigid, exhaustive, and regretful because we're not taking the decisions necessary to enable change – because quite often we just choose the easy way, seldom trust new ideas, and feel more afraid of our doubts than of life itself. This is why we must acquire a new awareness that can oversee our emotional states, detect their unconscious contradictions, and then make crystal clear decisions in favor of life.

*

We take on different roles throughout the day and, during each of their performances, pursue slightly different goals; sometimes, we act as individuals, sometimes as companions, parents, career people, students, teachers, or simply as friends. But the striving remains. Impulses reach our perception, influencing us from behind. Unconsciously, we sort our impressions of the world into categories: good and bad, beautiful and ugly, want-to-have and don't-want-to-have – depending on the prefer- ences that life taught us. Judgments arise automatically, which means without conscious thought, and conditionally, which means without objectivity. One plus one. We pronounce the result mentally. Purple. We judge whether we like the color or not. We have an idea and immediately interrupt the other person. Essentially, we don't decide at any point: It's all just happening.

And then, suddenly, you experience a negative feeling. "Something's missing." A wholesome life associates with needs that have to be fulfilled – but that's not it. In a society that no longer lacks food, shelter, and medicine, your striving isn't determined by needs but external stimuli. A spontaneous impulse may override decisions that were thoroughly considered. In an unconscious, automatic, and conditioned way, you suddenly believe "that something's missing" and want this sensation to go away. At this moment, a wish is born.

Human striving originates from unconscious thoughts that first invent a "lack," then set out to "eliminate" it and finally make us addicted to the "solutions." This addiction just goes on unnoticed as all of us have it. And so, we ignore that our wishes at first make us feel discontented, then take a lot of energy from us and, in the long run, don't even grant us happiness.

Worry

Many things in life can go wrong. Everyone knows this vague fear of potential problems. Worries may even cause our forehead to wrinkle. As if our issues could be solved merely by thinking, thoughts are chasing through the mind, turning in circles, growing into a hurricane that pushes itself in front of reality. The deeper meaning of life is concealed and blown out of our emotional world, up until we no longer even expect to feel peaceful. If deep inner peace should ever come to us, it usually arrives unexpectedly, and we already know that the everyday hassle will be returning soon. Thus, our worries come and go with the flow of time because our automatic and conditioned thinking remains unchanged. Any feeling of serenity will soon remind us of its eventual end. And so, our worries exist simply because we expect them to.

Life contains many certainties, but also many uncertainties because no one knows for sure what's going to happen either immediately or tomorrow. It therefore makes sense to organize everything essential and to prepare for particular eventualities. Excessive worries, however, worsen our situation, as an improbable future that may never happen impacts our life in the present.

If we believe that we have control over life, we're living in an illusion. And if we attempt to protect, strengthen, and expand this illusion, our influence on what's genuinely happening becomes increasingly smaller; mired in resistance, our life would become a cycle of anxious complaining, postponed decisions, and missed opportunities. Even humanity itself cannot comprehensively influence the upcoming events. We can, however, gain the competence to face the future confidently by realizing that the safest way to meet the unknown is without self-deception.

Uncertainty is a natural aspect of life; nevertheless, happy people have always existed. And so it's not a lack of certainty that causes unhappiness. Instead, unhappy people have made themselves miserable because the belief of "I lack happiness because I lack certainty" postpones a life that could really begin at any moment: A life in which "I am fortunate, and I lack nothing," except maybe a little practice, focus, and the will to pay more attention to my emotional world rather than waiting for external circumstances to change. And this ability to handle uncertainty with confidence brings an unexpected and intense joy of life and its opportunities.

*

All over the world, beautiful things are happening. However, the daily news is about deceptions, scandals, crimes, disasters, or wars. Based on this, we could argue that worries are fundamentally justified. Yet as anxious people, we have added another problem to the world because we aren't making better decisions. Now, worries, prejudices, and fears occupy our attention, making it increasingly difficult to see the good things in the world. We become a victim of selective perception. We may even feel that "looking at something good for too long" could be condemned as "naively looking away from the truth." And this prohibited perception is like a mental prison.

"VERY many men believe," explains Russian writer Peter D. Ouspensky, "that the fundamental problems of life are absolutely unsolvable, that humanity will never know why it is striving, or for what it is striving, for what it suffers."[a3] But the answers exist. We just have to take a close look and not just simply continue living. We can leave the cycle of striving and worrying – by recognizing our wishes, not instantly

---

[a] P. D. Ouspensky (Tertium Organum)

chasing after their fulfillment, but instead taking a shortcut to our actual goal.

Goal

Every wish has a superficial intention and a profound intention. The superficial intention is to achieve a specific situation: Finishing work early, having the housework done, passing the exams, buying a new car, or having that long-planned picnic in the park. The profound intention, on the other hand, is aimed at emotions and inner states we associate with having reached this situation: Freedom or harmony, for example, often also gratitude, connectedness, or serenity. We know many beautiful emotions! And these feelings are the "highest goal" of our wishes.[a4]

Probably, most of your wishes can come true rather quickly. You want to see the Grand Canyon? Then plan your trip. The feeling you experience when seeing the Grand Canyon isn't captured forever, though. You have to choose this feeling – or other feelings – again on future occasions.

Wishes serve as guideposts in the realm of our emotions. Winning the lottery promises freedom. Experiencing the Grand Canyon promises fascination. Picnicking in the park promises serenity. So the guidepost of a wish tells us: "This way will lead you directly to a feeling of serenity, and the opposite direction leads you to a feeling of potential *promise*." All pathways are open. In the pursuit of happiness, however, we believe that beautiful feelings may only be achieved (if at all) after an arduous journey, while bad emotions can simply be there. So we take *this path*: We choose a feeling of potential promises, even though what we had in mind was a completely different feeling.

Once you stop simply pursuing a wish but pause and reflect on its necessity, you find yourself right in the middle of a junction surrounded by guideposts. In which direction will you turn? Will you pursue the superficial intention or the profound one? The beauty is that your outer

[a] Michael Ray (The Highest Goal)

actions may be the same either way. Once you've identified the highest goal of a wish, all dependence on external situations ends, while your enjoyment of them doesn't. You no longer need a picnic to feel serenity. You no longer need permission for that! And from within this consciousness, you can hugely enjoy your picnic.

"His longings," says Lao Tzu about a striving person, "will never be exhausted. The only thing he ever finds is that he himself is exhausted."[a] Perfect happiness isn't a reward that comes after all of our wishes are fulfilled. It's a quality of simply existing in every moment. This natural state of consciousness can be learned. You must only *unlearn* the state of wantful unhappiness – by meeting real needs consciously, intercepting spontaneous desires, and then, when it feels right to you, reaching out to their highest goal.

✻

Human beings strive for happiness and are often unaware that they can choose emotions deliberately even without striving. All emotions are available, but unconsciously you choose: an emotion *other* than happiness. A few moments later, you choose: again, *another* emotion, but not happiness. And then, maybe right now, you choose: happiness.

Do you see how it is happening – how you choose your emotions consciously or unconsciously? For the most part, it just happens, without intention. But now that you know, you can learn to use this innate ability *consciously*. Roam through the vast parklands of your emotions, which hold infinite feelings. Here you will find everything you can possibly experience! Do you doubt this? Immediately, doubts are present. Are you waiting for proof? Immediately you feel great patience. Are you looking forward to it? You'll find the best shortcut of your life.

---

[a] Lao Tzu (Tao Te Ching, Verse 35)

+ You now know: why we're all striving for more, why we worry, and what our highest goal truly is.

You keep in mind:

A **choice** means choosing one of a number of foreseeable options. A **decision** means taking a path whose outcome is not predictable.

The **highest goal** is always an emotion. The highest goal may be completely different for every wish, while different people may connect entirely different feelings with the same intention. We can identify the highest goal as soon as a wish is born.

Δ *You now can: pay close attention to the beautiful things in life, discover the highest goal within your wishes, and immediately "jump" right into this emotion.*

2 Happiness

The meaning of happiness. The baseline vibration of our emotional world. Objectivity as something subjective. Society as handicap and help. Emotions as a free choice. Happiness through consciousness.

We strive for happiness, which brings to mind *being happy*, a feeling, and *being fortunate*, a circumstance. In our unconscious striving, we often lose sight of this difference and equate one with the other, even though there's no solid connection between "feelings" and "circumstances" whatsoever. If we had good fortune yesterday, there is no guarantee for happiness today – and if we are happy right now, we certainly didn't get there by good fortune alone. We therefore find ourselves faced with a contradiction because, should happiness truly depend on having good fortune, which would have us rely on favorable coincidences only, then what are we still striving for with our own innate powers?

Life consists of changes, which we divide into categories of "good" and "bad." We think of good things as "being just as planned," while bad things "put our plans in danger." Our emotions alternate in quick succession, making us rise high, fall deep, and feel normal in between. This normality differs from person to person. Some people feel content *as a baseline*; other people feel unhappy *as a baseline*. I would describe myself as happy *as a baseline*. In addition, you have a *baseline vibration* to which your emotional world always returns.

"What kind of people live in Athens?" a traveler wanted to know from old man Aesop. "Tell me where you come from," Aesop responded. The traveler told him: "I come from Argos, an awful place, full of liars and scoundrels and unfriendly people." So Aesop replied, "I am sorry to tell you that you will find the people of Athens are just the same."[a6] Our emotions easily prove themselves correct, while other possibilities pass by unnoticed.

Our personal baseline vibration has a tremendous influence on our life. More happiness is only possible by "enhancing" this vibration. We therefore need to take an *honest look* at where our emotional world has settled, followed by the *deliberate intention* to move this emotional world further up and beyond into the positive, no matter what.

What does it mean to take an honest look? If you look at "contentment" with honesty, then this emotional state doesn't feel bad, but neither does it feel great. You may get used to it – especially when considering that things could get worse. When you are being honest, though, *habitually* having "not a great time" is a poor choice as you may *voluntarily* abstain from a highly positive life.

What does it mean to have deliberate intention? You may think that feeling satisfied, dissatisfied, or even unhappy isn't *intentional* – and that it's quite unrealistic to be happy all the time. But this conviction isn't free, unchained, or deliberate; it's full of reasons why there can be no other way. In truth, therefore, you *knowingly* choose (at least from now on in) to take no actions concerning your mediocre baseline vibration and instead prefer to cling to arbitrarily *made-up* ideas.

Society

Community shapes us. We influence each other by living together. Our values, behaviors, and convictions are partially different but also quite similar in many aspects. Within this interaction, we develop a socially accepted worldview, which determines the type of life that is "objectively" deemed most meaningful. Deviations from this best possible existence are commonly condemned – if only by ourselves. Now we have to be rich, beautiful, and productive to experience positive emotions. Without ever questioning: rich in compulsion or excitement?

---

[a] A fable of Aesop.

Beautifully made-up or smiling beautifully? Productive from the perspective of others or from our own point of view?

So, what's happening is not objective but is, in fact, extremely contradictory. We strive to fulfill other people's expectations so that we ourselves can be happy. Subjective ideas define our emotional world. We may even give up particular life paths that *feel right* to us "for the greater good," which explains why the greater good feels impersonal, cumbersome, and wrong once too many people have joined in. As a consequence, apparent objectiveness can't help us in our search for happiness. The thought that "this matter is obvious because it's widely accepted" doesn't serve any logical argumentation, but rather indicates that we're wearing mental blinkers that keep us from seeing higher truths.

Today's society amplifies human striving, which in turn increases the responsibility of the individual not only to avoid being negatively shaped by society but also to shape it positively. In other words, this responsibility means that we must all start with ourselves and abandon our hypocritical, selfish, and contradictory demands on life before we can expect this from anyone else.

On the one hand, we want to be wealthier, more beautiful, and more productive – and on the other hand, we want "to be loved as we are." But how could any community function like this? People would have to love someone who "wants to be different," only to realize that however strong this love is, it apparently is neither accepted nor sufficient to break through our self-made problems.

At a more profound level, though, we don't only love successful, beautiful, and talented people. Last year's gold medal winners are long forgotten. We now value quite different people: people who shape us, accompany, and support us, people we feel at ease with, with whom we can drop any disguise, and experience enrichment. We remember those companions from beautiful or challenging chapters of our life, who helped us *to grow* in whichever way they could. This is real wealth, absolute beauty, and shared creativity, which absolutely deserves our happiness.

On a personal and global level, human striving isn't making our lives better, and *beyond that, it's not even essential for our survival*, because the fundamental human accomplishments – solidarity, passion, education, innovation, or art – exist independently of our trivial desires; they exist, in a manner of speaking, as autonomous *highest goals*. We may thus recognize society's standards as roughly placed guideposts and not as precisely prearranged directions. Being in a partnership may seem beautiful *in our imagination*, but that doesn't make every relationship beautiful. Having a university degree may seem useful *in our imagination*, but it isn't useful for every career. Even if certain situations *in our imagination* are firmly connected with certain feelings, it doesn't mean these feelings will automatically arise. We may end up waiting for happiness until we change our current ideas.

Present

Every sensation takes place in the present, even remembering something in the past or anticipating something in the future. This absolute certainty with all of its implications isn't part of our worldview. Instead, we often believe that the "perfect life" will begin soon: after work, at the weekend, when holiday season comes, after moving to a new house, on retirement, after winning the lottery, or once we've recovered from current health problems. And in this mindset, we'll realize on our deathbed that our real life never actually got off the starting blocks. Of course, life happened all the time, each and every day, yet we weren't really present. We were busy doing other things.

Emotions are like roads branching off a magical intersection, leading into all possible directions. We stand in its center and study its countless guideposts but can choose only one path at a time. We take some steps towards the *hope for a better life*. A little further, we take a turn-off towards the *worries about yesterday's shortcomings*. We may not like this path but mustn't judge its emotional trajectory. We did, after all, choose it, just as we always choose in the present, sometimes deciding on new paths without due care and consideration.

All EMOTIONS are always available – which grants a reliable insight: If we chase after superficial desires, try to escape from imaginary worries, remain unaware of beautiful moments, stay in unpleasant environments, or ignore feeling miserable, we select *negative feelings* from all the available emotions and so won't notice any happiness in our life.

However, it's time to give up this automatic and conditioned choice of feelings. Closely look at your emotions; really look at contentment, impatience, disappointment, exhaustion, or tiredness without wanting to change even one detail, without distracting yourself, so that you *simply* and *directly* experience reality.

The direct experience of an emotion demonstrates the dazzling, remarkable, sometimes painful, yet supreme and boundless diversity of feelings we are capable of. That's the human condition in all its abundance and the end of striving for more. Positive emotions make us happy; choosing negative emotions makes us unhappy. But even then, positive emotions won't just disappear – as their presence doesn't depend on external circumstances, but on *how we deal* with external circumstances.

The most beautiful moment passes unnoticed if nobody is aware of it. Without awareness, everything is nothing. Being aware or unaware changes a situation completely, which becomes clear in an instant – do we eat fast or slow, wait at the red lights impatiently or with composure, or brush our teeth crossly or cheerfully.

Everyone knows what makes them feel happy. For many people, that includes being by the ocean, experiencing its sights and sounds. The ocean and the sound of the waves, however, aren't what makes us happy: They make us more conscious, *and that feels like being happy*. Happiness is being conscious of LIFE. Being conscious is joyful, it fills us with joy. It indicates the clear realization that deliberately perceiving the present reality immediately liberates our emotions, brings us into our highest goal, and, without a doubt, makes us feel happy.

+ You now know: what happiness means, which paths lead there, and which paths will never take us there.

\# You keep in mind:

Our **baseline vibration** is the resting average of our emotional world, which we return to automatically – sooner, later, or after experiencing our highs and lows. This baseline vibration moves higher into the sphere of positive feelings through awareness.

EMOTIONS represent the infinity of feelings into which our consciousness can project itself. Their potential isn't created by humans.

LIFE includes all living beings in the universe, and in addition expresses the fact that there is always life and that, at the very least, a never-ending state remains in which life is able to arise again.

Δ *You now can: understand every feeling as your choice, choose to be happy any time you want, and support other people who want to learn about this.*

3 **Self**

Who am I? Our identification with body and personality. The nature of thoughts. The thinker and the mind. The unexplainable and the unthinkable. The discovery of the ego. Our unavoidable unconsciousness. The many kinds of consciousness. The hard problem of science. Consciousness as a feature of existence.

L earning new things takes time. We can't master something yet unknown right from the start, we first need to overcome initial troubles, and might even give up impatiently. But then comes a *breakthrough*, alongside with wonderment about how something now easy could have ever felt that complicated. And the same applies to the most meaningful question of all: Who am I?

At first, we neither understand what its answer could possibly bring us, nor would we believe that its answer will explain everything, from the meaning of life to the reason for all existence. "Who am I? What is my self?" As long as we haven't resolved or *broken through* this question, its answer isn't trivial or obvious. We could know all about the world – but would miss the most essential.[a7]

So, who are you? A first name and a last name? A human being? A pupil, a student, or a career person? A mother, a father, a senior citizen, a sportswoman, or an artist? Such answers describe external circumstances only, conventions, or self-images, but not the one who is doing the describing. "I'm certainly more than a description because obviously every description is made up by me. I picked it up at some point so that I can now identify with it." Or maybe your thoughts say: "Why should I bother thinking about who I am? I'm a human being, the crown of creation in the universe!" And at times, such excuses might suffice. But eventually, in a quiet or melancholy moment, while

---

[a] Gospel of Thomas (Logion 67)

wandering through an autumn forest, say, or waiting at a train station, or maybe sitting on a park bench, the question will catch up with you: Who am I, really?

Identity

Our body changes throughout our life. Its cells age, renew themselves, and are completely replaced about every seven years. This physical change somehow happens *around us*. We look at photos from our childhood, growing-up years, or last year's holidays, and acknowledge: "That's all me – I've just changed." But we've changed on the outside only, because then as now the same "I" remains throughout the many changes.

Our body. These two words indicate that "our" and "body" involves two issues which can't be confined to a purely physical reality. "I'm not only my body since, in a manner of speaking, I look out at the world from within it." Conditions have to exist in order for this to be possible, of course. We need sensory organs, a nervous system, and a brain – yet we cannot deny our I-perspective. "I exist and I won't be able to be just a body made of muscles, bones, and tissue."

There is more. Random images, thoughts, and feelings flash through our consciousness, often too fast to keep up. One thought says: "Inhale deeply!" and the body carries it out. Another thought says: "Exhale deeply!" and the body carries it out. We can perceive, reflect, and change the present because there are at least two forces at work. Without the body, our self wouldn't have a window to gaze out of, but without the self, no one would inhabit our body.

Time changes not only our body but also our personality. We've never felt as real as today, that's our honest impression because we keep learning with each experience, keep forgetting, too, and therefore not missing anything. While our body renews itself every seven years, the personality within finds itself transformed during a similar period. Our memories, priorities, and behaviors change, but the self-perspective remains. "I am therefore not my personality either, as I am able to look back on its changes to a certain degree."

✻

Thoughts convey an understanding that comes to us as images, feelings, and intuitions that are difficult to comprehend. When we think of a red rose, its picture appears in our mind. Thinking about holiday season reaches us more as an emotion. And terms like "global warming" or "government" trigger quite individual, often unclear images or feelings. We simply comprehend the words without being directly aware of the comprehension process. So our understanding of the world (or specific things within it) can't be called intentional, chosen, structured, reliable, or controllable; it rather arises from random, mood-dependent, and unpredictable "flashes of inspiration."

The attentive observation of thoughts reveals an appalling chaos of arbitrariness that (if written down) would shed doubts on our mental health – as the green polar bear demonstrates, which you'll think of right now until it disappears from your consciousness again in a few seconds' time. You have no choice in the matter. "I am evidently not my thoughts since I can observe their comings and goings, but can only influence this to a certain degree. I could concentrate on purple penguins in order to drive green polar bears out of my mind a bit faster. But still, it would remain unclear why I specifically picked purple penguins and not differently colored animals. Therefore, it's obvious that my self must exist *beyond* thought."

If you're wondering what might exist beyond thought, then that's a thought. As soon as this happens – when one thought reflects another, the illusion of a thinker arises; the impression of an intelligent mind arises, although thought just follows thought and is threaded on your attention like beads on a necklace. It's going to happen again at any moment. Your next thought will arise from infinite possibilities. Maybe it's a thought you've never thought before. Pause right here so that you won't miss it. Close your eyes for a moment. Which thought will it be?[a8]

∗

How long did you have to wait? Did you notice how the present was free from thought for a moment? This thought-free presence is our self. "So, I'm neither the thinker nor my mind because I exist without thought, I don't create thoughts myself, and remain unaware of what I'll be thinking next. I just perceive all of this."

The majority of life happens without thoughts. Reality also works like this – without prior understanding – as it surges against our consciousness, like waves onto the shore, washing up colors, sounds, and emotions *beyond description* plus bringing along a few *describable* thoughts. Our general philosophical knowledge of "I think, therefore I am"[b9] paints a distorted picture. Thinking does not make us to who we are. It's not a proof of existence but one of its potential consequences.[c10] "I am, and therefore, I can observe thoughts" because EXISTENCE and its contents are simply there.

Our perception of the world relies on sensory impressions. From these impressions, we can derive knowledge. We can then *share* this derived knowledge with others in a conversation or a book – while the original perception remains *unshareable*. We might tell our friends: "The sunset was beautiful," but the experience of the sunset remains something fundamentally indescribable, whose transmission exceeds the possibilities of language by far. Therefore, an inexplicable perception is not implausible but an everyday normality.

An infinite number of things exist in the universe. However, a language with an infinite number of words isn't practical. We are forced to summarize our sensory impressions in some tens of thousands of words,

[a] Eckhart Tolle (The Power of Now)
[b] Descartes
[c] Eckhart Tolle (The Power of Now)

establishing colorful plants as "flowers," and generalizing rose-like flowers as "roses" so that we can talk with one another about roses. Thus, the real world is scaled down by our language, by our thoughts, and by our knowledge. That's why all knowledge stays in the realm of the thinkable, which explains our longing for higher answers.

Our SELF is undoubtedly present as it experiences life right now; it exists. It just can't be explained. The unthinkable thus isn't a strange, illogical, or unworldly idea but a fact. "Who am I? Well. I still feel the need to answer this question with an intelligent sentence, although it's reasonably impossible. Any formulated answer would only comfort me until it disappears again. This search for me could make me lose my mind if only I knew who'd lose it."

We have in fact lost ourselves. This unconsciousness weighs heavily on our emotional world, pushing us down into negative feelings. But at the same time, the same unconsciousness hides our loss. We don't even understand that something is missing because we have found a replacement.

Ego

Our ego is the entire human illusion: Who we think we are, and everything that drives our unconscious, automatic, and conditioned mind. Of course, showing some *character* is required to connect with other people (on a small scale) or to work with others to shape a learning culture (on a large scale). There is nothing wrong with the ego in general. We are free to believe whatever we like as long as nobody gets hurt. Our ego, however, can't notice what's happening – and that, as the illusion within which we have lost and forgotten our SELF, it will cause suffering *at the very least* to ourselves. We are unconscious. And in this unconsciousness, genuine connections to other people aren't achievable. Also, genuinely shaping a learning culture is rarely achievable, as we primarily work on shaping ourselves. In the vast freedom of CONSCIOUSNESS, the ego creates a small prison, with far-reaching consequences for the community.

We let our ego react to the events in the world instead of acting ourselves. But our ego is only an imagination that's unable to feel the result of its reactions. We ourselves are feeling the results as emotions. This creates a great separation. We may feel bad, so the ego strives to satisfy its wishes hoping that we might feel better. But this hope is rarely fulfilled because striving doesn't make us more consciously aware.

Being consciously aware means to perceive things as they are, without preconceived concepts, without interpretation by the mind. An attentive view of the present moment would dissolve our current identification with thoughts. But the ego knows how to protect itself; it knows how to hijack thoughts and prevent our mindfulness. That's why we may spend a whole lifetime in our chosen identities, roles, or characters.

"A view of the present is all well and good," says the striving ego, "but it doesn't give me anything in return."

"Things don't get sorted by themselves," explains the planning ego. "I have to prepare stuff for tomorrow."

"Nothing's supposed to go wrong!" emphasizes the anxious ego.

"Although I don't fancy it," mumbles the lazy ego.

"It's the others. What would they think of me?" says the dependent ego. "Do I want to perform poorly or even be forgotten?"

"Of course not," concludes the frightened ego. "Who would want to live out their days unhappily and lonely?" This is how the many facets of the ego wrestle with each other, to then attack other people's egos, so that the stronger one wins, and the weaker ones crash and burn.

Our current general knowledge doesn't contain why we strive, what our real goal is, and that we are unaware, unconscious of reality. Many people accomplish an incredible amount of good with their unconscious striving, and their actions must be highly valued. But unconsciousness also creates suffering. Even good deeds may derive from negative emotions. One negative experience could turn all our faith in something or someone into its opposite. And each brief emotional betterment caused by fulfilling wishes might distract us from the real problem:

An unreal construct of thoughts determines our life in a very real way. In this *constructed life,* the ego feels perfectly normal and indispensable. From a cosmic perspective, however, the human illusion is a demented decision. We should know ourselves! We should know the difference between autopilot and autonomy without any need to study it. And this realization builds up the motivation to finally discard our burdens of the past, to welcome the shadows of the future as sunshine, and to discover the present without excuses.

Without excuses means to treat unconsciousness always the same, even if the motives behind it are good, or it shows good results. Any excuse for not wanting to be consciously aware requires of us an unyielding, yet curious and subtle exploration of: "What do I want in the outside world? What inner feeling does this promise to me? What's the specific thought which denies this feeling to me right now? And what's my most fundamental assumption that enables this thought to stay attached to me with such conviction?"

Your current ego won't survive this way of living, which isn't a problem. You've often started new phases of life, felt at home at previously unfamiliar places, and made friends with former strangers, to discover that there's an entirely unrestricted SELF beyond your self-image that will always find its way in the unknown.[a] "I'm not my ego either." So – what's left? All the previous considerations have been ruled out. Therefore, we'll continue ruling out until we arrive at the one that rules out.

Consciousness

Our perception of reality is vastly subconscious. We breathe, blink, and touch our faces but don't even notice. Also, the clothes on our skin constantly stimulate its sensitivity. The information is retrievable in our subconsciousness but has no priority.

---

[a] Paulo Coelho (Aleph)

By focusing our awareness, we can temporarily bring subliminal sensations into consciousness (just like you're becoming aware of clothes touching your skin right now). Our influence on sensory prioritization is low, though. Most of the time, we can't disrupt the way our body reacts, and we are utterly unable to prevent it reacting. The stove is still hot: Our hand backs off. A fly lands on our forehead: We wave it away. We sit at our weekly club meeting: Our thoughts come and go. As for our dreams, we can't consciously influence them, either. We can't wake ourselves up or stop ourselves from forgetting a dream in the morning. And once negative feelings make us strive for useless stuff, then most of what's happening is practically unchangeable.

The many non-influenceable paths in consciousness illustrate that most things in the universe just happen. Even our unconsciousness just comes and goes, which proves wrong a fundamental assumption of our worldview: Human beings *aren't* self-aware. We *can become* self-aware only occasionally, and for brief periods of time. We carry the ability to push our thoughts into the direction "which they would have in a moment of consciousness," and in this way, "we can induce consciousness"[a12] – which vastly transcends recognizing our body in the mirror. And this fact, that human beings are subordinate to consciousness, makes us less remarkable than we like to believe. But in return, the CONSCIOUSNESS *in* and *around us* gains a substantially greater significance.

A newborn reacts to its environment. A dog recognizes its owner. An ant avoids our finger. A flower opens its blossom to the sun. A stone is worn smooth by water over thousands of years. And atoms join to form molecules. All these events describe a basic awareness of the world, even if this wording sounds unusual, especially when relating to "inanimate" objects. Every interaction, however, requires an inbound influence, a compatible contact, a connected change – whatever we want to call it, which would be impossible without a fundamental perception of reality.

---

a P. D. Ouspensky (The Psychology of Man's Possible Evolution)

Nothing could happen without awareness. The things in our universe wouldn't do what they do. And that's the "hard problem of science."

We search for the source of our consciousness, but we search with our consciousness – or in scientific terms, we search with a perceptual apparatus consisting of countless interactions that are impossible without consciousness. We try to understand how our brain is working, but it's working for whatever reason, and in the precise way that we're trying to understand. We gain groundbreaking insights from our observations without getting any closer to the observer. And this significant presence of CONSCIOUSNESS in us and AWARENESS in the cosmos is scientifically inexplicable.

In our scientific worldview today, the "hard problem of science" receives little attention; if at all, it's considered as a spiritual exaggeration and removed from a scientific context, so remarkably we don't even miss a "resolution of the problem," which undeniably exists within us:

CONSCIOUSNESS is simply here as a fundamental feature of everything existing. EXISTENCE itself is conscious. And this CONSCIOUSNESS is our SELF.

*

Humanity shows that living without self-reflection is possible, for good or bad. Life doesn't need to be questioned but can simply be experienced. Our worldviews may overshadow us like mountains, restrain us from seeing the horizon, and block the sun's rays from reaching into our valley. Science will never take this limitation from us, as its view always reaches outwards into the world, away from our SELF. We get to know the microcosm (the smallest quantum effects) and the macrocosm (the most distant galaxies) but acquire only indirect insights about the CONSCIOUSNESS determining every part of it.

Therefore, kindled by curiosity, we have to venture out on our own to gain realizations about the SELF. Science does at least contribute a starting point for our journey: In reality, nothing at all is as we think it is.

+ You now know: that our identity exists only as a story in consciousness, that an infinite number of things can't be explained but perceived only, and that our self is one of them.

You keep in mind:

Self-awareness (in the sense of self-knowledge) is not a permanent human trait but an ability. We can be aware of ourselves at times.

The **hard problem of science** expresses that it's impossible to find the origin of consciousness through experiments.

EXISTENCE refers to the fact that undeniably *something* exists, that everything (that exists) belongs to it, that virtually everything could exist, and that in no case could there be a state of non-existence.

The **SELF** refers to our true unchangeable I, also referred to as WE – which is experiencing the present right now.

AWARENESS describes all potential nuances of perception, interaction, influence, change, or connection.

CONSCIOUSNESS is the AWARENESS within us, the attentive EXISTENCE behind our human eyes, and our SELF, as WE are nothing but EXISTENCE.

Δ *You now can: see the ego, resolve egoistic conflicts, and get to know the true I.*

4 Reality

The human perception. A filtered reality. Our views of the world before the world. Reality as the observer and the observed. Concepts and their consequences within the wordless. The direct experience of the real world. A higher logic.

D olphins recognize themselves in a mirror, can do math, and assign names to each other. The indications that dolphins are conscious creatures *like us humans* don't, however, satisfy the burden of proof in our eyes. The possibility of another species capable of thinking, learning, and realizing its SELF (maybe even earlier than us) is something we as a society won't consider. We assume that our perception is superior, more accomplished, and the overall benchmark. But this arrogance ultimately arises from an ignorance of how incredibly limited our human perception is.

Perception

Our eyes see less than *a ten-billionth* part of the light spectrum.[a13] Our ears only pick up sounds within specific frequencies. And our nose usually smells nothing. Also, the macrocosm and microcosm remain mostly hidden to us. Most information concerning reality simply passes by our physical senses unnoticed. Even information concerning our body, such as a mosquito bite, too much UV radiation, or the tearing of muscle fibers during weight training, doesn't reach our brain straight away but may only come to our attention later, as itching, sunburn, or sore muscles.

An incredible number of changes is taking place in the entire universe, all of which make our life possible – some more, others less. From this maximum amount of information, about 50 gigabytes per second reach our brain and are transformed into our perception. A passing car doesn't

---

[a] Electromagnetic spectrum = 10pm–10km | Visible light = 430nm–780nm

make any sound but produces sonic waves. The world isn't full of colors but full of light at different wavelengths. And the entire world, shining onto our eyes' retina is upside down. All of this information must be transformed – and is filtered through our entire human form like water through a thousand layers of rock, to eventually unfold its truly unique outcome within us. Once all this information has been processed, about 0.25 kilobytes per second reach our self-reflection as what we think about *right now*. This tells us that the filtering effect is massive. Reality is right here. It's just that our perception barely recognizes it.[a14]

As a consequence, explains Albert Einstein, it would be wrong to establish one's convictions on observational magnitudes alone.[b15] Our sensory impressions are no reliable measure. We observe a scientific experiment, a sunset, or a church service but only experience what we are *given to* experience as human beings, while reality vastly exceeds our available senses. Therefore, even as human beings, we mustn't place ourselves higher than REALITY but instead must examine *its effect* within our CONSCIOUSNESS.

*

Our perception of the world is formed by two sources: body and psyche. The body is our window on reality, which allows some information to pass but filters the rest, while the psyche stands at the window, looks out, and pays more attention to some things than others. As a result, our worldview is shaped by a number of habits – meaning, everything we've written, daubed, or painted onto our window facing reality.

The evolution of life could have produced entirely different perceptions and worldviews without us missing a thing today. Suppose we could see like an eagle, hear ultrasound like a dolphin, pick up smells like a dog, sense electromagnetic radiation like birds, see infrared like snakes, or perceive UV-light like bees, then this same world would appear entirely different to us. If we had no long-term memory, we'd lead an entirely

---

[a] Dr. Joseph Dispenza (What the Bleep Do We Know!?)
[b] Werner Heisenberg (Physics and Beyond)

different life too. And if humankind had learned to choose emotions deliberately, paradise on Earth would already be here.

Every worldview arises in the same EXISTENCE that provides us with body and psyche. So, no matter what we think we know about truth, this knowledge remains a worldview. All our imagination is part of it, as well as our impression that we explore the world as conscious living beings.

We aren't living *in* reality but we ARE reality, without being able to determine its beginning or end. We see our environment, but we're also a part of the environment. Everything is made of the same substance. We stare into our eyes with our eyes – and recognizing this duality grants us a simple but far-reaching realization:

REALITY, *on the one side,* is every phenomenon we perceive with our physical senses and, *on the other side*, is every body whose sensory organs allow this perception. CONSCIOUSNESS observes REALITY *through* REALITY and thus receives a unique perception of the world, depending on the capabilities given.

EXISTENCE is conscious. This CONSCIOUSNESS is always here, directly behind our eyes, underneath all the physical senses. These senses perceive REALITY. What's not perceived isn't REALITY but as yet one of the many possibilities in EXISTENCE and its CONSCIOUSNESS.

Your ego may now question the benefit of this knowledge: "What's the use of knowing that my perception isn't reality? A rose is beautiful just the way I perceive it! Why should I have this taken away from me?" And these words convey the truth. We shouldn't doubt a rose's beauty. The entire truth is greater, though, and beautiful too. In many instances, it's like this: Our ego recognizes a flower in passing, remembers a preset opinion, immediately thinks that "this flower is beautiful!" and doesn't even bother to take a closer look. The flower's beauty has become a set element inside a fixed worldview, as if we'd read a post-it on the window instead of looking *through* the window to see reality.

Unconsciousness can solidify the worldviews in our minds into dense convictions, which then intercept reality and imprison us inside our intellect. We obtain contrasting views of the truth, which may even lead to conflict, although windows with different inscriptions, paintings, or stickers surely imply *different worldviews*. First and foremost, we need awareness of *our worldview* so we may clean it *like a window*, open it from time to time, or even exchange it for a new one.

Thoughts are real. Their contents can, however, remove us from REALITY. If you're expecting friends, for example, but no one's coming, then your thoughts eventually ask: "Am I being let down? What's more important than me? Do I have to put up with that?" You get angry. But then you hear of the accident. Your anger turns to worry and reveals that the story you told yourself was an illusion with a very real effect on your emotional world. You got attached to imaginary thoughts. And this *attachment* removes you from reality, in good times or bad.

Concepts

Money doesn't rule the world – it's concepts that bind us. Coins or bills receive value merely by social agreements, ideas in our minds, concepts that only become valid by mutual acceptance. Two hundred years ago, people in many parts of the world still paid with shells from the beach, cowrie money, because it worked well as a currency. And something else worked just as well: You effortlessly had an image of shells in your mind right now.

Listing all the concepts would take as long as there are words in all the languages of humanity. Each word places another layer of imagination in front of reality, without adding anything to it. There's no left or right in REALITY, which explains why many people have issues discerning them. Also, there are no seasons, just phases in which Earth is aligned differently to the sun. And we all know this moment when we stop mid-sentence, in search of the right word, although its meaning is on the tip of our tongue. The real world isn't made up of concepts; instead, it requires habits, knowledge, and memory hooks to orient oneself in a realm of distinctions.

Concepts change our perception of reality. They paint patterns, connections, and relationships onto EXISTENCE, which otherwise wouldn't exist. Only then, a single sensory impression turns into a thousand causes and effects, so that within this we discover the sun, a beautiful forest, different kinds of trees, the rustling of leaves, and their dancing shadows. Every living being incapable of language and thus without vocabulary, experiences this world entirely differently. Without concepts, there wouldn't be *things*. There would only be CONTRAST. A cat doesn't see, hear, or smell birds, trees, or their shadows but simply experiences REALITY as one sensation without label that is replaced by new sensory impressions with every second and every step.

As human beings, we received the ability to condense sensations of REALITY into words. The sun's shining; we point upwards and formulate "sun." Now, we can think about the sun at night because its word triggers a reaction within the wordless. Language, concepts, and worldviews are intertwined. Each word automatically connects to one of our specific imaginations.

"Abundance" is a concept but triggers a reaction within you. Your ego likes to think of it as enough money to fulfill all wishes. But should you be unaware of this limitation that narrows your idea of "abundance" merely to "money," you will miss significantly wider meanings of abundance, which includes: An abundance of time while you're waiting for money. An abundance of missed chances. An abundance of independence from materialistic needs. An abundance of gratitude that perfect happiness needs no money. Or, from now on: An abundance of training opportunities to assign better or even no ideas to reality.[a16]

---

[a] Bashar (Quest for Truth)

Our perception conveys an incomplete picture of REALITY, that much we know. Nevertheless, we're facing a significant obstacle: Our perception feels absolutely complete to us. Mere knowledge won't change this belief. We'll need to add the curiosity of a child, great powers of imagination, and an increasing awareness to feel the presence of a hidden world at all times. The real world lies behind all concepts. CONSCIOUSNESS isn't setting us any boundary. Our thoughts and habits, even our body and ego could change, while WE wouldn't have any difficulties with adapting to those changes.

There is this moment of perception before thought. You look around your environment purely with your eyes – and *just then,* all sorts of labels flow into it, covering up the purely sensory impressions. Now the colorful spot has become a beautiful rose. The chirping sounds come from the sparrows. The wind blows from the west. Stress feels bad. And I need a coffee. But when you meet the moment before all the labels flow into it, when you perceive the difference between original and distortion, you'll briefly witness the world without a worldview obscuring it. You observe the real phenomena which exist behind all attachments.

Phenomena

EXISTENCE has no labels yet may assign labels to itself. We call ourselves "human beings," for example, although there's much more to us. In reality, we are not human beings but something far beyond what any description might convey. "Left" isn't really left. "In the morning" isn't really in the morning. All these are just concepts existing in CONSCIOUSNESS.

A newspaper can be rolled, folded, or crumpled as it lies on our doorstep, yet no matter its state or condition, it continues to be a newspaper because the same concept gets superimposed on vastly different sensations. The front page might even picture a snake or a wildfire, but we won't scare-jump back or dash off to fetch water, because (again) the same concept gets superimposed on vastly different phenomena. Even if we'd rip the newspaper into a hundred pieces, it would still be a torn newspaper to us. The REALITY changes, but our minds automatically (and unconsciously) push old ideas in front of the new reality to redefine what we see as real and thus *realize*.

∗

Our language has limits and doesn't even contain a word to explain this fact. Its potential is absolutely sufficient though, to prove false statements *as true*, to establish a new way of thinking, and to change our perception in this way.

You can pursue the line of proof for yourself, either in thought or in practice: Two plants are on the living room table, a rose on the left, a phalaenopsis on the right. But then, as you swap both plants around, you *can clearly see*: Some properties move with the plants, but others don't. The rose is still a rose but no longer the plant on the left, and the phalaenopsis, which previously stood on the right, you'd actually describe as an orchid. And so, the entire separation of reality into objects and their properties is dependent on you – and isn't within REALITY, but in the observing SELF only.

If you look closely at the rose now, as it stands next to the orchid, you'll realize what Chandrakirti, a Buddhist philosopher, discovered over a thousand years ago:

The word "rose" describes a specific arrangement of blossom, leaves, thorns, stem, and roots. Without these components, there wouldn't be any rose. Yet, the components don't exist *in addition* to the rose; they merely describe *the same* phenomenon in different detail, which is necessary because the phenomenon has no name by *nature*. Furthermore, you know for a fact that the phenomenon of the rose doesn't become a rose *by your naming it,* as letters or syllables don't change reality but simply put a concept on top of it. As a result, you uncover that a rose isn't *really* a rose but exists *as such* only as imagination in your mind.[a17]

---

[a] Chandrakirti (Introduction to the Middle Way)

"A rose is not really a rose." This realization grants us access to a higher logic. What seems like a contradiction in human logic, reveals itself as a greater truth. And this truth isn't a play on words but a new perception without mental blindfolds. The point is this: The reality *behind* a rose (the phenomenon) and the idea of a rose (the concept) are two entirely different things. A rose is beautiful, of course. But if you look attentively and directly at the phenomenon *behind* the rose – as through the eyes of children who haven't yet learned any names – and then realize it's not a rose at all, right then you're seeing the rose "in its fullest flowering."[a18]

A short-sighted person might perceive a rose at the back of the garden as some blurry spot of color. A person with healthy eyesight or glasses will recognize the flower in its familiar form. And a falcon will see it even better! But REALITY isn't blurry or different. Only our individual perceptions differ, so two principles always apply: Our physical perception can't be influenced because our eyes (and all the other senses) belong to REALITY. But our mental perception can be influenced because it's created by OURSELVES in our CONSCIOUSNESS. And as soon as we understand this physically unique perspective and this spiritually all-encompassing freedom, we flow into an extraordinary love for everything perceived.[b19]

✳

In a scientific, religious, or even spiritual context, doubts are often portrayed as something negative because doubts suggest a lack of understanding. Faithlessness may even be the cause of conflict. Yet, anyone who realizes that personal convictions, sanctums, and worldviews do not truly exist but are simply made-up and accepted, attains a sovereign state of *disbelief* in any knowledge – and so gains the utmost spiritual, religious, or scientific maturity. The truth above all truths – the ultimate truth – can't be expressed by words.

---

[a] Diamond Sutra
[b] Gangaji (You Are That)

This explains why "Who am I?" can't be answered by phrases. Any answer would be something conceptual. Therefore, the best description for our self is: "I AM, but not that! Am I someone who questions the world? No, not that. Am I someone who already understands a lot? No, not that." We observe the world and hold on to some of our discoveries for a little longer – it could be a shell, a spontaneous idea, or an entire worldview. Letting go of these discoveries doesn't mean that we don't appreciate their value any longer; it suggests instead that we are sharpening a thinking instrument that EXISTENCE uses for getting to know itself.

+ You now know: that our perception isn't reality, but that worldviews influence our lives for real.

You keep in mind:

Concepts are ideas in our minds that we put in place in front of reality. **Phenomena** refer to the substantial reality behind our concepts; meaning *that* which actually exists, even though we will never be able to perceive it in its entirety.

An **attachment** describes a thought stuck in our CONSCIOUSNESS, which unconsciously "hijacks" our emotional world. Attachments are all those things that make the human illusion feel real and provide arguments for its realness. It's like always holding a "mental photograph of the world" in front of the real world.

REALITY is that which (on the one side) constitutes all physically observed phenomena, as well as that which (on the other side) gives all living beings their physical form and sensory organs.

Duality embraces the two seemingly opposite *sides* of REALITY in a combined and correlating nature.

CONTRAST describes a perception without concepts – before any concepts are superimposed on our sensory impressions. EXISTENCE continually produces CONTRAST, like a revolving kaleidoscope, with the difference that we don't immediately discover familiar forms, things, or stories in a kaleidoscope.

Δ *You now can: experience reality directly, practice a higher logic, and leave every worldview behind (little by little).*

5 Matter

The atomic model. The search for the prime particle. Our invention of worldviews. The discovery of reality without deeply ingrained habits. A world full of emptiness. A first contact with quantum theory. Reality as mystery. The emptiness within matter. The vibrating cosmos.

O ur interest in existence inevitably leads to its substance: matter. We may well hope that this confirms our material worldview. But scientific findings reveal that nothing in our worldview – and nothing recognized by our senses – is in fact solid.

Atoms

The pages in a book appear to be smooth. A microscopic magnification, though, unveils a rough landscape, defined by fibers and hollow spaces. A special electron microscope shows that these fibers are themselves composed of molecules, whose connections determine the paper's properties when turning, tearing, or burning it. These molecules in turn consist of atoms, which quantum microscopy can only just vaguely detect. Direct observation is no longer possible at this depth of matter. Physical experiments merely observe reactions or indirect properties of matter (by using particle accelerators, for example). And the findings disclose even deeper levels of matter.

The "Periodic Table of the Elements" describes over a hundred different atoms that contain their individual constellation of protons, neutrons, and electrons. These subatomic particles again are formed by even smaller elementary particles, such as quarks, leptons, and bosons. The search for the smallest particle of matter still continues. And right now, we shall look at this "search" and its inherent problem.

Molecules, atoms, or electrons don't exist as such. A rose can be seen, but we can't *additionally* discover matter in it. A falling apple can be seen, but we can't *instead* observe something else. The individual particles of matter are just different conceptions of the same REALITY depending on how closely we look at REALITY.[a20] Therefore, the atomic model doesn't unveil anything real; it's merely the abstract result of centuries of efforts to forge many scientific observations into one coherent theory.[b21] To be clear, molecules, atoms, and all the other particles of matter were never discovered or found. They were defined and invented to explain the world. For this reason, matter always recedes from our view – because we can never see it *separately* from REALITY.

Classical physics suggests that there is an indivisible *prime particle* hidden somewhere within the depths of matter, which in its multitude forms our world like bricks form a wall. But does the universe necessarily consist of many prime particles? Or could it also emerge from *a single* prime particle that twists and rearranges itself like an infinite thread, shaping itself into our forms like a ball of wool? In any case, a headline of "Prime Particle Found!" wouldn't explain much. We'd still not know why the same material may behave like a book, a rose, or a human being. The origin and the intelligence of reality to form, manifest, and take shape would remain unexplained – although we already know about precisely this origin.

The search for a prime particle is based on three underlying assumptions: "The real world consists of an accumulation of matter. This matter exists independently of an observer. And its formation sometimes produces consciousness, as shown by human evolution." But these three assumptions are wrong, as we have deduced already beyond a doubt; instead, everything starts with EXISTENCE being ITSELF conscious. Its processes of consciousness allow for the creation, observation, and interpretation of REALITY. We'll never reach "an end of perception." And for these reasons, the search for the prime particle can be concluded today.

---

[a] P. D. Ouspensky (Tertium Organum)
[b] Francois Jacob (Imagination in Art and Science)

Although a prime particle may never be found, the study of matter doesn't become pointless, especially with regards to its technological applications. Future technologies will certainly change our life – but won't explain it.

*

It is generally accepted in society that science and religion are in some kind of competition, which will be won by whomever first proves the other wrong. But is the search for a prime particle still science – or rather the result of a strong belief? Would a clear definition of God be merely religious intention – or a highly scientific and analytical project? There is no clear demarcation. No matter which side speaks to us the most, we need to examine our point of view without bias. Science can't prove the universal laws of nature. And religion can't prove the divine laws of nature. Science and religion thus aren't contradicting one another but contain truths and contradictions within themselves. Within every discipline, experts hold opposing opinions. So, to rendezvous with REALITY, we mustn't withdraw into our deeply ingrained habits – and shouldn't just listen to "common sense" either.

Common sense contains and consists of convictions, which often obscure reality. As a consequence, we're capable of believing (first) that the outside world is more objective than our inner life, (second) that the outside world needs to change to make our inner life happier, and (third) that our inner life most certainly isn't mistaken regarding its outside worldview. These mental traffic circles demonstrate why some realizations never settle in, why we keep believing that winning the lottery will make us happy, or that atoms exist and *can even be felt* by knocking on a table – although we've never knocked on atoms, molecules, or a table but only on a spot existing in REALITY, which we then gave a name to.

Reality dissolves the closer we get to it. The pages of a book are mostly hollow; that's how the ink is able to seep into the paper and bond with it.

Likewise, all molecules and atoms primarily contain emptiness. The atom's nucleus consisting of protons and neutrons, *when scaled to human proportions,* is orbited by electrons at a distance of forty-four miles with nothing in between – just empty nothingness. From the viewpoint of a quark, *when scaled to the size of a human being,* these proportions increase. Now the outer bounds of the atomic nucleus lie about three miles away, which scales up the distance from quark to electron shell to over one hundred thousand miles of nothingness.[a22] A high-speed train would take around thirty days to traverse this distance. But as science already explains, even quarks won't turn out to be solid; they consist of preons, which in turn are *formed* by the minutest "strings" whose vibrations deep within the fabric of matter bring our perceptible world into being.

So how can our world appear solid and real? Why do we recognize objects when EVERYTHING consists of practically NOTHING? And why can the emptiness within our bodies hurt so bad when we bump our heads? The answers may still seem distant. But our questions are like a mirror in which EXISTENCE, eager to get to know itself better, is doing just that.

Quantum

Quantum theory is long confirmed, absolutely fascinating, and mostly unknown. Its insights give new meaning to old views and refurbish the classical worldview completely. Erwin Schrödinger coined the descriptive basis of quantum theory. His thought experiment requires a cat, a box, and some poison that may be activated at any time with a probability of 50%. He then asks: "If the cat is locked in the box with the poison, is it dead or alive after one hour?" Intuitively, we'd answer that the cat is either dead or alive, having in mind two different conditions. But this statement would be inaccurate. In fact, to us, the cat exists as *one* state of all possibilities and probabilities (for example, dead, alive, currently dying, immune, or escaped). Only when the box is opened,

---

[a] Proportions inside a hydrogen atom relativly scaled up to a 6ft. (1.80m) tall human being.

these infinite possibilities fall into one reality – which quantum physics has proven right concerning all things in the universe.

In the double-slit experiment, quantum particles (such as laser light) are shot through two slits onto a screen. The light's wavelengths pass through the two slits, overlap each other, and show a pattern of interference: brighter and darker stripes. If one slit gets covered, the pattern disappears. But not only then. The pattern also disappears if a measuring device counts how many photons take the left slit (or the right one). The explanation sounds unbelievable. If we find out that a photon passes through the left slit, reality has established itself. Now *the same* photon can't cross through the right slit, which it would generally do *as well.* As long as no one is looking too closely, the photons move through both slits simultaneously to superimpose onto themselves and so create a wave pattern.

The quantum world reveals facets of EXISTENCE that contradict our way of imagining the world. Our common sense is strongly put to the test. Any mistrust whether the "unexpected" explanations of quantum science are even "credible" would ignore the fact that, basically, we can't explain anything. Our current worldview has never been proven and so answers only few of the questions we have about life. We might more appropriately mistrust our intention: Do we even want to understand the world? Because this motivation inevitably brings to light previously unexpected insights and brings to mind one expectable certainty: If the laws of nature adhered to our imaginations, the universe would contain no life.

We think that light is reflected (or deflected) by objects or mirrors. But photons are not diverted. When light hits a mirror, it gets absorbed by its atoms, causes an excess of energy within, and triggers the emission of completely new photons. For this reason, the speed of light seems to slow down inside water, glass, or air. Photons move at the speed of light in a vacuum. But in a medium, including Earth's atmosphere, light and matter frequently collide (relative to the matter's density), so that light doesn't move slower but is absorbed back and forth more often. A photon created by nuclear fusion deep within the sun may remain in its core for ten-thousand years without making it to its surface. On Earth, too, we can observe the effects of light-matter-collisions with the naked eye: Light is not absorbed at the same rate in warm and cold air, which makes the air appear to flicker in the distance above hot road surfaces.

Our current experience of the world is a mystery that increases the more we learn about it. Richard Feynman, an American physicist and Nobel Prize winner, discovered that light doesn't travel in straight lines at all but instead travels on so-called probability paths; it may take chaotic and long detours without us, the recipients, noticing anything – just like postcards don't change depending on their delivery route.[a23] Our image in the mirror is thus created by photons leaving our face, getting absorbed by the mirror's matter, triggering the emission of new photons, which then travel back on any number of possible paths into our eyes, and still, every day, cause a remarkably similar perception in our brains.

*

Space and time have no meaning in the quantum world. Effects precede their causes, information travels faster than the speed of light, and things can be in two places at once. CONSCIOUSNESS, on the other hand, receives new meaning. The experiments show that the observer shapes REALITY: As long as no one is looking, all possibilities and probabilities exist simultaneously. But as soon as someone is looking, EXISTENCE falls into a distinct position.[b24] "In the beginning was the Word," says Jesus. "All things were made by this word [this vibration]."[c25]

Vibration

Matter itself is mostly empty, and yet, reality pulses with life. Asteroids orbit around Saturn, humans around their homes, and electrons around their atomic nucleus – to form almost impenetrable structures that repel

---

[a] Richard Feynman (QED – The Strange Theory of Light and Matter)
[b] Volker J. Becker
[c] John 1:1-3 (KJV)

anything approaching. Everything within matter is in motion, without ever stopping or touching each other. In this way, the matter of a stone, a rose, or our hands is reassembled several times per second without our eyes noticing it.[a26] We are never directly sitting on a chair or knocking on a table but are always kept at a distance by elemental forces.

One thing needs to be very clear: It's not matter that vibrates. It's not elemental forces that cause vibrations. The vibration itself creates those phenomena that we call matter, a rose, or a falling apple. The entire observable world, explains a German physicist and co-founder of quantum physics, Max Planck, originates and exists only by virtue of a force which brings reality to vibration.[b27] Without this VIBRATION, there wouldn't be any light, sound, matter, no solar systems, or even change itself. We wouldn't exist.

*

Any interaction, influence, or change requires CONSCIOUSNESS, but any *conscious perception* also requires an interaction, influence, or change.[c28] We see the stars shimmering in the night sky, but only because new light-waves are continuously streaming in. Our ears hear music as long as the instruments' soundwaves continue to stream in. But even when a star suddenly fades or an instrument becomes silent, more and more information streams in, allowing us to notice the absence of sensory impressions. CONSCIOUSNESS implies a constantly flowing CHANGE; the one isn't possible without the other, both are inseparable even from each other, and thus both are one.

The statements of science strengthen a realization of great significance: The matter that makes up a stone and the matter that makes up our fingertips aren't different. This is why we must treat everything in

---

[a] P. D. Ouspensky (In Search of the Miraculous)
[b] Max Planck
[c] Annie Wood Besant (An Introduction to Yoga)

EXISTENCE equally and – because we ourselves are alive – recognize LIFE and CONSCIOUSNESS in EVERYTHING.[a][29]

---

[a] P. D. Ouspensky (Tertium Organum)

+ You now know: that the cosmos ultimately consists of vibrations in consciousness, that reality is changed by its observation, and that the current state of scientific knowledge isn't yet part of society's worldview.

You keep in mind:

VIBRATION describes the fact that CONSCIOUSNESS and CHANGE are inseparable.

EVERYTHING contains every nameable fact in the cosmos; it's like an imagination that's continuously filling itself. **NOTHING** excludes every nameable fact; it's like an imagination that eternally empties itself.

Δ *You now can: let go of the classical scientific worldview, marvel at the mystery of your life, and change reality by gaining new perspectives.*

6 Time

Our invention of time. The beginninglessness of existence. The timelessness behind infinite time. Change as the foundation of existence. The present as the moment of every experience. The current creation.

We can feel the passing of time but can't explain its origin with any certainty. Our assumptions revolve around time as the fourth dimension, a universal quality, or a divine act. But time isn't a property of the universe, explains Albert Einstein. It's a human agreement. We just *say* that sunset is at seven if "the clock's hands point to seven" and the "sun touches the horizon" concurrently.[a30]

Our agreement of time doesn't apply to reality. When the sun sets at seven, it still shines further in the west. It's only six o'clock in the next time zone. And from the sun's point of view, day or night doesn't exist; Earth just rotates in the sunlight while all the clocks simply follow their mechanisms. Should we consider time as something real, though, then we have a "blind spot" within our worldview, which makes us miss out on reality.

Our sense of time is, in fact, the result of CHANGE that has no origin. And this realization has a massive effect on our worldview.

Origin

The scientific worldview explains the origin of the universe with a Big Bang. Religious worldviews refer to an almighty creator. So they both agree on a sudden point of creation. But every beginning needs a *before*, every identified effect has an identifiable cause, and every vibration depends on a change, all of which allows us to endlessly pose the question of origin: Who created God? What triggered the Big Bang? How could any event occur without time? Each answer can be questioned,

---

[a] Albert Einstein

again and again, thus invalidating every explanation before even attempting it.

A creation out of nothing can be excluded as well because "creating a universe" vastly exceeds the possibilities of nothing. If indeed NOTHING exists, nothing can start to exist. Since at least our present experience of the world exists, though, we can know that NOTHING never existed. EXISTENCE reaches back endlessly, longer than our mind may comprehend – because its concepts reduce each infinity into finite misconceptions only.

An infinite thing is not "a lot of one thing." An infinite road wouldn't be a "very long road" but it couldn't exist at all, for all sorts of theoretical and practical reasons. An infinite amount of money wouldn't be "a great deal of money" but in fact would lose any value; after such an inflation, it would be "worth no money at all." A permanently (thus infinitely) blind person doesn't permanently see *black*; he simply doesn't see at all, because our senses are unable to recognize an uninterrupted absence or presence of a sensation.[a31] For this reason, the unfamiliar and all-present (and thereby infinite) smell of a friend's apartment seems to disappear after a few minutes. The smell is still there, of course. But when our senses no longer notice change, we no longer perceive reality.

Infinite time likewise isn't a "very long time" but loses every temporal meaning, since an uninterrupted presence needs a *timeless place*. Water flows through a riverbed, the riverbed, however, isn't made of water but of stone, otherwise it would *itself* be washed away. A beginningless EXISTENCE thus can't depend on time. It can exist in a timeless space only.

The conclusion from these realizations is far too obvious to be readily accepted: EXISTENCE never came into being. The present universe, Earth, or human life came into being, but endless CHANGE exists since forever. Any estimated age of the universe, even an infinitely old past, would be a brief imagination only, arising in this present timelessness.

---

[a] Gevin Giorbran (Everything Forever)

The riverbed of time is CONSCIOUSNESS ITSELF: All impressions flow through there, which is why its presence stays hidden from our physical senses and oftentimes our mental senses as well.

Change

The human need for time, future, and past is deeply rooted. Our ego will cling to it and argue against the universe's timelessness: "The world is changing! Things aren't standing still! Therefore time passes!" But time isn't the cause of change, quite to the contrary; current time-independent CHANGE allows us to look up into the sky, invent twenty-four hours, and create a clocked worldview.

Even CONSCIOUSNESS gets time-stamped in our worldview. We learn that "physical sensations reach our awareness with a delay." If we step on a nail, for instance, the pain isn't immediately there: First, nerve cells need to react, send electrical impulses through the body and reach our brain to finally make us feel pain.

Anyone who believes in this kind of a delayed perception of the world falls victim to a great dilemma. Life would no longer happen in the present. All actions would appear to be lagging behind the present moment, based on events already past, and thus mechanically predestined. But such a fear, incapacitation, or resignation originates from a misconception which regards *the present* as the moment of physical contact.

WE are not our body. The PRESENT doesn't begin at the outer contours of our shapes but is always the moment in which WE OURSELVES become conscious of something. Looking from this inner perspective, the events taking place in the body belong to the outer world. Of course, our body's cells react to changes, too, because all things are conscious and accomplishing their tasks, but still: Our CONSCIOUSNESS can't leave its PRESENT. Every experience happens now, no matter how convincing other explanations involving past causes, future effects, and delayed chain reactions may sound.

A person without pain sensation would possibly not notice a nail in his foot until minutes later. Does that delay his life? A dwarf and a giant cry out in short succession. Did both of them step on a nail at the same time or with a time delay? You see, the PRESENT can't be divided into sequences of consciousness without creating relative, absurd, or contradictory interpretations of reality.

Our I and the PRESENT are inseparably connected. This moment right now is the same Now as earlier. And later will be the same Now as now, because equally our I will remain the same. And since we already know, without having as yet embraced it fully, that our universe can't have a beginning, we might as well surmise that the present moment has no beginning. Where does it originate? We are simply here. In other words: Nothing is preceding the PRESENT. All solar systems, planets, and living beings exist here in order to keep changing for all eternity.

Right now, it's happening again: On the quantum level, matter falls into position, new life emerges in nature, and our minds fill with new ideas, which sometimes seem old or repetitive – but undoubtedly belonging to the PRESENT. As a consequence, we can't relocate this world's creation into the past, as reality is created right now. CREATION isn't over but takes place all around us in this moment. The concept of time, too, arises in the mind. We must therefore learn to see through our *creation of time* so that, instead of the passing of seconds, we can experience the stillness of eternity.

$*$

Being human isn't our nature. "Existence precedes essence," explains Sartre.[a][32] We have to first *be* to then take on humanness. Our life originates not from cosmic coincidence but unconscious creativity. A timeless worldview (without past, future, and lack of time) isn't illogical in the least but merely unfamiliar. In the quantum world, time has

---

[a] Jean-Paul Sartre

already lost its meaning, as science explains – so that its withdrawal *from our worldview* announces a more accomplished perspective. We may live independent of the sensation of time. And once this occurs, something remarkable happens to us: We become more attentive, conscious, and happier while human striving, worrying, and suffering comes to an end.

+ You now know: that time is a concept in beginningless change, that your experience of the world isn't subject to any delay, and that EVERYTHING happens in the PRESENT.

You keep in mind:

The **PRESENT,** the **NOW,** is the only moment in EXISTENCE.

CHANGE describes the timeless nature of EXISTENCE and the eternally changing REALITY.

CREATION signifies that REALITY didn't come into being in the past but comes into being right now through VIBRATIONS in CONSCIOUSNESS.

Δ *You now can: discover the timelessness behind time, actively participate in creation, and shape eternal existence.*

7 Suffering

The conditioning of being. Human suffering. The two types of wrong. The human condition as a sleep. Thinking in probabilities. The Fail-Safe of Existence. Unconsciousness as a catalyst for awareness. Our development into an individual.

When humans, our great ancestors, gained awareness over body and mind, realized "I am" for the first time, and began to act with intention, it marked a milestone in evolution. But an equally astonishing shift has unfolded since within humans. We learned to divide the "I am" into qualities. "It's not only that I am. I should also be more awake, happier, or better somehow." Our *being* has been conditioned and no longer suffices by itself. Automatic thoughts limit us to a small part of our existence, focus our attention on just a few fragments of life, and attach us to ideas far off the present moment. And this unconsciousness is like a sleep, like a dream, in which many things happen, but few events are actively shaped.

Sleep

We realize this sleep by our inner contradictions: We long for harmony but like to complain. We look forward to the weekend but not the week's beginning. We feel low motivation for work but even less for being unemployed. We'd rather skip studying but don't want to be taken for fools. We yearn for being accepted "as we are" but pretend to be different for the outside world. We long to go to the gym when ill – and would rather be at home, relaxing, when at the gym. We want to be immersed in nature but drench ourselves in perfumes. We feel exhausted but don't want to sleep. We hope for better times but regret not having used our time better. And under no circumstances do we intend to disappoint other people, even if it requires giving up our own excitement. These inner contradictions carry with them the experience of suffering.

Humanity suffers. With a bit of luck, we feel quite content. But with sufficient tenacity and assistance, we can succeed in becoming deeply unhappy. Our suffering has become blind habit. We wouldn't actually say that *normal negative* emotions make us suffer, just as long as we are spared great misfortune. We would, however, state that physical pain makes us suffer and thus combine two different matters. An athlete feels the pain of his sore hamstring but *suffers* from training interruption, which feels worse than the pain because now his ego goes crazy, gets angry about the setback, and may no longer fulfill his unconscious desires. Therefore, our human suffering isn't caused by rare outer circumstances but represents our daily inner distance to happiness.

*

All humans are allowed to have whatever emotions they prefer. We must understand, however, that this freedom comes with great responsibility because emotions are the foundation of our next action. Lalla, a Hindu poet of the 14th century, reports: "For a moment, I saw a beautiful moving river. Then a vast water with no means of crossing it."[a][33] We look upon our lives quite similarly and frequently feel: "Life isn't easy. I'm its victim. And time, fate, or other people are the wrongdoers!" which then influences our next actions.

Yes – it's true that unfriendliness, deception, and crime are part of our world, but behind this lies the great unconsciousness about the two types of wrong. It all begins with the *imagined wrong* arising as a story in our minds: a story that's revealed by our innocuous complaining, our know-it-all attitude, or our everyday moodiness, which makes us feel that we have every right to be disappointed, jealous, or angry. And all these feelings end up in the *inflicted wrong,* in mistrustful acts we indeed inflict upon other people as a reaction to our imaginations – which then circle the globe like dominoes falling in a chain reaction.

---

[a] Lalla (Naked Song)

A teacher suffers under his students' lack of discipline. Eventually, even happy laughter bothers him. The students suffer under a draconian learning atmosphere, penalties, and nebulous ideas of discipline. Now it's challenging to create a meaningful learning environment, although both sides very much want this.

Parents worry about the future of their children and their choice of careers. Children worry about a future that appears to cause great concern to their parents. Now it's challenging to follow one's dreams, strengths, and also intuitions towards a true calling, although both sides very much want this.

An ambitious department manager strives for success. Everything must be done precisely according to his specifications. The employees are no longer allowed to pursue their creativity, and so get bored, or hope for a new manager. Now it's challenging to accomplish outstanding work, although both sides very much want this.

The two types of wrong are both cause and effect at the same time. Almost every word could be considered offensive. Every wrong inflicted upon us originated somewhere completely different. Stealing is an injustice, for example, but we can't deny that people who steal because of hunger are victims of an even greater injustice. A retrospective distinction is no longer possible in the advanced predicament we find ourselves in today. Nobody can distinguish cause and effect anymore or retrospectively relate a war to a bad dream. However, those who just assume the worst in humanity but don't realize the unconsciousness behind it, choose the unconsciousness in humanity and then spread the badness, inflict further wrongs, and miss the goodness within themselves.

∗

Our way of life could be entirely different. Just one volcanic eruption, one additional war a thousand years ago, or one scientific invention more or less, and our current worldviews would be vastly different, at least in part. But while this possibility is easy to understand, it remains hard to imagine. We can't easily comprehend that one particular moment is more beautiful than diamonds, that extraterrestrial life certainly exists, or how our life would be without mirrors – just like another humanity or extraterrestrial civilization couldn't imagine our way of living.

We can think in probabilities, though. If a car tailgating us on a winding country road is far too close, and (exceeding the speed limit) wants to pass – *how likely is it* that we accelerate? The probability is low. Now, we have to think for two drivers (ourselves in our car and the driver of the car behind us) and will probably even slow down due to the distraction. That's why being in a rush most often leads to a delay, more imagined wrong, and also more inflicted wrong because we did *not* think in probabilities.

The point is this: We need not be surprised at many things in life. If a superior at work has been acting as an all-knowing autocrat for years, it's very probable (and therefore not surprising or disappointing) that he will not change tomorrow – about as likely as a piece of cheese in the fridge turning into wine overnight. But it's precisely this apparent surprise about highly probable events actually occurring that causes most of our suffering. "I didn't win the lottery again! I still haven't found my life partner! I keep finding more and more gray hairs!" Consequently, *thinking in probabilities* helps us to see the world from an unbiased perspective that we don't choose *wrong-doing* but *right-doing* feelings, decisions, and actions.

An unbiased perspective on our life here on Earth includes one fundamental probability: the survival of our civilization isn't just a given. Evolution doesn't guarantee free passage. Humanity may well become extinct. At the same time, it doesn't help to conjure up this possibility and be afraid of it. Fear wouldn't create the required change in behavior. Our egos would only strive for safety, control, or isolation – unintentionally making the survival of humankind even more improbable.

A species that survives for thousands of years, colonizes distant solar systems, and even travels to new galaxies, would no longer carry an unconscious ego. Such a civilization requires significant technological progress – while at the same time dealing responsibly with the darker sides of such progress. A suffering ego-based society would therefore be unlikely to survive for centuries without setbacks, although it is likely to experience an evolution of worldviews before severe setbacks truly occur. That means: We shouldn't develop a fearful outlook to the future; to the contrary, we should cultivate a loving and grateful view of the CONTRAST.

Contrast

The Darwinian theory of evolution explains that "most flexible and adaptable species" survives and produces an even more viable generation. We have condensed these words into "the survival of the fittest" and commonly associate it with good performance, which, when focused on the best performance to adapt, ultimately conveys the same idea. Yet all these statements stop well short of any true understanding. The causes and effects of evolution are based on a much deeper principle:

LIFE wants to learn more about its SELF. EVERYTHING strives to perceive more REALITY. Plants develop more effective roots, petals, or leaves. Insects strive for mass, robustness, and the collective. Predators strive for speed, camouflage, or superior perception. Mammals strive for family, protection, and the first rudiments of a mind – thereby, as a side effect, "creating" more opportunities and fewer dangers, which then increases the chances of survival. And humanity strives for happiness, which it may only discover through greater awareness. As a consequence, we can explain that it's always the "more conscious one" who continues to *live* in EXISTENCE.

✳

Architects think of contingencies when planning buildings; they implement safety tolerances or fail-safe devices to ensure our wellbeing even during storms, earthquakes, or fire. In EXISTENCE, we find the same pattern. LIFE wants to perceive more of its SELF – and in case of failure, problem, or standstill, a countermeasure arises. Let's take human beings, for example. We're mostly unconscious. That's why we experience negative emotions – because what in the world could make us more conscious than negative feelings? Human suffering is a *Fail-Safe of Existence*, so to speak, which has been working all this time for our evolution.

Unconsciousness grants a fantastic variety of emotions. If our life feels troubled, unfair, or lousy right now, there's nothing actually going wrong. We're just in a particularly deep sleep, which creates more "fate" and accelerates our imminent awakening. The only unpredictable factor is how much stronger this "fate" needs to become, or in other words, how much louder the alarm clock must sound to finally spark our evolution into greater awareness. But even this rise in suffering is already taken care of because the consequences of unconsciousness intensify with time.

Our pursuit of happiness puts us into an imagined victim role, then causes us to inflict injustices on others, polarizes society, progressively generates further evidence of our negativity, and so increases the chance of an individual reaching a realization – namely, the point where *you decide* to no longer partake in this vicious circle, deciding that *you'll start with yourself* and work on your emotions. This then reveals itself in a sublime (but noticeably) growing awareness within individuals. In this way, our unconsciousness (and its consequence) acts as a catalyst, as a reaction accelerator that makes us perceive more REALITY and fewer illusions.[a][34]

Positive emotions tell us to "Carry on!" But negative feelings tap on our shoulder and whisper: "You are unconscious. You're asleep. Wake up!" The deeper we sleep, the harder suffering may hit us because the

---

[a] Ra (The Law of One)

universe sends out a louder wake-up call. For which we should be thankful. Even the most profound unconsciousness isn't enough to hide the *absence* of an attentive, conscious, and happy life from us. The idea of leading this life is already here.

*

EXISTENCE takes care of itself. Bitter food warns of poison, an initial physical pain prevents taking injuries from bad to worse, and an illness initiates a phase of rest. Body and mind are closely connected in both directions, which is of great help to us.

Our shoulders droop when too many worries weigh them down. But shrugging our shoulders three times makes those worries fall away immediately. Deliberate yawning overcomes hours of insomnia. And exercise releases our thoughts from fixed tracks. But we need to do at least *this*: We must let ourselves stop being a worried, restless, or brooding person, and instead choose a new voluntariness – with body, mind, or both of them together. Do we want to remain a victim of life? Or is being alive a blessing given to us?

Every evolution begins on a small scale, within one individual, with the first being that changes itself and sets the foundation for further changes. Therefore, we must not wait for others to change because we each can break the cycle of suffering for our SELF only, here and now, and then reshape the world with this attitude that's both selfish and selfless. "A wise man, recognizing that the world is but an illusion does not act as if it is real," says the Buddha.[a35]

The things within our perception, clouds, for example, don't exist individually but require an infinite number of circumstances – a planet, an atmosphere, a sun, heat, evaporation, wind, and an observer so that they can be perceived in their form. REALITY is never divided into objects; it's one composite CONTRAST regardless of what WE notice

---

[a] Buddha

within it later – just like a cloud remains a cloud regardless of what our vivid imagination sees within it.

LIFE consists of CHANGE. This CHANGE brings forth CONTRAST. And a life rich in contrast sometimes includes negative emotions that appear to us as *suffering*. A life devoid of any contrast would be inconceivable and certainly worse. Therefore, a joyful life isn't about avoiding negative feelings in advance or taking many preventive steps but to consciously perceive that *even our unconscious suffering* belongs to LIFE and its CONTRAST.

Through our actions and even our mere existence, we constantly throw pebbles into other people's lives, which sometimes, even with our best intentions, stirs up their emotions. Therefore, we not only need *kindness that looks forward*, so that we will inflict no harm upon other people, but also *kindness that looks backward*, so that we do not respond in equal measure to every wrong we think we have suffered. *Nobody wants to hurt us.* Everyone simply wants to be happy. Lalla explains: "If a few ashes fall on a mirror, use them to polish it."[a36] So if suffering falls into your emotional world, use it to polish your feelings and to make it shine all the brighter.

✳

The discovery that our suffering is our own responsibility strikes us like a shock – strong enough to change the human conditioning. We uncover the two types of wrong, let go of imagined wrongs, and may prevent inflicted wrongs from arising. We learn to communicate non-violently. We become much less hypocritical and instead become more aware of living by a good example. We no longer curse our problems but look for what causes them. We no longer count the reasons why we can't feel good in this moment but feel good wherever we happen to be! And this inwardly *undivided* state of consciousness means that we have become an *individual*.

---

[a] Lalla (Naked Song)

Attentively experiencing CONTRAST means that most self-made problems never arise because we encounter the challenges of our life with an entirely new competence, energy, and awareness. Previously undreamed-of results become possible. Above all, it's the mindful individuals who shape the future of humanity today, so that one day our descendants may travel to distant stars – not necessarily as a consequence of personal records, heroic deeds, or innovations but as a consequence of leading a responsible, enthusiastic, and infectious way of life that creates new confidence in lost certainties.

+ You now know: why we suffer, that this state is equivalent to sleep, and that evolution is working on our awareness.

You keep in mind:

Evolution describes the fact that conscious lifeforms are more likely to survive than lifeforms with less awareness of their situation. This observation can be attributed to one exceptional pattern in nature: LIFE wants to know more of EXISTENCE. In essence, REALITY can evolve to make better use of its CONSCIOUSNESS.

The **Fail-Safe of Existence** is a concept that describes a clearly discernable pattern in nature, namely that EXISTENCE supports itself and compensates its own "faults" to allow for an evolution at any time.

Thinking in probabilities implies not to be surprised by entirely probable events – or to avoid creating quite probable but unwanted events by acting mindfully. Given the fact that all LIFE comes from EXISTENCE, a direct connection *between them* is inevitable, for example – and that this connection may be described as cooperation, support, or some kind of fail-safe.

Δ *You now can: recognize the two types of wrong, appreciate human suffering as helpful contrast, and develop into an inwardly undivided individual.*

8 Faith

The diversity of human faith. The essence of religion. The definition of God. The signifiers of religion: indescribability, unity, name, prayers, altruism, commandments, and sin. The great connectedness. A faith beyond assumptions and knowledge.

We have faith – maybe in a higher power or a divine being, or maybe in believing nothing or being unsure about it. And even though this diversity of perspective promises interesting discussions, we rarely talk about it. We are reluctant to share our beliefs and exchange our views about faith, which prevents us from discarding outdated positions, from embracing new ideas, and from fostering three inner qualities: *attentiveness*, so that we do not become blind to our beliefs, *sincereness*, so that we always remember that we don't know everything, and *kindheartedness*, so that, amidst all the detail, we never forget our emotions, which are of prime importance. These three inner qualities give rise to a joyful life and have always been the fundamental essence of religion.

Without attentiveness, sincereness, and kindheartedness, even while we were standing directly before God, we would miss, mistake, or misunderstand "him." So the contradiction is perfect: The core idea of religion is to make us conscious. But because we are more involved in beliefs than reality, humanity has become more unconscious through religions.

Every conversation about religion must first clarify what we wish to discuss: the institution, its history, its traditions, or its central teachings and their application in everyday life. Any generalization would only lead to misunderstanding, accusation, and dispute. We should also consider the meaningful principles we have adopted for "ourselves" instead of attempting to process the pointless conflicts of "organizations." Organizations can't act and therefore can't commit ungodly deeds. Every act requires peoples' participation – as human beings may cause great injustice through their unconsciousness and, upon *realizing this*, would lose their beliefs immediately.

From a distance, we can only ever see the outer appearances. Services of worship require magnificent buildings, prayers need to point to a particular direction, and believers must adhere to specific times for their worship, which makes religions seem so rigid, unworldly, and contradictory. But we also need to consider the ground on which their teachings are falling. Our ego likes the idea of striving now so that we can become happy later, in paradise, by good karma, or after rebirth. To a certain extent, our ego also gains immediate confirmation when fulfilling religious duties: We briefly confess, pray, or interrupt our ordinary life and then, with a clear conscience, carry on *as always*.

A real encounter with God would look different. We would be transformed to the core of our being. Our unconscious striving, worrying, and suffering wouldn't just continue but would become vastly unnecessary after experiencing the highest form of attentiveness, sincereness, and kindheartedness.

The six major religions are Christianity, Islam, Hinduism, Buddhism, Daoism, and Judaism. As a widespread worldview, Atheism shall be mentioned as well. Many billions of people feel attached to these seven faiths, yet no two people share exactly the same faith. An impersonal faith (outside of a person) can be ruled out, just like the "one true religion." Each faith is something individual. This individual perception feels absolutely right, which is the same for everybody. This feeling of rightness doesn't stem from specific content, though, but from what we are accustomed to. And should we solidify our habitual perception of the world, this would be the end of our conscious life because new, unfamiliar, yet equally valid experiences – meaning: the PRESENT – no longer would attain any degree of veracity.

An atheist may not reject the idea of God since he does not know his own SELF. A devout Christian, Muslim, or Jew may not accept an imagination of God because any such image would signify blasphemy. And a person who just strives for the meaning of life may not consider himself a non-believer because he at least believes that his life currently has insufficient meaning and so is meaning less.

Human faith is always a mixture of wisdom and unconsciousness. Shamanism considers body, mind, and nature as supernaturally connected. In today's worldview, supernatural things are deemed implausible, although body, mind, and nature are genuinely connected beyond comprehension. And so, while we can always believe that specific details are *different* from other people's claims, how credible is it to use *this difference* to define ourselves, to strengthen our human illusion, and to pay even less attention to REALITY? The realm of what's natural is defined by human beings only, which means that supernatural (not defined by humans) things must exist. The truth will never be found in habitual worldviews. And for that reason, we will clearly notice realizations that are beyond our habitual way of looking at the world.

God

Each religion describes the *core truth* of its faith somewhat differently, explains its facets in hundreds of stories, and sometimes even refers to its indescribability. In the theistic religions, this truth is called God, while Far Eastern religions coined terms such as Anatta, Brahman, or Tao. It seems as if there is disagreement about the truth behind God, which is odd because all these words such as "God," "Allah," "Anatta," "Brahman," or "Tao" are nothing but an arrangement of letters circumscribing an idea, a meaning, or a *reality* – just like the letters that spell "rose" or "life after death." Consequently, we can clearly define linguistically what GOD *can't be* and what GOD *must be* to be GOD – regardless of whether GOD exists or not.

Religions commonly attribute three qualities to God: Omnipotence, omnipresence, and omniscience. So we begin by looking at these unproven *declarations*, fill all three divine attributes with meaning, and then compare the results with *reality* because *evidence* can be found going forward and backward. In the end, we have either confirmed or refuted our considerations – or perhaps even discovered another possibility.

GOD would have to be *omnipotent,* thus causing every change without exception and creating everything that exists right now or is arising – otherwise it wouldn't be GOD but just some powerful being itself bowing to greater gods. Our understanding of omnipotence therefore mustn't trigger the idea of an impulsive ruler who pulls strings from afar but must remain impersonal and universal. Even your hands would only turn the page because GOD is involved. And this leads us to the next quality.

GOD would have to be *omnipresent*, thus being present everywhere at the same time: in all galaxies, solar systems, on all planets, in every mountain, in humans, in you, in all animals, plants, T-shirts, atoms, and every thought. And this entire currently present reality would have to be omnipotent, meaning that GOD's qualities would be imbued into all things. So if we believe in an invisible God living in heaven, who has his own will, who issues commandments, or performs miracles, then we don't believe in GOD but an *imagination* – with this unconscious mistake also arising in GOD and through GOD. We would simply worship the thought of a powerful being yet miss the presence of GOD in the meantime. And this leads us to the final quality.

GOD would have to be *omniscient*, thus being aware of all things while they are omnipotently and omnipresently created. Every event would be deliberately chosen, even if its outcome feels like chance, fate, or coercion. Our understanding of omniscience therefore mustn't trigger the idea of a being with incredibly vast knowledge but must again remain impersonal. We mustn't associate omniscience with predetermination either because it contradicts omnipotence. GOD must be able to take new paths infallibly at any time and thus wouldn't be a one-time actor but the constant instigator of ongoing change in the present.

GOD must be *omnipotent, omnipresent,* and *omniscient,* and these three qualities include all qualities – none is left out.

✻

Proof of God can't succeed as long as it refers to many different ideas. But the *definition of God* changes matters. Now we know precisely what there is to prove. GOD must be all EXISTENCE, REALITY, and CREATION. And amazingly ... ALL THAT exists.

Perhaps this last statement needs to be repeated in other words. Our rational logic considers empirical conclusions as proof, facts, or truth. "In autumn, the leaves fall from the trees" may be regarded as "true" because although autumn, leaves, and trees exist only as concepts in our minds, something happens in REALITY that triggers precisely this perception of falling leaves. Also, the statements that water is liquid, that a rose belongs to the flowering plants, or that logic depends on human definitions, can be called "true." And if some hiker discovers an Osiria rose along his path, yet is unaware of its name, it can nevertheless be claimed that "the hiker discovered an Osiria rose," even though he needed to look up its name in an encyclopedia later.

The fundamental problem with truth is that we perceive it but can't capture it within words – because all words arise from the truth! The hiker might mistake the Osiria rose for a Moss rose and share his wayside discovery at home. But his neighbor says: "Moss roses don't grow around here. What are you talking about? We only have Damascus roses!" After which they might quarrel or become curious enough to set out to see with their own eyes. And as the hiker and his neighbor arrive at the "Osiria rose," both point at the same flower, look at each other in wonder, and gain insight. We can't prove something by assigning a name to it – or disprove something by assigning another name to it. Therefore, we may point at reality endlessly while shouting "Laws of nature!", "Coincidence!", or "God!", yet it forever remains the same thing.

We found out that our former ideas about existence, reality, and creation are inaccurate: Creation isn't a past act, reality isn't our perception, and existence isn't an accident. We were then able to expand our former conceptions into a new understanding: EXISTENCE describes the timeless present, REALITY describes the duality of observer and observed, and CREATION describes its eternal change. And finally, we defined what GOD must be to be GOD *indeed* and discovered that GOD is just another word for EXISTENCE, REALITY, and CREATION – so *rationally* the only option is to declare GOD as proven.

GOD as EXISTENCE, REALITY, and CREATION is, without a doubt, right here, right now. This clear perception can't be triggered simply by language alone. Language may only lead us to the edge of our mind by making use of knowledge, comparisons, or contradictions so that our SELF realizes everything else upon arrival. And since religion has been passing down knowledge, comparisons, and contradictions for millennia now, we suddenly value religious teachings with new-found seriousness.

Religion

Most world religions originate with one person: Jesus in Christianity, Mohammed in Islam, Siddhartha Gautama in Buddhism, Lao Tzu in Daoism, and Moses in Judaism. We cannot be certain whether these individuals existed and truly worked miracles. We can think in probabilities, though. One pebble in your shoe most likely got there by accident. A hundred pebbles in every shoe that you keep at home, however, indicates a coherent cause or even an intention. Similarly, the great pyramids were most likely built on purpose and weren't piled up accidentally by the wind. Religions give us similar indications. Jesus most certainly was not called "Jesus," as the letter "J" was first established in the 15th century. But all the anecdotes and deeds, or at least the idea of those deeds, which are included in religious writings, go back to an author. We can thus say with absolute certainty that *someone* indeed thought like Jesus, Mohammed, Siddhartha Gautama, Lao Tzu, or Moses, then shaped the *signifiers* of their later religions, and so changed the world.

✳

One of the core signifiers of religions is the inconceivability of GOD. Rumi, a great Persian poet, answers in the name of GOD: "If someone asks about my stature, stare into space with your eyes wide open – like this."[a37] And Jesus says in the name of GOD: "Split the wood, and I am there. Turn over the stone, and there you will find me."[b38] And Mohammed says: "Paradise is under the feet of the mothers."[c39] And the Buddha teaches: In still CONSCIOUSNESS, the truth will show itself, but never in imaginations – don't even *think,* because thoughts are like spoons that can't perceive the taste of truth.[d40,e41] The originators of these descriptions knew that GOD couldn't be described; they had *perceived* GOD and now sought to lead their students into the same perception by providing the best possible description of EXISTENCE, REALITY, and CREATION.

The unity of GOD is another signifier in religions. The Bible says: "And God spoke all these words: You shall not make for yourself an image in the form of anything in heaven above or on the earth beneath or in the waters below."[f42] For "I and the Father are one!"[g43] And the Koran says: "There is no god but God."[h44]

The monotheistic religions claim absoluteness based on these words. The higher logic of the signifiers was lost because when GOD is described as ONE, by no means does it imply one true faith among many false ones. *Don't be a disbeliever in the Oneness of the One,* the Koran

---

[a] Rumi (In the Arms of the Beloved)
[b] Gospel of Thomas (Logion 77)
[c] Mohammed (Islam: A Worldwide Encyclopedia)
[d] Mumon Ekai (The Gateless Gate)
[e] Buddha (Dhammapada)
[f] Exodus 20:4 (NIV)
[g] John 10:30 (NIV)
[h] Shahada (The First Pillar of Islam)

explains.[a][45] And if we look closely into the Bible, on "God spoke: You shall not make for yourself an image in the form of anything," we notice the contradiction that was consciously included – that a speaking God already evokes an image of God and therefore can't be GOD. We are supposed to get stuck on this contradiction, question our understanding, trust no single image of God without believing in a godless world, and in this way, arrive at the edges of our mind.

The monotheistic institutions thus stand in opposition to their teachings because either they teach GOD as ONE without excluding anything, or they teach simple idolizations without including GOD.

The name of GOD is yet another signifier of religion. Christianity speaks of JEHOVAH: Yahweh, I am, the Self. The Islam speaks of ALLAH: The Witness, the Observer, the True, the Creator who created everything from nothing, the Shaper who gives shape to every thing, the Permanent, the Eternal, the First without beginning, the Last without end, and the One. Hinduism speaks of BRAHMAN: The omniscient, omnipotent, omnipresent soul of the world, the infinite, eternal primordial cause, and our true self. Buddhism speaks of *Buddha-nature*: the true, enduring, eternal self. And Daoism speaks of TAO: "Something formless, complete in itself," explains Lao Tzu, "there before Heaven and Earth, tranquil, vast, standing alone, unchanging. It provides for all things yet cannot be exhausted. It is the mother of the universe. I do not know its name, so I call it 'Tao'. Forced to name it further, I call it 'The greatness of all things'. I call it 'That which is beyond the beyond'. 'That to which all things return'."[b][46]

The many distinctive words for GOD were never meant to be a name but simply to assign a word to the CHANGE that is eternal.

*

---

[a] Koran 6:14
[b] Lao Tzu (Tao Te Ching, Verse 25)

The mutual core signifiers of all world religions let us know, (first) that people from different cultures and ages chose a nearly identical way of expressing themselves, (second) that exceptional teachings originated from their realizations, (third) that these teachings sparked great devotion in men and women, (fourth) that all emerging wisdom, traditions, and sanctuaries later established a religion, (fifth) that these religions were passed down for thousands of years until today, and (sixth) that *coincidence* is the most unlikely explanation for this course of events.

All world religions originate from an identical EXPERIENCE that is conceivable at any time because EXISTENCE, REALITY, and CREATION (GOD) is the same for everyone at any time, too. We experience nothing else. And when CONSCIOUSNESS awakens to this EXPERIENCE, when it discards the human illusion, and looks at the universe through crystal clear eyes, a teacher is born who can give something of great importance to all those who seek answers: A faith that goes beyond assumptions and vastly beyond knowledge. Only rarely will this raise a new religion, yet always this will grow into an attentive, joyful, and extraordinary life.

The basis of a world religion is *realization*, not searching for knowledge or the desire to manipulate people. Without realization, there wouldn't be anything meaningful that changes our lives. If a "prophet" fulfills one hundred of our wishes, we would be impressed, though only briefly. But if a prophet takes away our human illusion, we would be *changed forever*. Therefore, people stay with teachers who live what they teach – whether in music, art, or mindfulness. And only if the students had never heard music before, had never seen the beauty of art before, had never before felt the depth of awareness – in such a case, the students could easily mistake amateurs for teachers.

In music and the arts, much is a matter of taste, but regardless – you will probably agree – we may perceive *signs* whether the work of an artist comes from inspiration or imitation. And these particular *signals* also exist in the teachings of awareness.

Signifiers

Humanity doesn't hold much knowledge about its origin. Our past lies in the dark. Even our family tree is lost going back just a few generations, and we don't really miss our ancestors' wisdom. We genuinely believe that in former times people *knew less about life,* be it two thousand or two hundred years ago, and that we've made steady progress in all disciplines since then. But our ancestors had more wisdom and *appreciable authenticity* than this belief would grant them. Confucius lived 2500 years ago, studied the writings of an even at that time already long-lost civilization, and gained great insights. Wisdom is possible anytime, as is its loss. And for that reason, we shouldn't consider today's world religions merely as accidentally long-lived phenomena but as the only *surviving* keepers of wisdom.

The EXPERIENCE of GOD is reserved for an inner realization. Words just remain imprecise paraphrases of a crystal clear perception, which explains why all religions seem different. The Bible, the Koran, the Vedas and Sutras, the Tao Te Ching, the Four Noble Truths, the Diamond Sutra, the Hermetica, and many other scriptures – they all sound slightly different in their narrative style. The Bible even comes up with different statements within its many translations. According to Luther, it says: "The Lord is my shepherd; I won't lack anything."[a47] King James says: "The LORD is my shepherd; I shall not want."[b48] And Young says, "Jehovah [is] my shepherd, I do not lack."[c49] And these differences shouldn't discourage us but spark our curiosity.

"Why do you speak to the people in parables?" the disciples asked. And Jesus replied: "Because the knowledge of the secrets of the kingdom of heaven has been given to you, but not to them. [...] This is why I speak to them in parables: Though seeing, they do not see; though hearing, they do not hear or understand. [...] For this people's heart has become calloused; they hardly hear with their ears, and they have closed their

---

[a] Psalm 23:1 (LUT)
[b] Psalm 23:1 (KJV)
[c] Psalm 23:1 (YLT)

92

eyes. Otherwise they might see with their eyes, hear with their ears, understand with their hearts and turn, and I would heal them."[a50]

We shouldn't wonder which translation of the Bible may be the correct or the best one, and then mentally switch off again. Even if *Jesus himself* were to preach on the mount right in front of us, we'd still need to learn how to grasp his words because his intention never was for us to understand his words simply as *commonplace,* as *it fits our ideas,* or as we think we should comprehend his words. Instead, the preaching is supposed to spark CONSCIOUSNESS within us, which makes us perceive the world directly with our senses while not believing anything – because it's this belief of *having understood something* that makes us blind to reality and blind to the EXPERIENCE of SELF.

Another signifier of religions is prayer. That is an original translation of the Lord's Prayer: "O Birther! Father-Mother of the Cosmos, focus your light within us – make it useful: Create your reign of unity now – Your one desire then acts with ours, as in all light, so in all forms. Grant what we need each day in bread and insight. Loose the cords of mistakes binding us, as we release the strands we hold of others' guilt. Don't let surface things delude us, but free us from what holds us back. From you is born all ruling will, the power and the life to do, the song that beautifies all, from age to age it renews. Truly – power to these statements – may they be the ground from which all my actions grow: Amen."[b51] And these words were chosen purposefully to inspire consciousness within us.

Awareness isn't just some placebo effect but a nearness to reality – and in this understanding, a conscious prayer literally brings us closer to GOD. The more peaceful the surface of our perception becomes, the more we recognize the reflection within. Some religions refer to this shift as meditation, but the immersing mechanism remains the same. Any thankless, angry, or stressful prayer worsens our emotional state. A conscious prayer, on the other hand, has the power to open our eyes, to

---

[a] Matthew 13:10-15 (NIV)
[b] Neil Douglas-Klotz (Prayers of the Cosmos: Meditations on the Aramaic Words of Jesus)

reach our arms out wide, and to heal our hearts, so that we see the miracles that make our lives possible at all times.

The strongest signifier of religions is altruism: "Whoever loves others has fulfilled the law. [All commandments] are summed up in this one command: 'Love your neighbor as yourself.' Love does no harm to a neighbor. Therefore love is the fulfillment of the law," explains the Bible.[a52] "None amongst you believes (truly) until he loves for his brother – or for his neighbor – that which he loves for himself," explains the Islam.[b53] Everyone who wants to practice these words faces an obstacle, though. It is difficult, if not downright impossible, to love strangers and unfriendly people as one loves oneself. We might therefore believe that God will reward us for merely trying. But Jesus didn't talk about the effort of trying but explained that loving one's neighbor first of all requires knowledge of SELF. Of course, the ego cannot love anyone, not even itself, as it only distinguishes ideas and stays in unconsciousness. In mindfulness, on the contrary, life would follow the unspoken principles of the heart. So, "if you need rules to be kind and just," Lao Tzu explains, "if you just *act* virtuous, this is a sure sign that virtue is absent. Thus we see the great hypocrisy."[c54] We shouldn't be prevented from lying, stealing, or killing by the threat of punishment but, in the first place, shouldn't become so unconscious that we would want to inflict wrong upon each other.

Divine laws don't serve as a moral instance but provide a humanmade test of awareness, so that we can reflect their contradictoriness. Such laws would be credible only if we were to believe in an image of God that we should not subscribe to. Also, admitting that we, as human beings, need instructions to tell us what's good and bad, would openly declare that we are not responsible. And should we believe in a *commanding God* while fully aware of our irresponsibility, this would ultimately make our unconsciousness even more apparent. "But how can we be so

---

[a] Romans 13:8-10 (NIV)
[b] Sahih Muslim (The Book of Faith, Hadith 45)
[c] Lao Tzu (Tao Te Ching, Verse 18)

unconscious?" That's what contradictoriness wants to show us. "How can my thoughts be so convincing? And who exactly am I?"

The Ten Commandments of Christianity are not describing divine laws but a divine state of consciousness in which the question of "Who am I?" is answered – which makes us live in the here and now without striving, worrying, and suffering. Buddhism explains: Loving kindness (Metta) and caring compassion (Karuna) describe a heavenly state of consciousness in which we perceive all people and beings in their true nature, admire their consciousness, and help them to let go more and more of their unconscious suffering.[a55]

A universal power lets our lungs breathe, and this divine power is present within us NOW. In Christianity and Judaism, we find its vast and incredible signifier – the name of God: Jehovah, which goes back to Jahwe, Yahweh, and ultimately YHWH. And YHWH declares: "I AM THAT I AM; [...] this is my name for ever, and this is my memorial unto all generations."[b56] These words could certainly call forth the idea of a heavenly being referring to itself as God. But the *signifier* evident in these words resolves this misunderstanding. GOD is the SELF and YHWH, and the SELF and is pronounced like a breath: like an audible inbreath followed by an audible outbreath.

"Be still, and know that I am God."[c57] For "God created man in his own image [meaning: with all his abilities], in the image of God [meaning: within his SELF] created he him."[d58] The EXISTENCE, REALITY, and CREATION, which makes us breathe, think and observe, didn't construct us, put us aside, and forgot about us, no, WE OURSELVES, HERE and NOW, are all its MOSAIC.

✳

---

a Thich Nhat Hanh (Old Path White Clouds)
b Exodus 3:14-15 (KJV)
c Psalm 46:10 (KJV)
d Genesis 1:27 (KJV)

The connectedness of all world religions changes our understanding of GOD. But in the end, it all comes down to voluntariness whether we want all images of Gods or non-Gods to be taken away from us, so that we come closer to GOD. The Bible teaches us: "Every kind of sin and slander can be forgiven, but blasphemy against the Spirit will not be forgiven.[a59] "If anyone corrupts the temple of God, God will corrupt him in return; for the temple of God is holy, and it is you! Nobody shall deceive his self!"[b60] In Christianity, a life separated from God is considered a sin. And this "sin" is a *signifier* for unconsciousness, *another word for it* because all sins and suffering originate from *unconsciousness*. Thus, the Bible says that as long as we deceive our SELF and don't live in CONSCIOUSNESS but dwell in the past or future, our emotions of suffering won't cease.

Jesus declared: "Let any one of you who is without sin be the first to throw a stone"[c61] because above all, awareness means not to judge unconsciousness, neither in oneself nor in others. And this awareness begins with remembering that we aren't unconscious as a human being. WE are not human beings. CONSCIOUSNESS is just briefly looking in a direction that feels like a human illusion. Therefore, Jesus assures us: "There will be more rejoicing [in CONSCIOUSNESS] over one sinner who repents than over ninety-nine righteous persons who do not need to repent."[d62] And the Buddhist Diamond Sutra explains: "If someone were to offer an immeasurable [treasure of an entire universe] as an act of generosity, the happiness resulting from that virtuous act would not equal the happiness resulting from a [person] who gives rise to the awakened mind and reads, recites, accepts, and puts into practice this sutra, and explains it to others, even if only a chapter of four lines."[e63]

We have discovered more than enough signifiers of religions to leave no doubt: The signifiers give a new dimension to the history of humanity.

---

[a] Matthew 12:31 (NIV)
[b] 1 Corinthians 3:17-18 (MENG)
[c] John 8:7 (NIV)
[d] Luke 15:7 (NIV)
[e] Diamond Sutra

Jesus was no Christian. Mohammed was no Muslim. Siddhartha was no Buddhist. Their intention wasn't to propagate a religion but rather a conscious, truthful, and kind way of life.

+ You now know: why today's religions came into being, what the meaning of God is, and that the core teaching of religions is connected with the search for our SELF.

\# You keep in mind:

The **definition of God** distinguishes linguistically what GOD is and what GOD can't be in order to qualify as GOD.

GOD, also JEHOVAH, ALLAH, BRAHMAN, or TAO, is a word for the combination of all qualities of EXISTENCE, REALITY, and CREATION; it thus describes a real actuality, which may be perceived once WE discover the SELF.

The **EXPERIENCE** is a moment of mere perception, without interpretation, thoughts, or concepts; it's a total dispersion of the SELF in the PRESENT, which provides the answers to all questions made up by humans.

Δ *You now can: see the great unity within human realizations, decipher the hidden signifiers in religious teachings, and develop a faith beyond assumptions and knowledge.*

9 Purpose

The meaning of life. Meaning and meaninglessness as ideas. The origin of purpose. Our attachment to otherness. Self-being. Excitement as nearness to our self.

A human life passes quickly, and time fades memories – of us, of entire civilizations, and one day even of humanity. So what great purpose could there possibly be in our little lives? We fear that, as we approach the end of even a long life, we may have no answer, or that we may have lost any momentary purpose again *by then*, and this fear has its justification. Society talks about success, wealth, and power as if they contained great significance, but there is no value in unconsciousness. We might well believe that all of us need to find our own individual answers, do good deeds, and search for the one true love – but how convincing could it be to make a higher meaning dependent on the lowly ego, which has a different mood for every hour of the day?

Human beings can't create lasting meaning. Everything we create will fade again and also take along the feelings associated with it. Therefore, the "purpose of life" can only be found beyond being human.

Meaning

Our ego feels that nothing is more important than the current thought, and thus moves seamlessly through vastly deviating layers of meanings without being able to maintain a sense of proportion about them. There are moments when truly important things in life matter, for example, that nobody got injured in an accident. And there are other moments when every little detail matters: the napkins must match our tablecloth, the car must befit our career, our CV must suit society. This is how we first fabricate an arbitrary framework from which LIFE may deviate quite easily, then question the meaning of all these deviations, and finally expect answers in an equally illogical language.

In REALITY, these problems don't exist. Expectations and disappointments arise only in our CONSCIOUSNESS. Just like interior decorators design an apartment, we choose the meaning of concepts, get tired of them over time, or daydream about affording something better, while our apartment or the world, which is making our creative arrangements possible in the first place, does not change.

A bee in the garden may delight or annoy us. A lazy day may feel like a senseful pause or a senseless waste of time. Our whole life can seem meaningful or meaningless. Our attachment to *just one single* concept, however, indicates our attachment to *all* concepts. Once we select one possible meaning for ourselves, we simultaneously accept all other possible meanings. The point is this: Anyone who believes that life is meaningless assigns meaning to this idea – which in itself proves the belief as false. The idea of "meaning and meaninglessness" only exists in combination as one concept in our mind, but never separately.

In REALITY, there's neither meaning nor meaninglessness, but this fact must not be accepted casually. In fact, human striving, worrying, and suffering makes no sense. But CONSCIOUSNESS creates every sense at will, to then assign significance to the CONTRAST. That's why no drop of water, no ray of sunshine, no breath of air existing in the PRESENT is truly meaningless because WE decide its meaning right NOW. And if we believe that our life is too short, that we shall die before long, and be soon forgotten, then it's a senseless (wrong) interpretation but a quite senseful (necessary) experience, so we may learn from this painful mistake and be awakened by it.

You know the saying "everything in life happens for a reason." This basically means that *everything in your life* happens *for your reason*. Your life doesn't take place *with* you; it takes place *through* you. And once you realize *that*, no further purpose needs to be added to you and your life.[a][64]

---

[a] Bashar (Quest for Truth)

Some experiences spark amazing and uplifting feelings within us and make us know very clearly why we consider some things to be *meaningful*. The external trigger of these emotions isn't what matters. If a bee would spark the *same feeling* as the Grand Canyon, then it's *the same feeling* and doesn't become more or less significant based on its smaller or larger catalyst.

We nowadays say: "Love is a very meaningful feeling," as if there's an alternative to this statement, as if this sentence makes it true, or awards love a seal of quality. But in the early days of humanity, as our language developed and things or feelings received their names, the emotion that was named "love" was the benchmark of all meaning. Without ever having felt water, *wetness* cannot be understood. And without having felt love or other uplifting feelings, *meaning* cannot be understood. Without emotions, all things would have the same meaning. It would be impossible to recognize something as precious or to question the purpose of life today. So it all comes down to this: that we don't look for meaning in concepts but choose uplifting and thus meaningful feelings.

*

Most people think they are different from others. Our genes can't confirm this otherness. The genetic framework of our bodies is 99.9% identical. The atoms and molecules that piece us together are also fundamentally constructed similarly. The closer we examine ourselves in the microcosm, the more similar we become. And the same is revealed the farther away we examine ourselves in the macrocosm. Our life phases of birth, life, and death are identical. Our potential emotions and thoughts are too. And from a cosmic perspective, humanity just counts as one brief, collective flare of life. It's merely our unconscious mind that considers us to be different from each other – which in reality is not the case.

In EXISTENCE, EVERYTHING has the same origin. We are that which WE ARE – meaning: We aren't what we should be, want to be, or somehow cannot be but genuinely are our SELF. In most unconscious moments, this SELF-BEING is taken over by emotions that feel different, as if we were *not* ourselves. Yet, once we learned and realized that feelings are chosen deliberately, we initiated an exodus: a migration out of slavery and back home. External circumstances no longer decide how we feel. And this state of consciousness shows itself best in the emotion which, in our language, we call EXCITEMENT.

Excitement

SELF-BEING is inspiring; it fills us with spirit. We feel *ex-cite-ment*, which implies that the *moment moves up*. We become conscious. EXISTENCE is more observer and less the observed for a moment. So, whenever we experience an emotion of EXCITEMENT, it tells us that we are close to our SELF.

Society doesn't make it easy for us to find and follow our EXCITEMENT. University degrees are somehow "more valued" than high school degrees. We subconsciously question why anyone would want to become a gardener, bookseller, or mechanic when it's possible to build a career as department manager, managing director, or millionaire instead. People who are excited by gardens, books, or cars begin to doubt themselves. Someone who is a baker at heart becomes a teacher, while someone who is a doctor at heart may become a baker. And so, we leave our true calling – or stay in the wrong one, because we keep on waiting for the "right" moment instead of finally following our *inner compass* and its *guiding voice*.

EXCITEMENT is a significant emotion: It tingles like a strong intuition, beckons us to leave the warm nest for an even greater comfort, and takes us by the hand to lead us onward even in stormy times.

Your EXCITEMENT shows itself in the smallest of ideas and the biggest of life's dreams, which seem to have an existence of their own, represent their own highest goals, and even now make you highly attentive. Maybe you feel EXCITEMENT about walking through the rain right now or lighting some candles tonight; you may feel EXCITEMENT when you think of selling some old belongings at a flea market (instead of just

104

throwing them away); or maybe you decide to repot the overgrown plants on your balcony or to plan a trip to places you've not been to before. Others may not understand our motivation or they may have quite different ideas about our life, possibly caused by worries or fears, and that's fine, as long as we ourselves take the final decision. We won't always comprehend other people's motives, either, or keep them company at every turn along the way.

Jesus taught: "When you enter a town or village, look for someone who is willing to welcome you. [...] Greet those who live there. If that home welcomes you, give it your blessing of peace. If it does not, [let your peace return to you]. Some people may not welcome you or listen to your words. If they don't, shake the dust off your feet when you leave that home or town."[a65]

The universe does not mind human beings who discover and follow their EXCITEMENT. You may well doubt this. "I can't just do whatever I want!" And that's true. You shouldn't do what you're unconsciously *driven to* but what consciously *excites* you! Your ego does whatever it wants, which is staying within its illusion – this will almost never excite you. But your SELF follows a path of pure creativity, which helps you to overcome all self-imposed obstacles and to fulfill your dreams without effort.

A falcon that wants to take off from the ground must orientate itself for a moment, then lift off with a mighty leap, and merge with the air, until suddenly strong updrafts carry it upwards *without effort*. In a similar way, our EXCITEMENT first needs *attentiveness* so that we don't mix up unnecessary stuff with matters of the heart, then *readiness* so that we don't falter leaping into the unknown when the moment has come, and finally *integrity* so that we don't inflict injustice onto other people – so that then we are being carried onwards by EXISTENCE ITSELF.

*

---

[a] Matthew 10:11-14 (NIRV)

The meaning of LIFE is SELF-BEING, not with the ego but way beyond – so that we sense that, despite all human faults, doubts, and weaknesses, we rest in a whole and indivisible CONSCIOUSNESS.

"Are you excited about it?" – *Yes.* – "Then move on!" – *No.* – "Then turn around. At first, just with your thoughts, then in your feelings, and finally, maybe even in your actions."

The more we hear this whispering voice with increasing clarity, the less we will be diverted from our life path by unexpected crosswinds or negative influences. In the beginning, we need to listen carefully. But at some point, our intuition exceeds our old conditioning, the one that finds us via the negativity of media, the expectations of society, or the opinions of others.

There's so much to experience in the world! There's so much worth doing. Our decisions will impact humanity, its problems, and its future one way or another. And the *most meaningful option* we have within our power is to follow our EXCITEMENT. That's the first stone, which causes an avalanche and proves not only to ourselves but also to everyone else that there are more meaningful worldviews to discover than the one currently held.

+ You now know: that nothing is meaningless, why we call some things meaningful, and what comprises a life full of purpose.

You keep in mind:

SELF-BEING means not to try to be something other than the PRESENT – which also includes stopping all efforts to be PRESENT right now.

EXCITEMENT means doing what we *truly* want, with attentiveness, readiness, and integrity. It's the safest thing in the world, the greatest wealth of a human being, and the strongest guiding principle during the search.

Δ *You now can: observe how the mind assigns meaning, discover the self-being underneath, and within this freedom, follow your excitement.*

Consciousness

Now you know. Life's big questions have been answered, the answers have given new meaning to some of the words in our language, and enabled the discovery of an extraordinary reality. You are home again – or are you? All the answers are there, but is that enough for you? As long as a feeling remains that something is missing, your search for higher consciousness will continue. In which case, you are now in class as a student. And so, the next part of this book addresses the deeper application of the reliable realizations we have made.

The Bible contains a parable that explains what's about to happen here. When the farmers cultivated their lands, some seed fell on stony ground, got burned in the sun, or were eaten by birds, but some seed fell on fertile soil and bore fruit a hundredfold.[a66] The *realizations about our life* have sown an awareness within you, which through cultivation may now grow into a mighty tree, allowing you to look down on past selves from increasingly greater heights. The Tao Te Ching presents these possibilities rather directly: "When the best seeker hears of Tao, he strives with great effort to know it. When an average seeker hears of Tao, he thinks of it now and again. When the poorest seeker hears of Tao, he laughs out loud. Tao is always becoming what we have need for it to become. If it could not do this, it would not be Tao."[b67]

We may begin with a single certainty: Realizations far beyond words, thoughts, and ideas will in turn lead to a life far beyond words, thoughts, and ideas.[c68]

---

[a] Matthew 13:3-8 (KJV)
[b] Lao Tzu (Tao Te Ching, Verse 41)
[c] Diamond Sutra

10 Awakening

The missing recollection. Awakening as an analogy for a real experience. Our retrospectively complemented worldview. The Law of Unknowing. Questions and answers through creativity. The support life gives us.

Dreams are real experiences with distinct qualities. We may forget a dream as soon as we wake up or still vaguely remember it, experience a dream through the eyes of a completely different person, perceive it as convincingly real or even a perfectly lucid experience. Upon awakening, our CONSCIOUSNESS then returns into a *human being*, into another real experience with distinct qualities.

Recollection

We go to bed at night, fall asleep, and forget our life. Our ego is forgotten, too. The process of waking up then makes all the memories return, just as if the dreamer were to put on his clothes again. We snap back into our ego, return to human striving, worrying, and suffering, and everything again seems to make perfect sense; as if indeed the ego had experienced a good night's rest (or a bad one) and therefore is entitled to be in a good mood (or a bad one). But something is not quite right. *Everyone who is awake should know himself.* Within the dream, we have forgotten our self, that much is clear. But even awake, we do not know: "Who am I?" Our I exists, but the recollection of it is missing. And so the dreamer realizes within the dream that he is still asleep – that a story is being told in CONSCIOUSNESS right now while waking up could happen at any moment. AWAKENING to the SELF isn't a spiritual idea but an event that is possible, real, and ultimately inevitable.

A child doesn't know that "two plus two equals four." From primary school onward, this fact becomes real in retrospect, meaning that "two plus two" has always equaled "four." As adults, we quite naturally accept living within such a "retrospectively complemented worldview." You read an article about "suprafluids ignoring gravity" and accept this piece of information as a universal fact. You notice the first snow of the year as you open the blinds in the morning, and retrospectively your worldview is supplemented by "snowfall last night." The previous state of unknowing gets no further attention because newly perceived information does not require feelings of guilt.

Similarly, AWAKENING from the human illusion to the SELF is a retrospective realization. Even though descriptions of AWAKENING sometimes sound like an epiphany, you are unlikely to call out: "Wow, I finally found my self!" Instead, you'll retrospectively recognize that the SELF was always there, understood everything correctly all the time, and voluntarily chose a perspective of unknowing. It's as if you're walking through a beautiful landscape on a wonderful day, and after several hours, you suddenly realize: "What a wonderful day, and what a beautiful landscape!"

*

The Western worldview considers AWAKENING as some kind of spiritual exaggeration and thus as moving away from our understanding of reality. Which is exactly how we should understand it: as moving away from a great limitation. The world is made to be observed without worldview.

A dream may contain multiple things, maybe "ourselves, a beach, sunshine, other people, a sandcastle on the shore, and a small ice cream parlor up in the dunes," but on waking up, we realize that *all this* existed in our consciousness only. Our life may also contain many things, "ourselves, sometimes the beach, sunshine, usually other people, and very similar things like sandcastles on the shore, or ice cream parlors up in the dunes," and with AWAKENING, we realize that ALL THAT exists as one EXPERIENCE in CONSCIOUSNESS only. So every attachment to ideas, concepts, or thoughts tells us, as the Buddha explains, that the SELF isn't awake yet.[a69]

The analogy of spiritual awakening helps us to understand what awaits us in AWAKENING because we already know what happens each morning: Once sleep ends, we may explore life in vastly more authentic ways.

The AWAKENING to the SELF is no more complicated than perceiving the sound of a D minor fifth, than looking at a dalarna-blue wall, than experiencing the taste of a cherimoya, than smelling the scent of chicory, or touching the bark of a meranti-tree. We may not know what these experiences feel like, but we can trust that they will arrive in CONSCIOUSNESS. Further preparation is not required. And the SELF will feel as it has always felt, including this present moment.

Veil

EXISTENCE will always observe itself from some angle, will always experience itself from an I-point-of-view, and thus will always have a *limiting horizon*, which prevents other experiences in the same moment. As a consequence, a living being may never have the feeling of knowing everything, as, by implication, an observer with an unlimited horizon would not be a living being. *Unknowing* is a universal law of LIFE: when EXISTENCE feels like a *living-being-experience*, other areas of EXISTENCE remain inaccessible. And only this unavoidable VEIL in front of the MOSAIC grants us curiosity, creativity, and free will.

Some questions cannot be answered because the answers are not part of ordinary life. A broken heart asks: "What's wrong with me?" A sleepless night asks: "Is everything going to be okay?" A doubting ego asks: "Will I ever understand my life?" And when we pause in these moments just briefly, we can see what's truly going on: Questions don't just float around the cosmos like dandelion seeds and, therefore, they are not *found* but *invented*. A question, however, may only be invented in

---

[a] Diamond Sutra

combination with an answer, which means that along with our questions, we already *possess* their answers.

EXISTENCE isn't determined by questions and their resolution. When a curiosity arises and is joined by an interest to solve it, both emotions simply drift through CONSCIOUSNESS without the necessity of putting them both together. Therefore, our potential suffering is not caused by our unsolved questions. The problem is our unconsciousness regarding their answers. It's easy to uncover an infinite number of details in reality, but this possibility does not need to kindle an uncomfortable feeling of unknowing within us.

Answers like "two plus two equals four" are based on memorized concepts. Questions like "What will happen a hundred years from now?" only distract from current events. And variations of "Will I ever get ahead of my problems?" are not questions that have answers, but thoughts that require self-reflection – about this "I," about the "details" that turn life into a problem, and thus about the unconscious focus of our full creative potential, because: It's this unobserved creativity of CONSCIOUSNESS that puts questions into our field of view and positions their answers seemingly *out of reach*.

When children play in a sandbox, creativity is what makes them build a sandcastle and then tear it down again, maybe with a shovel, their feet, or a toy excavator. Creativity *itself* innocently plays with CONSCIOUS-NESS. And with equal innocence, creativity creates the impression within us that "finding answers" is beyond our abilities.[a70] Our questions thereby highlight our position in CONSCIOUSNESS, just like knocking signals that, depending on whether they sound *near* or *distant*, indicate the position where earthquake victims are buried.

*

What causes a human being to AWAKEN? The answer is: everything. EVERYTHING in LIFE helps us to awaken.

---

[a] Bashar (Quest for Truth)

We may believe that physical health increases our awareness. What could be easier than being aware without worrying about the transience of life? But then, it could also be the other way around. What could be easier than being aware while certain of our mortality?

We may believe that material wealth increases our awareness. What could be easier than being aware while realizing that we feel dissatisfied even when surrounded by abundance? But then, it could also be the other way around. What could be easier than being aware with the freedom of not having to worry about unnecessary possessions?

We may believe that extensive knowledge of philosophy, spirituality, or religion increases our awareness. What could be easier than being aware through understanding the timeless wisdom of past cultures? But then, it could also be the other way around. What could be easier than being aware when in a vacant state, without any pre-set ideas forged into our chain of thoughts?

We may believe that long-term relationships increase our awareness. What could be easier than being aware while having dinner, or fooling around, or falling asleep together? But then, it could also be the other way around. What could be easier than being aware when you are alone, in authentic solitude?

We may believe many things – that tranquility, spending much time in nature, and going on exotic journeys would increase our awareness – and that may very well be true. Then again, we might require the exact opposite. EXISTENCE sets everything in motion for us. Yet whatever arises, AWAKENING just happens. You won't contribute anything to it. Or do you actually think that, as a human being, you contribute in any way to opening your eyes in the morning, so that you can continue your search for new experiences?

+ You now know: that we can truly awaken from the ego, and that spirituality is connected with both the origin of religions and our search for the self.

You keep in mind:

The **Law of Unknowing** explains that no living being may ever know or perceive everything, thus always perceiving a limited horizon. An observer with an unlimited perception and horizon cannot be considered a living being.

The **AWAKENING** describes the possible, real, and ultimately inevitable state when CONSCIOUSNESS feels like ITSELF again and "wakes up from the ego."

The **VEIL** expresses that, *on the one side,* no living being can know or be aware of everything, and that, *on the other side,* only this Law of Unknowing arranges the PRESENT into what we perceive. The VEIL grants us curiosity, creativity, and free will. If all paths were to lie "within our horizon," then where could we go? If all creations were to exist "within our horizon," then what could we do? And if all questions and answers were to reside within our field of vision, how could we still make any kind of decision?

Δ *You now can: observe the creativity behind your questions, feel the constant support life gives you, and search for the recollection of your self.*

11 **Search**

The discovery of origin. The states of being. The phases of humanness. Ascending within consciousness. The traps of unconsciousness. Overcoming the gap between knowing and feeling.

A human being is like a river, asking itself: "Who am I? Where do I come from? And where am I going?" The river comprehends that it originates from distant springs, but unraveling the past in all its detail proves impossible. Its existence has no explanation. The future is equally uncertain. The only certainty is the approach of the unknown ocean. And so, the river flows with a feeling of homelessness, without knowing its place in EXISTENCE. "If only I could find the origin and meaning of my life."

One night, the river has a dream. It dreams of being a small spring in the high mountains, longingly asking itself: "Who am I? Where am I going? And where do I come from? I wonder if the creeks, the mountains, or the rain might know the answer." And in this moment, the river AWAKENS. It realizes that a tiny spring is *its* beginning but not *the* beginning. A spring surges up through the bedrock, the underground watercourses fill up with rain, the rain falls from the clouds, the clouds rise from the seas, and the seas take in fresh water from the rivers – from itself!

In this EXPERIENCE, the river loses all sense of separation and itself becomes a beginning, an ending, and the in-between. How could we think that an endless cycle isn't at some point an endless cycle but only a river? Within this discovery of originlessness lies the perception of origin. All is sometimes cause and sometimes effect in one united WHOLENESS.

The purpose of life is not our human striving – that's why we strive for happiness while *seeking* the end of our striving: our AWAKENING. We may be entirely unconscious of this *search*, or may only be aware of some of it, but that doesn't alter its nature. Our humanness, meaning, our identification with an ego, mandates that we shall continue to search until finally we have left the human illusion behind.

Ascent

The MOSAIC may be compared to a high mountain range: Although all things exist along its slopes, the world looks different from "further up" than from "further down." As we ascend in CONSCIOUSNESS, our view on the horizon widens and grants an expanded self-conception. The same world feels different when we are a child, an adult, or a Buddha. We can discover different "states of being"[a71] in EXISTENCE, both through our own experience and the accounts of others, turn these into a trail map, and along the way provide recommendations to all wanderers on their ascent.

(△1) The first state of being is consistent self-unconsciousness. A stone knows nothing of its existence. And micro-organisms, insects, fish, or some mammals probably are also incapable of self-awareness.

(△2) The second state of being is emerging self-awareness. A living being may now learn to solve specific problems, apply tools, or use language to some extent. But life remains governed by instincts, conditioning, and feelings, while thoughts play minor roles only. We realize that ascending (from the first to the second state) is possible and quite common. An infant is born consistently self-unconscious but soon moves upwards into self-awareness and beyond.

(△3) The third state of being is sleeping consciousness: the human being. We learn to recognize our body and reach a point where we no longer need to think about this. Self-knowledge is possible but occurs only rarely, briefly, and coincidentally. We can shape the world but may also lose ourselves in illusions (for example, believing that we have already reached the summit of creation). The perception of the world is divided into knowledge, those who know, and those who don't know, which favors an ego-society. But a shaking up of these beliefs, whether

---

[a] Maharishi Mahesh Yogi (The Seven States of Consciousness)

through fate, self-reflection, or coincidence, can initiate a vastly more conscious life.

(△4) The fourth state of being is transcendent consciousness and commences with one question unthought of before: "Who am I?" The ego becomes transparent while, beyond all physical and mental form, the SELF begins to shine through. Stillness returns to CONSCIOUSNESS. All of REALITY is realized as being aware. We learn to deliberately choose our feelings, which may be labeled as perfect happiness. Our heart opens up to the whole world as there is no longer a need for masquerade. We feel our EXCITEMENT, entrust ourselves to it, and follow it. We have seen the unconscious behaviors of being human (△3) as what they truly are. Former worldviews are left behind as we discover and apply a higher logic and a new language. However, WE aren't fully awake yet; perfect happiness is no permanent emotional state. An echo of the human dream is still hanging on, fading only upon reaching the states of being that follow (△5-7).

Phases

Life necessarily includes phases of preparation. And *being human* is a preparation for AWAKENING, consisting of many phases, such as (first) to suspect a higher truth, (second) to discover the ego, (third) to become aware of the search, (fourth) to work consistently on the duration, frequency and intensity of our awareness, and (fifth) to feel increasingly whole, healed and pure as a result.

The first phase of our conscious search – that's how I call it – is the gathering of information. An entirely new world opens itself by way of books, movies, and so-called satsangs, in which students and teachers search for truth together. In this phase, we receive a great deal of wisdom within a short period of time, discover the unity of all things, and feel how *meaningful* it is to be fascinated by LIFE.

The search for more information, however, can turn into a phase of suffering: We might believe that we are becoming more intelligent, more mature, or somehow better. We might think of all the knowledge we still lack and translate this into a lack of happiness. And finally, all the information gathered might serve to strengthen our ego instead of our awareness, so that we merely imagine that we have become more mindful while, in reality, we have become more unconscious.

Our ascent *through the states of being* thus requires a steady letting go of all ideas about it, just like hikers steadily let go of the ground beneath their feet, no matter how hard the journey has been so far.

Socrates said, "I know that I know nothing,"[a72] which today we consider a philosophical wisdom. But Socrates actually describes a fourth-state-of-being perception ($\triangle 4$): That our mind contains nothing but its own inventions – or in other words: That the mind can't understand the mindless nature of CONSCIOUSNESS because it is *itself* just a limited phenomenon within CONSCIOUSNESS. Philosophy (the love of wisdom) is also just a phase of being human that Socrates had long left behind; he knew that the "thoughts we love" prevent us from discovering the truth. It's these beloved attachments, maybe to wisdom, our ego, science, God, or other matters, that lay out the traps of unconsciousness in which we are currently caught.

An atheist may be attached to science, but as soon as he discovers the gaps and misunderstandings it contains, understands its dependency on the human mind, and recognizes the non-analyzability of REALITY, something within him changes forever. A religious person may be attached to God, but as soon as he discovers the gaps and misunderstandings in the concept of God, understands its dependency on the human mind, and recognizes the necessary qualities of GOD, something in him changes forever. These irreversible changes indicate having mastered a phase of life.

---

a Socrates

The final phase of the spiritual search – that's how I call it – is to overcome the gap between knowing and feeling: You may well have uncovered every secret of the universe but still believe that this has no impact on your emotions.

The *gap* can be compared to a three-dimensional street painting. From the right angle, the painting looks like an impassable canyon. You're standing at this precise point, looking "down" into the canyon, paralyzed, and no longer realizing that the gap is actually *flat*. From any other angle, this illusion would fail. You could easily cross over to the other side. But from the *viewpoint of knowledge*, it seems impossible to get across to the *viewpoint of feeling*. The key insight here is: When you feel that you don't know enough to be able to feel enough, as if the "right emotions" haven't arrived yet, then *this feeling* is the right feeling because it's *really there*. It only contains the illusion of a gap, of "not fully being there yet."

In fact, we often have emotions with a fake depth of perspective. One sudden bad mood may spoil ten joyful years of our life. But these negative feelings genuinely have no depth, no past, and also no truth regarding their contents; they merely possess tremendous persuasive power as there's no other more significant feeling present at the time. EMOTIONS always occupy the entire PRESENT. So if something is still "missing" in our search for AWAKENING, then it's not because we are actually missing something but because we still aren't *directly* looking at our feelings as though they were street paintings.

*

The search ends without any intention or effort, without regard to how long a person has been searching or even had the notion of being able to find something. We leave our habitual perception for a moment and don't go back. This evolution is possible because the "construction plans" are already complete. More awareness is already there. More CONSCIOUSNESS already exists without wanting to hurry us along. Nobody needs to rush because *what we are searching for* is forever available to be searched for. I AM here. Therefore, it doesn't matter what exactly we're doing in our search, as long as we don't, on the one hand, wait for things to happen on their own, and don't, on the other hand, prevent things from happening on their own.[a][73]

[a] P. D. Ouspensky (A New Model of the Universe)

+ You now know: how our access to consciousness might be arranged into states, that humanness isn't the peak of evolution, and that we are therefore searching for our awakening (higher consciousness).

You keep in mind:

The **search** states that all human beings strive for happiness but ultimately seek the end of the ego. This search may last an entire lifetime without us becoming aware of it. The *conscious search* begins once we ask "Who am I?," once we suspect a higher truth, and work on our awareness.

The **states of being** are a model describing different conscious ways of living, showing us the evolution that is possible for humanity, and thus serving us as a guidepost towards CONSCIOUSNESS.

WHOLENESS stands for the perception that everything is the source of everything else – which is revealed to us when the mind no longer divides the infinity of LIFE into beginnings or endings. This perception is accompanied by an intense feeling of communion, which may be described as *complete healing*.

Δ *You now can: evaluate your ascent in consciousness, watch out for the traps of unconsciousness, and experiment with overcoming the gap between knowing and feeling.*

12 **Portals**

The portals to our emotions. The touch of reality. The meaning of our feelings. The emotional weight. The human being as a happening. The readiness to change immediately. The right perception for us now. Awakening as our first act. Help in the moment of becoming aware again. The highest surrender.

C onsciousness is like a palace. Holding its keys, we can roam all the rooms and corridors at our leisure. The ocean waves open our eyes to the beauty of our incredibly ancient planet. A crackling campfire directs our attention to the fleeting beauty of a spark. And a moving song immerses us in the beauty of human talent. Not much needs to happen in the world to change everything in our emotions, as though we were traveling to new worlds through magic portals.

The portals and keys are just symbols, of course. In reality, we're already living in a new and magical PRESENT. But because our life doesn't feel that way and is often filled with distractions, we should try to understand the *mechanisms* that open our portals, so we can deliberately roam our palace not just sometimes and briefly but everywhere and anytime.

Some portals open through techniques such as meditation, breathing exercises, or energy work; others open through experiences of exceptional emotional depth. You can begin learning them today, taking a first step or what might feel like the thousandth. Endless possibilities are open to you: You can dance to a silent melody at home, take invisible leaps into the air while walking, deeply inhale good emotions, immerse your eyes in the structure of bread, surround your body with energy, send light to a loved one, search for and find something beautiful, pay attention to the rustling of a blanket, or see the world through the eyes of a newborn.

Seeing means that photons touch our retina. Smelling or tasting means that molecules collide with our smell or taste receptors. Hearing means that sound waves reach our eardrum. And touching means that the vibrations of matter are getting closer to each other. In summary, we can say that all sensory perceptions are a *touch* of REALITY. And therein lies a significant change in perspective.

REALITY doesn't plan that a red rose primarily appeals to our sense of sight, a juicy lemon particularly impresses our sense of taste, or tired legs somehow exhaust our sense of touch. The phenomena in EXISTENCE aren't *subdivided* and broadcast on "specific channels only" but are always *completely* here, in all aspects of REALITY. The division into seeing, hearing, smelling, tasting, or feeling thus exists only in our perception. And that means: Beyond our perception, only one sense exists – the CONSCIOUSNESS that perceives the touch of REALITY.

The red of a rose, the taste of a lemon, the feeling of tired legs, where are they? Your answer may be "within the rose, within the lemon, or within my legs," but these are projections only. If you explore where your sensations are, you won't find them anywhere else but in your CONSCIOUSNESS.

Emotions

Positive thinking is a well-intentioned recommendation. But if you feel the need to think positively, you're *currently feeling negative* and recognize how all new thoughts quickly take on the colors of your prevailing emotions. Thoughts themselves have no colors. "I'm fantastic" can mean anything. And "Oh, my God!" sounds completely different based on your emotional state. Therefore, we shouldn't rely on contradictory recommendations when we're in a bad mood, but just need to remember to *feel* positive.

The inner glow determines the radiated heat. We may pray with high hopes that "please let today be great" or positively think that "today is definitely going to be great," but in both cases, the result is that this great day hasn't actually begun yet. That's why an honest intention unconditionally focuses on the present: "I look forward to today. A lot. And I'm excited about the wonders that await me!" This way of thinking, speaking, and feeling is called "affirmation" and makes use of an influential connection.

Words, ideas, and feelings are connected. The word "tree" unavoidably triggers an imagination, but which one? Do you see a mighty lush tree full of songbirds? Or do you see a bare, dead tree in the icy wind? All imaginations are possible. Yet while unconscious, these imaginations are chosen by habit and decide whether "tree" makes us smile or shiver.

In medical science, improving or worsening our health *by emotions* is described as the placebo effect. We can go one step further, though, and acknowledge CHANGING the PRESENT not as a placebo effect but as CREATION. Should we decide to live a very mindful, cheerful, and joyful life for one week, the impact would be felt clearly, in our mind and body, in our diet, our leisure activities, and even our conversations. And if "fake pills" help us to make this decision, it would only demonstrate the power of our emotions even more clearly.

Medical technology enables us to record and evaluate brainwaves. Sensors pick up electrical impulses and display the results on screens or data recorders. Stress – an area of the brain lights up. Fear – another area flares up. Love – and a different region of the brain is set ablaze. "But what's first," we ask ourselves, "our emotions or the impulses?" And the fact that such questions gained an aura of scientificality should make our brains flicker with amusement. Apparently, as a society, we must re-learn what EMOTIONS truly are:

E1) Emotions aren't located in our brain but are VIBRATIONS of CONSCIOUSNESS, which sometimes seem close to the heart, sometimes seem close to the gut, and often seem to linger in our head. Our brain only functions because its cells have AWARENESS. So whenever brainwaves change, CONSCIOUSNESS was present first. Thus, what the electrodes measure in our heads are *no feelings*, but *biochemical reactions*, which *either* were triggered by a previous EMOTION *or* might cause us to choose a new EMOTION afterward.

E2) A picture is worth a thousand words, but one word allows for thousands of imaginings. The word "emotion" can refer to many matters, so we need to define it precisely.

Should you notice a snake crawling out from under your seat right now, you would probably experience a great fright and might later describe it as an "upsetting emotion." But this description lacks precision. The snake didn't trigger a mental emotion but a physical reaction, which you rated as "upsetting" *after the fact*. By contrast, should you notice right now that you've missed a crucial appointment, you would probably experience a great fright, which can be quite accurately described as a "distraught emotion," as you'll now spend hours pondering the consequences and feeling its physical impact on your heart rate and body.

We must not equate physically triggered sensations with mentally triggered ones. Sometimes the biochemical processes in our body influence our emotions, and sometimes the present emotions influence our body.

E3) EXISTENCE can't be divided into cause and effect. In our language, action and reaction appear to be regulated. Cold air causes goosebumps, for example. So, if scientists claim that "cold air leads to goosebumps," we would immediately agree and firmly reject the reversed statement: "Goosebumps don't lead to cold air."

But if scientists claim that "dopamine leads to well-being," you should think about it first because, in this case, cause and effect aren't hard-wired. *Well-being from dopamine* would only be one kind of well-being, along with countless other kinds that aren't triggered by dopamine, but which (in reverse) might trigger an increase of dopamine in the body.

We must not, therefore, assign predetermined origins to our EMOTIONS as different causes may lead to the same effect.

E4) In reality, EMOTIONS have no names. We certainly have assigned words to some *emotions* – such as fear, joy, or love – so that we can talk about them. But each of these emotional directions resembles an entire "octave" of sensations and may also refer to quite different "tones." Speaking about "joy," looking forward to the *next vacation* is quite different from looking backward at the *last vacation*, and both are quite different from a *pure joy* that permeates our entire PRESENT – all these are different experiences that we haven't named or even felt yet.

What's this feeling that *resonates in us* when our eyes wander across a vast landscape? What's this feeling of spending Christmas under palm trees? What's this feeling that *resonates in us* after we've tidied up our home or decorated it? What's this feeling of being welcomed as a foreigner? And what are these feelings of enjoying a cup of coffee, starting a weekend of book reading, stepping into a new phase of life, sitting on an empty bus, or making the most of a rainy vacation day?

Our everyday life is filled with EMOTIONS we never talk about because we don't have words for them. Some emotions are beautiful and refreshing, while others are unpleasant and disruptive, but this difference doesn't limit their observability. The reality of a feeling isn't revealed by its name, but only when we feel it attentively and without generalizing it.

E5) Our ego strives for more *good* and less *bad* feelings. In the religious domain, a similar distinction is made between righteous and sinful feelings. EXISTENCE, however, doesn't contain feelings of different value but is always genuine, original, and pristine. We must not judge EMOTIONS. We should only evaluate the *unconscious impulse*, the direction in which a feeling pushes our thoughts because it's *these thoughts* that either contaminate our awareness (and our window on reality) or let it become pure again.

Laziness could be a negative emotion. But if you're too lazy to go on a drinking spree, you might have ascended in awareness. A sense of duty could be a positive feeling. But if you dutifully serve the wrong thing, you might have descended in awareness.

A moth burns to death in a flame because it just follows the light. Similarly, a human being may fall into great suffering when blindly following the idea of good or virtuous feelings. And our considerations should take this into account. We mustn't judge emotions as such but only the effect on their observer.

E6) Sometimes, the ego says: "I'm stressed," but WE aren't this feeling of stress. We are only its observer. We're listening to a tune that we ourselves have selected, turned up in volume, and set to repeat. *Stress* can be reliably chosen by attaching to a great many details. *Boredom* requires attaching to the shallow notion that nothing in the world deserves our attention. And *well-being* would only require the realization that both stress and boredom might be fascinating tunes as long as we can unselect them deliberately.

Each EMOTION has a particular VIBRATION, which never changes. Stress, boredom, satisfaction, fear, or love will forever be found in their own specific place, in their own particular vibration. The only thing that changes is our life, according to the tunes we are choosing.

E7) Modern humanity believes in rationality. But a purely rational insight is impossible because, without an *emotional element,* we would be unable to believe that our understanding of something was correct. Thoughts cannot determine their value among each other. Every insight and decision thus builds upon an *emotional weight.*

Not once in your life did you get up for a logical reason. It has always been an emotional weight such as a thirst for action, a sense of duty or boredom, back-ache, or being hungry that made you get up.

"Two plus two equals four" feels right, although it's just an agreement. Being lazy sounds tempting at times, but our experience warns us that we'll regret the consequences later. A sense of duty sounds demanding but promises a later gain. A garden plot sounds like hard work but also like recreation. And so, some thoughts feel wrong, right, or even intelligent depending on the time of day, our mood, or our prior knowledge, but these feelings do not confirm the thought's contents –

they are just the VIBRATION of EXISTENCE at the time of our interpretation.

At the end of the most rational argumentation, the most substantial emotion wins. And knowing this, we can slowly come to understand our nature, our responsibility, and our work.

Act

The ability to lead a fulfilled life doesn't stem from vast knowledge or compelling logic, but purely from learning how to choose the right emotional weight. Should we genuinely believe that emotions are triggered by coincidental biochemical activity in the brain, this would give us an emotion of incapacitation; not because our brainwaves suddenly switch to "incapacitation" but because now, our inner attitude colors our entire perception. We would have incapacitated our SELF.

The human illusion fundamentally involves feeling a sense of separation more strongly than a sense of connection. In awakening, we recognize the cause as OURSELVES and thus change everything. The PRESENT loses all explanations of why things are as they are; as if a hundred sticky notes were torn off from our window on reality. The EXPERIENCE of the world, which arrives in our CONSCIOUSNESS, isn't a result of the PRESENT anymore but IS THE PRESENT as it is unfolding right now. And should we doubt this, we mustn't attribute these doubts to reasoning or great intellectual achievements, as doubts are not a result of the PRESENT either but simply belong to it, without depending on logical explanations.

The cause of human unconsciousness is easy to explain but difficult to accept: A human being doesn't act. A "human being" isn't even able to act, which does not entail disenfranchisement but a correction of perspective. WE are not human beings. In reality, CONSCIOUSNESS is constantly refocusing: Attention is bound and set free and, in our case, feels like a human life. A double-check confirms this: If we were to act intelligently, mindfully, and independently as human beings, then *we would not* consider our thoughts and their contents as our creation, use them as a basis to strive for happiness, and perpetuate a cycle of wrong-doing. But all that is taking place – because, bound in human unconsciousness, we neither do something *for* nor *against* it – which leaves only one possibility. The human state of being is just a HAPPENING.

*

The PRESENT means CHANGE, and this CHANGE includes everything. As human beings, we can't *additionally* add another layer of change here and there. Everything that changes is one layer. Every blink, breath, or smile unfolds together with all of EXISTENCE, just as a butterfly opens its wings in one single motion.

The idea of psychosomatic effects illustrates our erroneous thinking in multiple layers. We declare that the spirit influences the body, making it sick or healthy again. And although that's true, we must take this train of thought through to completion. Without spirit, we couldn't perceive our bodies. Our physical body is therefore a perception in spirit. And as a consequence, every power of the spirit is also contained in the body. We need to appreciate both body and spirit as one layer in whose HAPPENING we can search for healing actions only in a holistic way.

When we throw a thousand pieces of confetti into the wind, this act triggers countless events. EXISTENCE works in quite a similar way. CONSCIOUSNESS chooses an EMOTION, and ten thousand events take their course, some visible to us, but most concealed. Once everything HAPPENS, it's impossible to intervene. We can't make anything undone in retrospect. As long as no new EMOTION is chosen, and no further ACT follows, WE wait in the wind empty-handed, watching.

If the PRESENT feels excellent, why change it? We only need to act to change something. And this ACT requires that we "as human beings" connect with CONSCIOUSNESS, discover our actual preferences, and then find our *readiness to change immediately*:

A master of meditation becomes highly attentive at will, even in everyday situations, and deliberately chooses his feelings. A beginner of meditation, however, waits for a quiet moment, sits down elaborately, closes his eyes, struggles for control, and is torn apart by the effort. And this effort, the most intense feeling within the HAPPENING, must disappear from CONSCIOUSNESS *just like that* – because an ACT by the SELF is never triggered by human intentions but always by letting go of human intentions.[a74]

Surrender

The restless mind, which reveals itself in meditation, isn't an enemy. Water flows along a riverbed *because it exists*. And perception flows through CONSCIOUSNESS *because it exists*. Those who find this exhausting, complain about existence itself, with one thing seemingly not yet accepted:

We can neither stop nor pause our thoughts. Any attempt to try would still be a thought. Any thinker who might want to try this would also remain a thought. As a consequence, our ascent in awareness isn't about mastering thoughts but about admiring their overall impression like confetti in a street parade, and via this change in emotion, awakening to our first conscious ACT.

Meditation teaches us specific ways of letting go of human HAPPENING – to "surrender": by concentrating on our breathing, by cultivating loving-kindness, or by paying attention to our walking. These different techniques increase our expertise in the *perception currently right for us,* as an unchanging perception creates different feelings in changing situations.

In sunny weather, we may gaze off into the distance with delight, enjoying the warmth of the sun, and being aware of contrasting bright colors. But when it rains, this perception would lead to disappointment, so that we shouldn't look for colors but switch to our close-range perceptions and discover an equally intense pleasure: lively water drops

---

[a] Jeanne de Salzmann (The Reality of Being: The Fourth Way of Gurdjieff)

on window panes, leaves dancing and swirling, and all those concentric circles intermingling in the slowly expanding puddles, all of which invite our mind to immerse itself within. Similarly, meditation isn't about experiencing the world passively or actively, but *really* experiencing it with our senses in a multitude of ways, without being distracted by names, concepts, or explanations.

We sit down to meditate, close our eyes, inhale, and exhale deeply. A short while later, we feel something tickling. Inhale deeply. Yes, my little toe tickles. Exhale deeply. What does it feel like, this tickling? Inhale deeply. It feels like something I want to get rid of before I know what it feels like. Exhale deeply. But what does it feel like without wanting to eliminate the sensation? Inhale deeply. It feels as though the need to scratch is steadily increasing! Exhale deeply. But how does it feel without believing in this desire? Inhale deeply. Without attachment, it doesn't feel that bad. Exhale deeply. Now the tickling is a stimulating vibration in consciousness, which currently conceals other possibilities. I'm observing it. Inhale deeply. Now it's gone to make space for other sensations.

*

The realization that our feelings determine our life instills the motivation to choose them deliberately. The hope that our life might change any other way, or merely through external circumstances, would compare to waiting for sand in an endless desert. Everything we need is already here. We already have the aptitude of putting ourselves in any mood through thoughts, colors, sounds, or smells.

Selecting good feelings is like ventilating your home. When the air quality in the living room is poor, quite a few options are available for selection: We might not even notice. We could promptly open the patio doors *without a second thought* and allow fresh air to stream in. We could think about the best sequence in which to open the windows but then not open even one of them. We could think about it for a moment and then tilt some of the windows. Or we could develop a habit of airing our place thoroughly every morning. The point is: When we are aware, without thoughts, positive feelings will come quickly. But when we can't be free of thoughts *immediately*, then the right thoughts can help us *get there*.

Meaningful emotions don't arise from meaningful details but by withdrawing from wanting to know every detail. And when we step back from our thoughts briefly, enabling consciousness to arise, we can choose the next thought ourselves before it happens by itself.

We can spin our thoughts into a direction that brings us closer to a positive emotion, and then practice this direction until we arrive at that emotion. We can *think more generally* and *feel more precisely,* which sounds like this: "I sometimes feel frustrated because things aren't going the way they could. I seem to care about the result, and that's fortunate. Indifference would not make my life better. Motivation is more desirable. I am grateful that I have this motivation. Indeed, I am thankful for being able to feel something like gratitude, because it's a great feeling. I'm incredibly grateful for not having to long for motivation but to have it. And I am thankful that gratitude, just like love, sometimes hurts, when its experience had to wait a long time for its discovery."

Sed Bayu asked his students the following questions to practice general thinking and precise feeling: "What is the greatest of all lights? What is the greatest pilgrimage? Which relationship is best? What is most comforting?" Lalla was the first to answer: "There is no light like that of the sun, no pilgrimage like that to the Ganges. There is no relationship closer than with a brother, and no ease like a wife." Sed Bayu responded: "There is no light like that in the eyes, no pilgrimage like going down on your knees, no relationship like that with one's own pocket, and no comfort like a blanket." But Lalla raised the bar again: "There is no light like that of knowing God, no pilgrimage like a deep longing, no relationship except the one with God, and there is no peace that isn't gratitude for that."[a75]

---

[a] Lalla (Naked Song)

Surely you know sleepless nights full of sorrow, indecision, or guilt. And you may briefly encounter frustration, disappointment, or dissatisfaction in the coming days. But maybe you'll decide on something else: on balance, confidence, or gratitude. We are here to practice it until positive feelings come easy.

Unconsciousness will always contribute negative emotions. Even the best seeker is unconscious from time to time, experiences negative emotions then, and might ask, "Why can't I remain conscious? Why am I not making any progress? Why do trivial problems trap me for hours?" These negative feelings drop off when we accept our contribution to their negativity – and replace it with *this acceptance*. Nobody needs to make a monster out of unconsciousness and thereby become even more unconscious.[a76] What's so wrong with the ego? Who has a problem with it? And don't all emotions, even the ones that feel negative, require our fully conscious presence so they can be perceived?

We seem to regard unconsciousness as a loss of control, as if we need help *before* becoming unconscious, to prevent it just in time. But this isn't true. We need help in the moment of BECOMING AWARE, help with where our gaze is turning to right NOW. And this realization triggers a great surrender, a falling upwards, a letting go of all resistance, and an acceptance that we cannot act as human beings.

This EXPERIENCE will CHANGE the HAPPENING and will let OUR SELF ACT.

---

[a] Friedrich Nietzsche (Beyond Good and Evil)

+ You now know: that being human is a happening, that all meaning lies within our emotions, and that there's a perception that's right *for us* in every situation.

You keep in mind:

The **emotional weight** describes the "winning feeling" in a consideration. In every decision-making process, the option that triggers the "weightiest feeling" within us ultimately wins. Without this emotional element, all choices or decisions would be impossible.

HAPPENING explains that our LIFE as human beings only *happens* because (and as long as) the SELF is unconscious. That's why humans aren't able to act. Only CONSCIOUSNESS can act.

An **ACT** describes an intervention into the HAPPENING by sparking a conscious emotional change within CONSCIOUSNESS (which is caused from beyond the ego). Such an ACT requires our total surrender, which involves that WE drop all imaginations, let go of all resistance, and accept that we cannot act as human beings.

The **portals** stand for techniques or experiences that help us to become very attentive and to choose our feelings deliberately. The biggest portals are the Now, Death, and Love.

Δ *You now can: look for help in the moment of becoming aware, find the readiness to change immediately, and select the emotional weight in your life more attentively.*

13 Now

The proof of the eternal Now. Our use of contradicting systems of logic. The anthropic principle. The present as a mirror. Walking in the Now. The idea of hidden knowledge. The past as a road or tower. The Now as the only original. The nature of memories. Coincidence and synchronicity.

Whenever misfortune strikes us, it had to happen "right now, today of all days." Something beautiful or even ordinary happens "right now" as well – we just don't notice it in the same way. And this principle doesn't change. The NOW never passes, it never elapses, but stays HERE forever, to create a continuous story from continuous impressions. No matter how convincing the illusion of the past, the future, and its chronology may seem, it is created NOW without ever being able to leave its PRESENT.

"I kind of understand that past and future are conceptions in eternal CHANGE only," we might feel right now, "yet unquestionable evidence would help."

This unquestionable evidence has long been given but competes with the impression we have that it isn't sufficient. Letting go of a deeply ingrained illusion seems unbearable to us. As a consequence, the evolution of our worldview doesn't need more facts but rather the permission to adjust to higher truths.

The proof of the eternal NOW is, (first) that neither future nor past was ever found in reality, (second) that all units of time, be they minutes, hours, or eons, are human creations, (third) that we would interpret the PRESENT quite differently without the concept of time, (fourth), that we also experience memories only in the PRESENT, (fifth) that our impression of the past doesn't prove a past *in this exact form*, (sixth) that EXISTENCE has no beginning and no end and thus is *timeless*, and (seventh) that the PRESENT and its endlessness are proven by this moment "right now."

Mathematics demonstrates that using contradicting systems of logic is standard. Within finite numbers, "A = A" is a certainty, while within infinity, "B ≠ B" becomes quite possible. Yet if logic A is only valid in the morning (and not in the evening) and logic B is only valid in the evening (and not in the morning), then both thought-systems are invalid when based on a full day. Therefore, we mustn't consider the axioms of mathematics as absolutely solid truths but as "locally valid tools," which, despite contradictions, are of great use in the hands of experts. A carpenter's hammer is made for driving nails into walls and also, if necessary, for pulling them out again.

In a similar way, our mind isn't made for thinking exclusively in terms of "past and future." We should think "in time" only when required and then, when it isn't necessary, rest in the timelessness of CONSCIOUS-NESS, without feeling that setting this *tool* aside is wrong or conflicting.

Mirror

The anthropic principle states that humanity can only look into the starry sky because the universe is compatible to the creation of life – which ultimately implies that otherwise, if incompatible, no observers would exist. But this view of life forgets one fundamental axiom: EXISTENCE is always present. And that means: The PRESENT and CONSCIOUSNESS cannot cease. A non-presence, a non-existence, or *pockets* of life and non-life belong exclusively to our imagination, yet have nothing in common with reality. The universe doesn't need lucky coincidences to allow for sentient life because, in the PRESENT, there's always an observer looking at the starry sky, reading a book, or just experiencing LIFE. Within this sensation, EXISTENCE holds one *absolute* and an infinite number of *relative* components: We don't know what's being experienced, but we know that it's happening due to the absence of alternatives. So there is no anthropic (human) principle in reality; instead, there is a *cosmic axiom* stating that consciousness is *always present*.

EXISTENCE looks into ITSELF and sees the EXISTENCE. We see nothing other than us. The PRESENT is a mirror, so to speak. Its reflection is mostly incomplete, veiled, in constant motion – and therefore looks like a physical reality with height, width, and depth; it also seems to contain memories, experiences, and knowledge. But wherever we look, we inevitably look straight into a mirror.

✳

I would like to suggest an exercise for you called "Walking in the Now." It only requires a stroll and works like this:

"I'm going for a walk. My gaze is on the ground, and my attention is directed inwards. The path ahead and behind me somehow symbolizes my life because, honestly, I often think that the past is behind me while the future comes closer with every step.

I remember, though, that both past and future exist only as ideas in the PRESENT. With this in mind, I imagine that there's *nothing* behind me *anymore*. With every step, the last moment and everything lying behind me drops into a void, into nothingness. As soon as my foot lifts from the ground, there's no going back. The nothingness follows me now and dramatically affects my feelings. I even feel slightly scared to turn around and directly look at the emptiness, but there is also something compelling to it. I feel that my thoughts about the past don't stay behind but come along *with me* and that emotions associated with them weigh heavily on my shoulders, like a backpack I hadn't bothered to sort out for years.

I stride forward and understand that we're leading a life on an *eternal wave*. The present never falls apart. Then I slip off the backpack and let it fall. It disappears in the void behind me, together with my past. My shoulders relax and grow surprisingly light. I become acutely conscious and enjoy the Now, in which one foot is continuously placed in front of the other.

Soon, I have the feeling that a sense of time is wanting to return. My unconscious and automatic mind pleads for me to do something meaningful again, like chasing my desires – but I push aside these thoughts and slowly raise my eyes. Nothing lies behind me, but what lies ahead? NOW I AM HERE; I feel that. But where will I be in a minute? I examine the path in front of me and then imagine my future self very clearly, how it walks ahead and has already reached that gnarled tree by the side of the path. How is it going to feel? I decide to pay close attention once I reach this waypoint.

I reach the waypoint and sense into myself. NOW I AM HERE. Strange but not unexpected. I and NOW haven't changed. No matter how many times I repeat this: No future me will ever feel different. And having arrived at this attentive state of mind, I'm no longer walking through the world as a person. I'm moving through a person as the moment."

Original

Human illusion arises from a blend of consciousness and unconsciousness. The unconscious part of our perception indicates that we miss certain truths about reality – more than we actually should miss. And this fact reveals that there is *hidden knowledge for human beings*. The idea of occult, supernatural, and concealed knowledge is entirely rational, not in the sense of shady secret societies, but in the sense of hidden knowledge becoming accessible through our increasing awareness.

Take material possessions, for example. We may blindly strive for our possessions or identify with them. We may discover through more mindfulness that possessions aren't making us happy, but only slightly shift the reasons for our suffering. We may understand that we truly own nothing in the world. We may understand that we will lose all attachments with death. And in a moment of even greater awareness, we will see that *right now*, we aren't taking anything with us into the PRESENT, either.

CONSCIOUSNESS alone exists in the PRESENT, forever refocusing. Who knows what significance we'll ascribe to our material possessions next year? Their value may appear quite different then. But even if all possessions lost their value by next year, we would still have everything that gives time, money, or diamond rings their importance. I am still here.

∗

Attentiveness means an instantaneous letting go of thoughts, concepts, and attachments, including letting go of the future, past, or our memories thereof. The ego doesn't want these identifications taken away. It's going to interpret *letting go of the past* as a "denial of reality," which will then prevent more profound attentiveness. For this reason, one phase of the search is acquiring a parental mind mode, in which the random calls of the ego no longer distract us.

Our ego says, for example: "I was born many years ago and have experienced a lot. My memories of the past show that all these things happened for real." And this statement is conceptually correct. Nobody questions this description of reality. But since we want to experience the PRESENT without concepts, we've already moved one step ahead: It's no longer about concepts and their correctness.

Who is this "I," and what do these "years" mean? We could question our concepts endlessly. We could prove that, in reality, "years" don't exist, that an "I that was born" only refers to our body, and that our true I was certainly not born just some years ago. But we've already moved one step ahead: We don't want the ego to get defensive and then argue to "have spoken in concepts only" while in fact getting more attached to its concepts. We want to spark an unprecedented change of perspective and perceive EXISTENCE highly attentively without a single concept.

If a person generally feels unhappy, it's essential for him to *realize just once* that he is not unhappy by nature but that he *chooses* this feeling deliberately – then, every future experience of negative emotions will be entirely transformed for him. If CONSCIOUSNESS generally feels like a human being bound in time, it's essential for CONSCIOUSNESS to *realize just once* that it isn't bound to past and future by nature – then, from this moment on, WE may talk about our past and future as always, but its experience will be entirely transformed for us.

Human beings (△3) conceive the past like a road extending *behind them*, whose length they've traveled. But the transcendent consciousness (△4) conceives the past like a tower *within itself*, whose floors it may visit. The step *out* of human time *into* the eternal PRESENT raises the horizontal understanding of time vertically, so past and future suddenly stand firmly in the PRESENT.

Our ego feels that it is ever-changing. But our SELF doesn't change. WE are HERE NOW, along with memories and intentions that accompany us through the PRESENT. Yes – our memories are real. Our plans for the future are precious. All information, all our knowledge, all our wisdom is only available because we have acquired it. Our whole life is based on it. We must use this experience and *learn from it* – but without *rehashing negative emotions yet again*. Because the decision for recapping our past suffering or envisioning our future sorrows would inexcusably take place in the PRESENT.

The PRESENT is never the result of the past. *In its result,* it is always the current interaction of consciousness and a greater or lesser degree of unconsciousness.[a77]

*

Memories are real experiences in the NOW, which recap the REALITY we've experienced, at least when telling the truth. If I tell you that yesterday's rainfalls turned all trails into mud tracks, you'd likely agree that it's best to wear sturdy shoes today. And if you tell me that you have traveled the world ten years ago, then I'm unlikely to doubt that but will listen to you with interest. Yet:

---

[a] Bashar (Blueprint for Change)

If five people recall the same situation and all five memories are different, have there been five different realities? Did things that no one remembers anymore never actually happen? And are memories always based on actual courses of events? The answer is: We can't assert to know REALITY by referring to our memories. We can only assert to know our *human perception* of REALITY. And that means: We can remember our experiences even without attaching to the past.

Our memories aren't permanently present; they aren't like photos at an art exhibition but only appear in consciousness upon thinking in specific directions; they often contain just fragments of the original experience and might even trigger quite different feelings in retrospect. Previous problems become funny stories. The downsides that ended a relationship are forgotten faster than the upsides. And above all, it's the repetition of anecdotes that keeps our memories fresh – not because memories are literally refreshed but because we now keep additional "new repetitions" in our mind.

A rose is not really a rose. Considering this, we shouldn't be surprised that the past is not really the past.

Every moment is an original that can only be perceived once, even when it's seemingly composed of an everyday experience, a repetitive sensation, or a continuing situation. It's as if the *Mona Lisa* appears for a moment and then disappears forever, as if the *Last Supper* and then the *Starry Night* and then the *Girl with a Pearl Earring* show themselves and then disappear forever. The EXPERIENCE of EXISTENCE doesn't repeat itself, it "doesn't bring back even one thing" because something past can't just wait outside of the PRESENT to be brought back later.

We may deal with the uniqueness of CONTRAST as always, of course. "The weekend was excellent, as always. Tomorrow I'll get up, as always. My worldview remains unchanged, as always." But the basis of these statements is that they are spoken out *right now* and shift our original experience into a different context. We may also consider the uniqueness of CONTRAST as something coincidental. But in the end, every experience means that *something coincides with us*, namely, a unique incident impossible without us.

Our world is comprised of events, which are never coincidental or repetitive but rarely reveal their unique and coexisting nature.

We regard something as "synchronicity" when the connectedness of everything reveals itself to us – when events occur just after we think of them, and we ask ourselves whether this was merely coincidence or whether we somehow foresaw the future. And no matter how strange our considerations may seem in these moments – we should know that we're not acting as a little human being. EXISTENCE always acts as a whole, even if one aspect of these actions consists of not-noticing the connectedness.

*

The NOW can't be contemplated enough. No matter where we are: Our eyes can turn in ten thousand directions. We can follow one direction and take a closer look. And from any point along this path, we can look in another ten thousand directions, constantly keeping in mind that CONSCIOUSNESS is always present, the PRESENT is always now, and the NOW is always original – which makes EXISTENCE into an eternal simultaneity. The present in which I am writing these lines is the same present in which you are reading these lines. The Now, in which you're putting this book aside, is the same Now, in which you're opening it again. And the moment of your birth is the same as ten million years from now.

But even though we are using several words to describe the NOW as eternal, always new, and simultaneous, it shouldn't suggest several properties. EXISTENCE is simply here, without beginning or end. And if we recognize within it a chronology between yesterday and today, a blossom emerging from a bud, or that our life unerringly moves towards death, then this is nothing but our present explanation.

+ You now know: that even contradicting tools have their purpose, that some realizations may only be discovered through greater awareness, and that every evidence first has to conquer our emotions.

You keep in mind:

Synchronicity describes simultaneous events that, from a *logical perspective,* can't be connected but, from *our perspective,* appear directly connected. Regardless of whether we believe in this connection or not, our thoughts won't uncover the truth. All things in EXISTENCE are definitely connected. And for this reason, as our awareness increases, our discovery of "coincidences that can't be coincidences" also increases – or in other words, we discover magic.

Walking in the Now is an exercise you should try.

Δ *You now can: look into the present like into a mirror, appreciate the present moment as the only original, and perceive your sense of time as a "tower in the Now."*

14 Death

Our fear of death. The soul and the self. Beginnings and endings as observations in life. The big mix-up. The five phases of death. Awakening as resurrection from the dead. Rebirth as the continuum of life. The search for the end of the ego.

D eath accompanies us throughout our life. We fear our *end*, ignore the possibility of losing a loved one, and even avoid thinking about its significance. We have won a journey but now feel troubled by the wind in our hair. Human beings, Lao Tzu explains, are too entangled in their living to contemplate death.[a78] This ignorance shouldn't be whitewashed as a voluntary decision or a positive way of thinking. Every positive, voluntary, and honest life includes the certainty that we will die, that no evil motives reside in this natural process, and that a world without death wouldn't add more purpose. And *after* these certainties have been sincerely received within our being, we'll still have enough time for the latest sports results, the latest gossip, increased stock prices, the scratch on our car, fabulous fashion, a weighty book, mail that needs filing, or the best remedies for imminent boredom.

Fear of death has many facets, origins, and intensities, which you'll hardly notice while quietly reading right now. But you know which fear we're talking about because the brain does not distinguish between reality and imagination. "You only have two days to live," your doctor just said. Did he really say these words? How would it feel – no, how *does it feel* when only days, months, or years remain? And most significantly, would it be okay to die right now? Oh, how the ego wants to flee from these imaginings, only to postpone the realizations that we will gain.

---

[a] Lao Tzu (Tao Te Ching, Verse 75)

Hoping for a life after death is a widespread phenomenon with diverse expressions: that our soul ascends to heaven, that our soul is reborn, or that medical progress embeds our soul into immortal bodies. But as inventive as human beliefs may be, we must put our trust in *something more than that*.

Our SELF is not our body, mind, or personality; the SELF is free from all things. In our imagination, however, our soul has our personality, as if memories, habits, and aspirations were stored within it. So two possibilities arise, both leading to the same realization. Either we consider our soul and our SELF as two different things, which renders the soul a bland fantasy. Or we consider soul and SELF as identical – and detach our personality from it. In a terrifying way, this means: Our personality won't survive death. But in an uplifting way, this means: Our SOUL certainly continues to exist. CONSCIOUSNESS is always present. And this fact challenges our worldview to the limit. We no longer know what death is meant to be.

Death isn't an experience but the description of an experience. We see that a change ends because the CHANGE doesn't end. The hourglass runs empty, and someone shouts "Stop!" because the observation continues and recognizes no more sand crystals trickling down. Speculating what to expect in death is therefore unnecessary. Should we continue to experience something, we wouldn't be dead – and *experiencing nothing* would be an impossibility in itself. Every living being originates from something real: EXISTENCE. And nothing real can cease to exist because going elsewhere is not a possibility for the PRESENT. Therefore, an inwardly observable death can be excluded. The MOSAIC is entirely immortal.

We only know an outwardly observed death, the departure from an embodiment, the end of an original form. These words aren't meant to diminish our emotions of grief, loss, and love; they are profoundly justified. Our considerations merely put things into perspective. All concepts that "move into the world through the mind" will one day "move out of the world through the mind" again. A day begins and ends, yet in reality, no day has begun or ended. It was but a concept. Sometimes, we may describe this movement as birth, sometimes we may call it death, and talk about them like opposites, but their direction stays the same.

When a human being dies, we should never forget (first) that the concept of a human being consists of much less than what was truly present, (second) that a whole world ceased to exist, (third) that the value of a world cannot be measured, (fourth) that whatever ended was not the SELF, and (fifth) that without human finiteness, human experience would have no meaning. And if we can already see this higher truth now, that death takes away less than we thought, and life gives more than we previously thought – then our emotional world significantly deepens. We discover that there are more important things than immortality.

Every fear requires a known, felt, or imagined threat. But death can neither be known, felt, nor imagined, which reveals that our fear of death is a great mix-up. We are not able to fear it at all. What we do fear is the question: "If I die now, when have I lived?" And the realization of this mix-up leads to a shock. Our fear of death is the fear of never having lived. We knew this all along. EXISTENCE didn't abandon ITSELF but made us feel quite clearly that human striving, worrying, and suffering does not yet constitute LIFE. Consequently, we must replace all "hopes for a life after death" with the "intention of living before dying."

Anyone who thinks that life is short, dreary, or empty could say the same about piano scores. White paper with black lines and dots is awfully dull. But piano scores aren't made for the eyes but for making music, which then unfolds its beauty: in a melody, in chords and verses, joined by other instruments or voices, in a dance, or quiet enjoyment. And just like that, LIFE isn't made for the ego but for SELF, which then unfolds its beauty: in an incredibly intense EXCITEMENT of being here, in LIFE.

*

Our understanding of human mortality is illustrated by the "five phases of death," which evaluate whether we are in denial, anger, negotiation, depression, or acceptance while facing death. These phases represent an increasing withdrawal from the human illusion because it's only our *ego* which denies reality, gets angry about it, suddenly wants to negotiate with fate, or lets us fall into depressive feelings, but then slowly dissolves on our way to acceptance.

The first phase, denial, has two parts, namely the time *before* and the time *after* realizing that we're already in the process. Our dying has already begun. We won't turn into a "dying being" sometime later but are born as such. And only denial (the first phase of dying) would explain not knowing this very well.

We can spend an entire life in denial. Our life could well end in anger, bargaining with fate, or overwhelmed by negative feelings. But it could also end in deep awareness.

People who have accepted their death and surrendered all fear, report that they perceived the world with absolute clarity like never before, that suddenly the leaves magically rustled in the wind, the birds sang their most beautiful songs, the sun softly caressed their skin, that water tasted like wine, or a deep breath turned into the highest pleasure. Both body and mind shifted into a direct perception of reality. This awareness, however, wasn't caused by being close to death, but by being distant to the ego. The ego strives for extraordinary experiences that make us happy for a short time. But the realization of life's shortness and exceptionality fulfills us in eternity.

Resurrection

The highest surrender, the letting go of the ego, is both death and birth. A dream ends, but EXISTENCE ITSELF opens its eyes. "The one who believes in me [in CONSCIOUSNESS] will live, even though they die," says Jesus, "and whoever lives by believing in me [in CONSCIOUSNESS] will never die." "I am the resurrection and the life."[a79] And these words unite the Christian resurrection and the spiritual awakening into one and the same experience. Jesus doesn't speak of a resurrection after a physical death. He speaks of an immediate ascension to GOD with the crucifixion of the ego. "No one can see the kingdom of God unless they are born again." And when Nicodemus asks how a person can be born when they are old, Jesus makes it very clear: "Surely they cannot enter a second time into their mother's womb to be born! Very truly I tell you, no one can enter the kingdom of God unless they are born of water and the Spirit. Flesh gives birth to flesh, but the Spirit gives birth to spirit."[b80]. And Rumi explains: "Our words and actions take place on this side of the veil. O soul, when the veil is gone, we are gone."[c81]

"Tell us, what will be our end?" the disciples asked. But Jesus replied: "What do you know of the beginning, so that you now seek the end? Where the beginning is, the end will also be. Blessed are those who abide in the beginning, for they will know the end and will not taste death."[d82] "Therefore keep watch, because you do not know on what day your Lord [the AWAKENING to SELF] will come. But understand this: If the owner of the house had known at what time of night the thief [unconsciousness] was coming, he would have kept watch and would not have let his house [awareness] be broken into. So you also must be ready, because the Son of Man [the AWAKENING from being human] will come at an hour when you do not expect."[e83]

The "return" of Christ as the Messiah isn't about the second coming of one human being but the migration of humanity out of its suffering, other-directedness, and self-suppression.[f84] This migration is our task.

---

[a] John 11:25-26 (NIV)
[b] John 3:3-6 (NIV)
[c] Rumi (In the Arms of the Beloved)
[d] Gospel of Thomas (Logion 18)
[e] Matthew 24:42-44 (NIV)
[f] Bashar (Blueprint for Change)

Jesus teaches: "Be passersby."[a85] Pass by your own story! The illusion of a living person must die, so the LIFE behind it may be discovered. And when WE live then, we must die again in every moment. Every identification must be given up again, whatever it contains, even if it's the fear of never-having-lived even once.

"Blessed are the poor in spirit," says Jesus, "for theirs is the kingdom of heaven."[b86] And this *signifier* of possessing nothing in spirit doesn't imply poverty, loneliness, or stupidity but expresses the fundamental Buddhistic idea of being without attachment.[c87] Buddha explains that whoever wants to achieve the highest, fully awakened spirit needs to abandon all ideas, must not even rely on ideas about sounds, smells, tastes, feelings, and thoughts yet without ever believing that their perception doesn't exist, is an illusion, or doesn't belong to life.[d88]

In the vastness of the universe, in a small solar system of the Milky Way, on a blue planet called Earth, a child is born, but this doesn't create new CONSCIOUSNESS – instead, a new perspective is created in EVERYTHING THAT IS. LIFE is continually being reborn in the MOSAIC. This rebirth doesn't suggest a reincarnation in the future; it can be understood as a continuum with infinite possibilities of entering, as nothing travels from past to future, but all things remain right in the PRESENT.

✻

Death is one phase in our search, where we voluntarily or forcibly let go of all attachments until just the SELF remains. As seekers, we are initially unaware and wouldn't understand the need to steer towards our ego's demise. One day, though, we will reach the edge of our mind and look down into EVERYTHING and NOTHING. And in that moment, our ego gets scared to the core, wants to flee, and wishes it never had

---

[a] Gospel of Thomas (Logion 42)
[b] Matthew 5:3 (KJV)
[c] P. D. Ouspensky (A New Model of the Universe)
[d] Diamond Sutra

ventured out on the search, but it is too late. We've gone one step too far and recognize the infinite voluntariness within EXISTENCE, in which being human is an experience we would choose again immediately.

+ You now know: that existence is immortal, that we're seeking the death of our ego, and that this loss of attachment is a resurrection to life.

You keep in mind:

The **fear of death** is the fear of never having lived.

Δ *You now can: accept your inevitable outer death, take a closer look at what you fear about it, and progressively let go of the illusions that seem to be your life.*

15 Love

Her presence. The near enemies. Our separation and combination of existence. Unconditional love. The duality of the One. Letting go of mental objects. The cosmic nature of love. Altruism as nearness to reality. The secret of our tears.

L ove – will we ever meet her through contemplation? Can we touch her face merely through physical closeness? Can we embrace her full magnitude with just our arms? You need to confirm something *within yourself* right now: Any attempt to reflect about love requires an emotion that is *near to her*. You can't encounter love while angry, tired, or agitated, right after a disappointment, when falling asleep, or working with full concentration. You must feel at home, arrived, and aware of what's important in life.

Rumi explains: "If someone asks, 'How does it feel to be slain by love?', close your eyes and tear open your shirt, like this."[a89] Eyes see what's in their field of vision. And the heart feels whichever sensations flow through your consciousness. You should thus confirm how close you feel to love or, in case she seems distant, perceive her presence right behind you.

Duality

Love is regarded nowadays as understood but often not yet attained. We think we know the feeling of love *because it's missing*. Society even provides standards of where to search for love, be it in marriage, at parties, or through dating sites, which can't guarantee and could indeed stop us from discovering LOVE in all her depth. Of course, we know those butterflies in our stomach when falling in love. Of course, we know that shortness of breath in the heart when going separate ways again. But this understanding rarely allows us access to a much greater reality.

---

[a] Rumi (In the Arms of the Beloved)

Our ego can't love anything: It merely leaves us clinging to imaginations held dearly. Only when truly "rooted and grounded in love," Jesus explains, will we comprehend the true meaning of space and time and realize what transcends all knowledge, so that GOD completes us.[a][90]

*

Every emotion, as they say in Buddhism, has a near enemy that may cause great harm if undiscovered.[b][91] Indifference could be mistaken for serenity, blind ambition could seem like motivation, and pity might suggest compassion, even though each of these emotions are fundamentally opposite in their sensation, *sound,* and *tone:* Indifference excludes, whereas serenity remains open. Blind ambition is selfish, hectic, and rigid, whereas motivation leads in a mutual direction. And pity elevates oneself over others, whereas compassion remains at eye level. The difference reveals itself in the "algebraic sign" of events. Negative emotions, the near enemy, separates people from each other, while positive emotions bring us closer together.

LOVE also has near enemies. There is, for example, the idea that love must follow a preset path instead of revealing itself in its uncontrollable nature. There is, for example, the expectation that partnerships require a constant giving and taking rather than being a deliberate journey. And there is, for example, the dependency to hold on even to questionable relationships instead of plunging into life without hesitation.

But the nearest enemy of LOVE is FEAR, which is why we often associate love with suffering. In an unconscious way, we already know that one day we'll be deservedly disappointed by our ego's strange imaginations – for as long as our true intentions remain in the dark. FEAR clings on, polarizes the environment, and ignores the truth. But LOVE embraces, calms the environment, and looks beneath the surface of things. For this reason, discovering LOVE is directly connected with discovering the SELF.

---

[a] Ephesians 3:17-19 (KJV)
[b] Jack Kornfield (Meditation for Beginners)

*

All CREATION appears to be full of contrasts because we have creativity. Just like water *knows* how to freeze when it is cold, and ice *knows* how to thaw when it is warm, we know how to *create* mental objects and *let them go* again, to fill EXISTENCE with more differences or similarities.

A rose can be divided into a stem with thorns, leaves, and a blossom. The blossom can be subdivided into a receptacle, sepals, petals, stamens, and carpels. And the carpels, also called pistils, can be further separated into ovaries, stigma, and stylus. But equally, one hundred roses become one garden, many gardens become one suburb, several suburbs become one city, one region, one country, one continent, one Earth, one solar system, one galaxy, and finally an entire universe. This unfolding and collapsing of the world arises within the same truth. REALITY doesn't change because of this. All divisions, combinations, and oppositions are purely within us.

Everything *that's created* requires learning; this includes our language, for example, all our knowledge, or the ego. We don't inherit it just by being born. Yet everything *that's creating* is just there within us, it acts, it happens. But why?

EXISTENCE experiences ITSELF; on the one side, it's the *observer*, and on the other side, it's the *observation*; both are facing each other (as symbolized by Yin and Yang), and yet both are complementing, creating, and sustaining one another forever. That's the duality of the One. But the *observer* may come up with the idea of further separating his *observation*: into an objective outer world and a subjective inner life – into a cosmos and a soul. That's the Trinity of the One. Christianity describes it as "Father, Son, and the Holy Spirit." Buddhism describes it as "the truth, its manifestation come true, and its possibilities still unfulfilled." We may understand it as the I, the body, and the psyche, which create a *mind* and its dialogue within us. And this mind then lets us discover ten thousand differences within the MOSAIC.[a92]

Some people identify more with the "bad things" in life, while others identify more with the "good things." But ultimately, our love must belong to the possibility of identifying with all things. The entire creative process *unconditionally* deserves our gratitude – because just by using it, we can change everything without pre-conditions.

"You will only ever have two choices: LOVE or FEAR. Choose love, and don't ever let fear turn you against your playful heart."[b93] Unconditional love never means simply to accept everything that happens in your life; it suggests quite to the contrary that you unconditionally feel which emotions are presently there and then act in LOVE.

*

Our *separation* of CONTRAST into many differences doesn't create a reality in which some things deserve less love or more hate. All opposites exist on one level, just like the colors of a painting. The canvas may show a person engrossed in reading a book, but this doesn't make the colors indicating the human silhouette more valuable than the colors making up the book and environment.

So if you think you are currently reading a book, then the EXPERIENCE consists of precisely this situation but without any difference between you, the book, and your environment. Even if your thoughts say otherwise, the principle doesn't change. The canvas *you now look at* shows an environment from ego-perspective, a book in your hands, and thought-bubbles arising in front of it.

A child who learns the basics of multiplication must first get used to a lot of information; it has to create *inner formations* of mental objects like thought-bubbles because numbers aren't a natural part of reality. First of all, the spoken "five" is quite different from the written "5," and

---

[a] Lao Tzu (Tao Te Ching, Verse 42)
[b] Jim Carrey

neither is in any way equal to "2+3." Getting used to mental objects is an unavoidable part of the process of learning. Even as adults, we'll continue to create new concepts within our minds, or (with just as much energy) close off our minds to avoid getting used to them.

Using mental objects can be compared to juggling. Even a perfect juggler still requires some level of concentration not to drop any balls, torches, or swords. So if you need to buy tomatoes, milk, cheese, butter, ciabatta, olive oil, red wine, and eleven roses for this evening, then this intention *creates* quite a familiar information in your mind but nevertheless requires concentration not to forget any of it. You need to continuously juggle all the information (or write a grocery list) so that you don't *let go* of any details earlier than necessary.

Letting go of information doesn't mean that you lose or forget knowledge, but that the contents of an information currently play no role in your consciousness (such as "tomatoes are nightshade plants" or "red wine is best enjoyed at 16°C, which is 61°F"). The *creation* of information means the opposite, namely that mental objects are pushed in front of the PRESENT and potentially play a significant role. You step into a flower shop, look at a white orchid, and immediately start to think: "Oh, what a beautiful flower, so white, soft, and nicely shaped. And its sweet scent. I want this flower in my living room!" so that all your newly created information has long moved in front of the flower and has moved yourself away from its true nature.

Nearness

Permanently having *many attachments* in mind makes life more complicated. The best example: We create the mental object "Other people are more beautiful, wealthier, or more influential than me," and immediately, our life has become more complicated. EXISTENCE has removed itself from ITSELF, so its PRESENT is now filled with negative feelings of insecurity, helplessness, or sorrow. The mental object "I'm better than others" brings arrogance, unconsciousness, and separation into our life and prevents us from getting to know other people. And even the mental object "I have the most amazing life, friends, and holidays" fills the PRESENT with ever-increasing expectations. Such a complicated life, in which we're consistently attached to many thoughts, is often overshadowed by FEAR.

Having *few attachments* in mind makes life easier. The SELF doesn't divide ITSELF but remains near to EXISTENCE, so its PRESENT is now filled with positive feelings. A life in which we let go of many attachments, therefore, is often imbued with LOVE. In these light-hearted moments, we can forget a disagreement, discover common ground, or create something for the pure joy of it, even if it's writing an epic story of a thousand pages.

In the outside world, moving between opposites is normal. Water freezes, ice melts. The fireplace warms the room, an open window brings in fresh air. We plan holiday trips down to the smallest detail, but unplanned moments make up the most abiding memories. With regard to our inner life, this poses the question: Can we accept both polarities, the *creating* and the *letting go* of mental objects, as normal, necessary, and even meaningful?

I'm asking because human life is complicated. We hold on to many attachments. We lack LOVE. You probably understand now what that means. In human striving, "creating information" plays far too big a role, and "letting go of information" plays far too small a role. Reality thus moves into the far distance, imaginations *twist* in its place, and make *twisted* ideas seem plausible.

We may sometimes say that love "is blind." But in this world, nothing sees more clearly than LOVE. It's only our awareness that's blinded and distracted at times. We may also believe in a scientific way that love "only contributes to the survival instinct of a species." But does the sun shine for the sole purpose of our survival? The sun was here before us. The survival instinct of life was here before us. And in the same way,

LOVE was always here, waiting for our conscious discovery, so that we may evolve into a civilization that's about more than just surviving.[a94]

But our most twisted idea might be that we somehow *let go* of love and now need to *create* it again. We expose this idea by looking at the ego, how it goes treasure-hunting for love, how it tries to dig out love, and then wants to polish it like a rough diamond. But it's not LOVE that comes and goes like this. It's you. You leave or enter LOVE.

EXISTENCE is conscious. Once its CONSCIOUSNESS perceives this, once it recognizes itself *in the next person*, an infinite mirror effect arises in its emotions, an absolute resonance emanates from the SELF, and this VIBRATION resounds in concert with all creation – that is LOVE: deep and dear, reviving and overwhelming, stunning and moving, gripping and uplifting, captivating and liberating, healing and tearing, like "a wound where the light enters you,"[b95] reducing all human attachments to insignificance.

✻

Love is the most powerful emotion. It incorporates great closeness but also great separation and grief. When we love someone, we were given an irreplaceable jewel to take care of temporarily. But this treasure isn't ours. It's the experienced enrichment that belongs to us.[c96] And in this honest vulnerability, we discover a long lost secret: The emotion we call "love for a person" and the emotion we call "mourning for a person" are *one and the same feeling*. The difference only lies in the story we're telling, which either talks about "self-pity for a loss suffered" or "gratitude for a gain received."

The PRESENT is made to be felt without story, protection, or distance, which requires great courage. LOVE shows its enrichment in gain and loss – joy and pain. Our ego merely looks for a twisted love *without pain*

---

[a] P. D. Ouspensky (Tertium Organum)
[b] Rumi
[c] Paulo Coelho (Like the Flowing River)

and thus receives a love *without gain*. Consequentially, we need to go beyond the ego to feel which things we can trust, and which things we need to mistrust. A rose is not really a rose. Any preconditions for love are not really preconditions for love. We shouldn't trust concepts. But LOVE is LOVE – you can trust in that unconditionally.

Selfless love ultimately means letting go of the ego. But along with the ego, all attachments to loved ones must be dropped as well. That's why we doubt. The task seems contradictory. How could we possibly surrender our attachments to loved ones? Yet if our connection to CONSCIOUSNESS, PRESENT, and EXCITEMENT doesn't come first, we have nothing to *give* to our loved ones. Jesus teaches: Who loves the idea of a daughter, a son, a father, or a mother more than reality, isn't able to feel their true value.[a][97] And the Buddha teaches: Who wants to give rise to the highest, most fulfilled, awakened mind should perceive that all beings need to be led to the shore of awakening, but that after all beings have awakened, in truth, not a single being has been awakened.[b][98]

You must accept at great risk and without safety that LOVE requires a constant *letting go*, while any FEAR of letting go reveals a *creation* of attachments right now. And when the SELF realizes that it stands just *in between*, you'll finally feel the natural state of your heart, as it opens up like the greatest of all portals and invites the entire cosmos in.

---

[a] Matthew 10:37-39 (NIV)
[b] Diamond Sutra

+ You now know: that love represents nearness to reality, that her sensation is a cosmic potential, and that the human illusion removes us from it.

You keep in mind:

FEAR is a VIBRATION that makes us feel as if we're not "really" alive. It's an intense attachment to thoughts, and thus it's the cause of all human striving, worrying, and suffering. FEAR is also the near enemy of LOVE, when we confuse separation anxiety with deep connectedness, for example.

LOVE is the most powerful VIBRATION and, therefore, the most powerful ACT in the universe. It changes everything. WE OURSELVES feel like LOVE when CONSCIOUSNESS is entirely free, and all attachments are let go.

Δ *You now can: pay attention to the near enemies of positive emotions, let go of attachments that make life difficult, and hold in your heart the experienced enrichment, even when crying because of love.*

16

This chapter is empty. It should be entirely empty to be honest, without words, meaning, and realizations, but how would that be possible? The next chapter would follow without a gap, leaving no trace of the emptiness. Therefore, these letters give you some time to observe how you look at pages filled with symbols, how these symbols form words, how these words trigger familiar imaginations, how these imaginations automatically decide on the color of a rose, and finally how a sensation arises of knowing a rose or understanding these words. But you haven't understood a thing. You are just observing. Because as soon as familiar imaginations fail to appear, as with symbols such as 玫[a]99 or ῥόδον[b]100, it becomes unmistakably clear that words have no inherent meaning.

WE exist and naturally observe what happens in EXISTENCE. *That includes* our thoughts, whose forms, shapes, and contents sometimes seem like intelligent insights yet remain pure observations nobody needs to understand. Perception isn't based on understanding but on presence. It's just that our language contains no word able to trigger this *present perception* within us right now. Students and teachers therefore must take detours and use words (that have no inherent meaning) to drag our attention to the PRESENT (that is perceived all the time).

A blind man doesn't understand colors. This statement sounds logical. A sighted person, however, has never understood colors either, because he simply perceives them without any schooling, effort, or alternative.

---

[a] Chinese: 玫 [méi] Rose.
[b] Ancient Greek: ῥόδον [rhódon] Rose.

And this fact destroys any purely scientific approach because we are unable to notice a missing sense of perception, or two, or even thirty of them. And even if we were to suspect such a lack, we would be unable to emulate a perception inaccessible to our body.

Right at this moment, too, you can't know how much information your senses receive from reality. But at the same time, you realize an absolute certainty: Every single worldview is ultimately based on the perception of your given senses and the non-perception of your non-given senses. In this respect, all worldviews are incomplete, like houses built without windows.

If you feel convinced of your worldview, then this is the current HAPPENING, which means that it's not *you* who is convinced of your worldview. The overall unconscious situation just feels that way. You yourself *would know* that being convinced of an incomplete truth is contradictory. But when the HAPPENING has taken over, it means that EXISTENCE currently just follows the paths it's well-acquainted with.

*

Our ascent in CONSCIOUSNESS can be arranged into states, so to speak. The first state of being (△1) is consistent self-unconsciousness. The second state of being (△2) describes the emerging self-awareness, becoming conscious of body and mind. The third state of being (△3) feels like the human being: sleeping consciousness. And the fourth state of being (△4) stands for transcendent consciousness, the willful and accelerated search for enlightenment.

A disciple of Patrul Rinpoche, his name was Lungtok, still hadn't realized the highest, fully awakened mind after years of practice. One night, Rinpoche asked his student, "Can you hear the Monastery dogs barking? Can you see the stars shining?" Lungtok nodded. Rinpoche then said, "Well, that's it." And at that moment, the student awakened.[a][101]

---

[a] Matthieu Ricard and Trinh Xuan Thuan (The Quantum and the Lotus)

The AWAKENING happens unexpectedly. The PRESENT no longer contains different sensations but shows itself as the EXPERIENCE, which makes all divisions possible. WE ARE THE EXPERIENCE HERE AND NOW but discover in it a monastery, dogs, stars, students, and a teacher. WE ARE THE EXPERIENCE HERE AND NOW but discover in it a room, a book, a myself, hands, and the necessity to turn the page soon. WE ARE THE EXPERIENCE HERE AND NOW but discover in it an experience that *feels different*. That's why Jesus explained to his disciples: "When you make the two into One, when you make the inner like the outer and the high like the low; when you make male and female into a single One, so that the male is not male and the female is not female; when you have eyes in your eyes, a hand in your hand, a foot in your foot, and an icon in your icon, then you will enter into the Kingdom."[a]102

(△5) The fifth state of being is cosmic CONSCIOUSNESS. EXISTENCE AWAKENS to ITSELF. The I recognizes itself as ONE in the cosmos. All attachments fall away, taking the ego with them, and leave behind an immeasurable liberated emptiness; as if our view turns away from a *photo of the starry sky* and rises to the endless starry sky itself, sparking a novel way of thinking and feeling beyond imagination. The cosmos doesn't contain life but is LIFE! We're completely overwhelmed by eternity and infinity, while time, space, and their previous influences depart from our perception. Inner sensations and outer sensory impressions merge into one level of EXPERIENCE, and when we move, it feels as if EXISTENCE is moving *through itself*. The inner dialogue of thoughts ceases. Fear of death fades. All striving, worrying, and suffering ends, to reveal instead the most comical performance we've ever experienced. A loving joyousness bubbles out of us and towards all people, creatures, and events, even towards all egos that currently play their roles. The SELF remembers everything. In one moment, we learn infinitely much; not in a human way of understanding, but in understanding *all possible* ways of living. The destiny of every human

---

[a] Gospel of Thomas (Logion 22)

being, the insights of science, and the teachings of religions lose their outlines and reveal the MOSAIC, which connects all cultures, all ages, and all living beings. It has always been like this and always will be. The PRESENT just briefly felt human, to now lead an awakened life.[a103,b104]

✻

We are on a journey through EXISTENCE without knowing right now which peaks lie behind the peaks at the horizon. Sometimes, however, we may catch a glimpse of distant, even higher mountains. Even in an awakened life, there are ways, possibilities, and phases to learn more, to become more attentive, and to continue *ascending* in CONSCIOUSNESS without any hurry.

(△6) The sixth state of being is GOD. CONSCIOUSNESS discovers itself as CREATOR. The world is no longer experienced: The world is specifically chosen instead of other possibilities. WE learn to change REALITY purposefully through our VIBRATION, which naturally occurred in the previous states as well – just mainly unconsciously. This ACT unfolds as an expression of LOVE – just as a mother acts out of love for her children. But these words (or other words) aren't meant to transfer understanding into you. The words aren't meant to raise questions, either. The words only give you time to observe how you look at symbols and create a world at the same time.

(△7) The seventh state of being is ONENESS. Every meaning collapses. All ideas and thought-patterns are surrendered, even those of a creator. The states of being were only interpretations that never existed. Everything is let go. The PRESENT has become "Anatta," the Not-Accepted, which doesn't even perceive itself as SELF but simply *is*. INFINITY stands at every point of perception and expands into new infinities. That is the beginning *in* which GOD creates heaven and

---

[a] Sogyal Rinpoche (The Tibetan Book of Living and Dying)
[b] P. D. Ouspensky (Tertium Organum)

earth[a][105], in which an observation falls out of the observation and feels like our life.

Right now, as you read these lines, LIFE exists in all states of being. Determining this state for another living being is impossible. CONSCIOUSNESS cannot be proven *for others*. We may only classify ourselves to some extent: Humanity resembles the third of the seven states, where we believe in many concepts – that dolphins have less consciousness than humans, for example, or that ants have even less consciousness – even though ONENESS is everywhere, has no highs or lows, and always denotes being *right in the middle*. So, if the "states of being" suggest that we can ascend into awareness, this presumes that, previously, EXISTENCE did descend into the MOSAIC.

You may look up at the starry sky, plunge into its endless expanse, and drown in the question: "Where do we come from?" But when you stand at the shore and see a wave rushing up to your feet, where did it come from? The wave is created by naming it. And in this sense, EXISTENCE, as the giver of all names, holds all possibilities to journey *selfward* in every direction through *clarity* of perception.

---

[a] Genesis 1:1 (KJV)

+ You now know:

You keep in mind:

Δ *You now can:*

17 Clarity

Trusting in certainty. The Law of Attraction. Our expertise in visualization. The secret of our desires. The possible evolution of human beings. Entering a new culture from the inside-out. Our primary responsibility. Emotions as our vision.

C onfucius asked one of his students: "Do you regard me as someone who learns extensively and thereby knows much?" His student replied: "Indeed I do. Is that not so?" And the Master said, "No. I penetrate all with one thing."[a106] The only mystery within the universe is the mind. Our questions will never be exhausted or resolved, not even by ten thousand answers, as long as understanding simply means assigning names to EXISTENCE. Who am I? A human being. What are we made of? Molecules, atoms, and elementary particles. Why do I like the sunset? Because it paints beautiful colors onto the landscape, the clouds, and the sky. Answers do not bring understanding but becalm us due to their creativity.

Many people know that reality is quite different than they think, but few people trust this knowledge. The thoughts are rumbling like thunder but haven't become a lightning flash of insight yet because one thing is missing. When we realize something with absolute certainty, we must also trust this certainty at a time when the feeling of trust is absent. And once that happens, we gain the clarity that penetrates all.

Attraction

Isaac Newton studied how cannonballs fall to the ground, derived mathematical equations from it, and formulated the laws of gravity – as an approximate description of the world, which may be refined by more advanced measurements and formulas. But no matter how precisely we will describe gravity in the distant future, a cannonball falls to the

---

[a] Confucius (The Analects of Dasan, Volume 2)

ground as always. REALITY just *works*, no matter how well we understand it. And the same applies to our ATTRACTION.

EXISTENCE consists of VIBRATIONS in CONSCIOUSNESS, which remain set until changed, just like the selected frequency on a radio. As long as nothing changes in the current situation, meaning, energy is neither added nor subtracted, the existing VIBRATION remains stable and maintains itself as such. We experience these VIBRATIONS within CONSCIOUSNESS as EMOTIONS. Our feelings cannot end all of a sudden but remain set until inner or outer impulses shift their "frequencies" into the positive or negative. WE thus *receive* what WE *radiate,* as the EMOTION we radiate right now *is* our NOW and maintains itself as such.

As long as our PRESENT sounds like [contentment][a107], this [contentment] will persist and attract more reasons for [contentment] because we interpret the world accordingly, these interpretations provoke subconscious reactions, and these reactions in turn bring hard evidence into our life, which fully rationalizes our [contentment]. So as long as we effect no change, the [contentment] remains stable – which, from our perspective, seems like reliably "attracting more of the same" and characterizes the *Law of Attraction.*

Such law and regularity can of course be challenged. You could argue that emotions don't change the world. "The world is the way it is! What possible difference could my emotions make?" This may just be the way you think – yet this viewpoint changes your world, which implies that your world could be entirely different. Nobody wants you to believe that *human* emotions have some kind of extraordinary power; such an interpretation would confuse cause and effect. EMOTIONS aren't created by humans. EMOTIONS create the human illusion. For *this reason,* you should trust in their extraordinary power.

In the third state of being, within human logic, the Law of Attraction cannot be entirely understood. We may only notice its reliable operation,

---

[a] You may insert any other feeling here.

which we commonly tolerate in our everyday normality. GPS navigation guides us to our destination – without us knowing or even having any interest in its technical details. And the Law of Attraction deserves the same pragmatic application: We need not understand it but we can rely on it.

Jesus teaches: "Whatever you ask for in prayer, believe that you have received it, and it will be yours."[a108] "Whoever *has* will be given more, and they will have an abundance. Whoever *does not have*, even what they have will be taken from them."[b109] "For he spoke, and it came to be; he commanded, and it stood firm."[c110] And Lao Tzu explains: "Those who flow as life flows know they need no other force."[d111] Allah says: "I am as my servant thinks I am. [...] If he makes mention of Me to himself, I make mention of him to myself."[e112] And C. G. Jung states that we act *magically through the soul*, once we become aware of the synchronicity of all things through time and space.[f113] With this in mind, you need to wrestle with your worldview. Is our ATTRACTION merely a dreamy desire for magic or a perfectly logical law within the universe that explains our entire life as human beings?

ATTRACTION *works* for one simple reason. WE aren't exclusively physical living beings but facets of EXISTENCE with access to all its possibilities. So guess what's happening when we try to improve our life in a physical way only? Our ego jumps forward to act "over there," while our SELF stays back and acts over HERE for real. And these unconscious ACTS explain why the events in our life frequently surprise us.

Every EMOTION in EXISTENCE triggers an ATTRACTION, no matter the circumstance, be it consciously or unconsciously. Thoughts do not trigger any ATTRACTION because their contents have no connection to REALITY. The thought "It's Monday" can feel good or bad and may also

---

[a] Mark 11:24 (NIV)
[b] Matthew 13:12 (NIV)
[c] Psalm 33:9 (NIV)
[d] Lao Tzu
[e] Sahih Al-Bukhari
[f] C. G. Jung (Synchronicity, An Acausal Connecting Principle)

be thought on a Friday. The thought "I have to go to the hospital" may announce cheerful or dire events. And the statement "Yesterday, my wallet and my chronic headaches disappeared" cannot be universally understood without background information. Every loss is simultaneously a gain of its opposite, which is why the PRESENT is given meaning solely by our emotions of "good" or "bad."

A lonely single person habitually recognizes happy couples. A pregnant woman sees young families everywhere. A bitter employee finds no pleasure in whatever task. A stressed-out person achieves little, an indifferent person is slow to comprehend, and an exhausted person doesn't sleep properly. Things we frantically strive for require frantic efforts, but things we approach lightly just happen. Our attitude towards life manifests in facial expressions, body posture, and choice of words. Those who wait for every hour to pass will have more reasons to wait. Those who hope for a dream job will continue to hope. And those who want wealth will continue to want because the vibration of poverty cannot feel abundant. To sum it up: If *that-which-is* isn't enough for us, it'll stay that way until our attitude changes.

A conscious observer realizes this as the most logical thing in the world: An unchanged VIBRATION equals an unchanged LIFE. LIFE can't change if its VIBRATION doesn't change. Cause and effect are always in harmony and explain something otherwise impossible. Our worldview contains countless paradigms, contradictions, and gaps in knowledge, and yet the correctness of this worldview is regularly confirmed – which only works for one reason: Our ATTRACTION is effective. We perceive our perception as *right,* and this provides us with more of *feeling right* – albeit mostly without bringing more happiness.

∗

Law of Attraction has gained some fundamental publicity through books and films because it points out that we can improve our lives. But such an idea could well trap us. "Happiness" brings more "happiness" into our life, that's true, but it's true for all feelings. The ATTRACTION always stays true to its principle. The "hope to improve life" results in more "hope to improve life" and makes life worse in our view.

This logic is simple but requires a careful study of present emotions and their accompanying events. Our ego doesn't know how WE feel. It can't identify the "near enemies of emotions" and may even mistake fear for love. It makes us believe that the *wrong* things are happening – things we didn't *want* to attract.

When we feel enriched right now, we receive more enrichment in the form that is *right for us*. Materialistic acquisitions are side effects only. A feeling of joy doesn't necessarily attract winning the jackpot, as material wealth might even take us away from happiness – and so doesn't occur. When we do not feel enriched right now, though, we attract more lack of enrichment, make our life worse, and become all the more dependent on the *Fail-Safe of Existence*.

Should our life slide down into a self-destructive routine, the CONTRAST we attract begins to destroy the self-destruction, be it with physical or mental problems, and thus initiates our reorientation.[a114] In good times or in bad, the ATTRACTION gives *evidence* that WE are not helpless, weak, or incapable but can create better situations through our EMOTIONS.[b115]

Human striving, worrying, and suffering multiplies negative emotions. Moreover, our ego believes that negativity can improve life without understanding that it makes life worse right from the start. A person primarily living with negative emotions thus needs to realize a great many things, namely (first) that he's mentally disordered, (second) that the cause of his negative emotions is unconsciousness, (third) that his negativity is primarily rooted in imitation, (fourth) that his natural state wants to be within positive emotions, (fifth) that positive feelings can only arise when negative attachments don't occupy the present, (sixth)

[a] Bashar (Quest for Truth)
[b] Bashar (Blueprint for Change)

that only awareness can help him, and (seventh) that it's a beautiful feeling to offer awareness for others to copy.[a116]

*

Having established that you can't generally dismiss the regularity of our ATTRACTION any longer, especially since the "indifference regarding a life-changing possibility" would promise a quite "indifferent life," it's time to initiate an experimental learning phase right now. That's where your thoughts come into play, so that you *first* navigate within EMOTIONS and *then* observe their impact on your ATTRACTION.

We plan our day with great depth, contour, and precision, which explains many of our déjà vu experiences. In the evening, everything is set out: Get up early the next morning, go to the bathroom, make breakfast, assemble everything you need, commute to work, add two hours of overtime, take care of errands, return home, tidy up, maybe read a bit, watch TV, or engage in a leisure activity, then turn off the lights. And all this time, our ATTRACTION is effective while we mostly follow our fussy thoughts and blurry ideas.

Our "hope for a beautiful day" doesn't contain a clear-cut picture of what's making a day beautiful but rather a recallable list of things not belonging to it: like the traffic jam in the morning, a doctor's appointment in the afternoon, or rain in the evening. To practice our ATTRACTION, we need to redirect our blurry absorption into a *clear-cut visualization*. We have to regard our thoughts as less interesting in their content while considering our EMOTIONS as more compelling in their sensation, like this:

I'm *glad* that rain in the evening became one of my concerns because it means I'm fine. I *see* before my inner eye that some clouds are breaking up, rays of sunlight shine through in beautiful contrast, and puddles slowly turn into calm mirrors. I *hear* in my mind how the rustling of the rain is lessening, how the last drops of water are running off rooftops

---

[a] P. D. Ouspensky (The Fourth Way)

more slowly, and how passing cars are splashing through the run-off. I *expect*, as I open the window, how a fresh breeze is greeting me, how the sun's rays warmingly touch my skin, and how the weather couldn't get any better! And at this moment, my whole life has changed. Therefore, I don't *visualize* for something to happen, but for the joy it brings me.

The impact of our visualization on the external world can't be predicted with precision. We don't know what the Law of Attraction physically brings into our lives. But for what reason would we need this prediction? The impact on the emotional world is already there – or can be chosen again at any time. And that reveals the secret of our desires. As long as the world supports our emotions, we are in harmony. But once harmony is lost, we receive a signal – a wish – which helps us return to it.

Wishes give us ideas on what to visualize next, in order to then carry us "like rockets to our highest goal." The profound intention of a wish is fulfilled immediately. The superficial intention is no longer required. *And in that moment,* our EXCITEMENT may take over – which then attracts the physical manifestations of our visualization. So we must not enjoy the material world only but should also, in a tangible way, experience a visualized idea in our awareness, so that we create a PRESENT that couldn't be any more real.

Exodus

Our realizations about EXISTENCE, CONSCIOUSNESS, and LIFE include the possibility and the responsibility to rethink and transform our society. This evolution begins small, with only a few people who work on their awareness and initiate a great awakening. One mindful second can save our life in a dangerous situation. One mindful minute could set our life on a new path. And one permanently mindful lifestyle will transform its entire environment – because tuned-in people realize that being unconscious is not enjoyable. Awareness is more meaningful. This insight just required some initial help. Our civilization today, which has everything but awareness, is therefore no obstacle to our evolution but a promising foundation for our exodus.

*

Psychology, it is said, reveals the emotional processes in humans. But in reality, being human is a process within EMOTIONS. Sartre said: "Man is nothing other than his own project,"[a][117] a design, an illusion, or a story. And indeed, our SELF projects and designs the ego. We believe that we live in REALITY as a "person" and that we must somehow "improve" as such.

Helpful psychotherapy doesn't focus on getting our problems under control but on letting go of the *design* that creates our problems in the first place. Human striving, worrying, and suffering only ends when we leave its cycle. The search for AWAKENING only ends upon surrendering. The SELF only remains awake when letting go of attachments again and again. And in this ever-expanding orbit from which we observe our earlier designs, something incredible is revealed: Psychology means to study the possible evolution of a human being, that is, what EXISTENCE can design *beyond a human being* regarding language, worldview, and understanding.[b][118] Psychology, therefore, isn't a science but our power of observation.

*

The human design enters a particularly defining phase during the school years. In this phase, we are supposed to get ready for life and find our place in the world. Little of this comes about in class. And yet, the initial idea of *cultivating oneself* was never lost. Teachers, students, and parents are willing to dance; it's just that they are mired in the educational system, which makes their dance seem like a fight. In reality, there is no education system, of course. That's just a concept. We primarily look at the symptoms of unconsciousness: That our egos are continually creating the two kinds of injustice, and that our EXCITEMENT systematically receives too little attention. Changing this

---

[a] Sartre
[b] P. D. Ouspensky (The Psychology of Man's Possible Evolution)

situation lies in the hands of the people who are more mature, who start with changing *themselves*.

Teachers should feel their EXCITEMENT for helping students discover their own EXCITEMENT. This mindset creates an individual beyond the system, which puts "teaching an attitude" above the curriculum and respects the protocol only if meaningful. A perfect vocabulary test doesn't bring us any closer to LIFE. Questions born of curiosity, a voluntary year abroad, or (if need be) repeating a grade will.

Students, for their part, should feel that behind all the formulas, vocabulary, and poetry lies a much higher intention, namely that they learn to discover their excitement, follow it, and play the leading role in their lifetimes. Once students and teachers change in this way, begin to notice the changes in the other, and engage at eye level, they begin to "look up to each other."

*

A great suffering in our society stems from the assumption that one can be happy in partnerships only. Law of Attraction reacts to our emotion of "not being allowed to feel happy whenever," and brings us more of it, even if at some point we do find a partner. And now, we don't want to lose the emotion of "being allowed to feel happy right now." As a consequence, our relationships demonstrate that a strong desire for couple-based happiness creates conflict, that physical presence doesn't imply spiritual connectedness, and that every joyful partnership ultimately needs two joyful individuals.

EXISTENCE contains all things as one thing. In reality, everything is here together, without distinction or division. It's our mind that makes *many things* out of it, to then feel *separated* from them. Separation from other things or even from other people thus is an illusion accompanied by real feelings, because WE are close or distant to the SELF. "There is only one reason to get married or enter a public commitment with another, [...] when you're conscious," says social psychologist Michael

Ray, and that is "to go to the highest goal together."[a][119] Only when two people support each other in their EMOTIONS, when they make each other more aware, is it meaningful in regard to SELF-BEING and LOVE to remain in a relationship.

*

Our culture, especially the work culture, demonstrates a strong psychological dependency on "those higher up in the chain of command," which leads to a great loss of responsibility and authority. The "inferior ones" feel like empty shells waiting for inspiration, while the "superior ones" feel like horns of plenty that can only pour out but not fill up. The bosses' ego can indeed determine the success of an entire department, can inspire, or impede, at least when the employees have no *firmly grounded perspective* yet.

When our ego experiences negative behavior, it feels mistreated, looks up plaintively towards all that injustice, and desires less of this behavior; but when our ego experiences positive behavior, it feels correctly treated, smiles down happily at its achievements, and desires more of this behavior – rather than remaining firmly grounded in its own *center*. Undeserved criticism should leave us unscathed, and so should undeserved praise, because the truth we know doesn't change by virtue of other people's perception.

Nevertheless, it can't be our goal – especially in the business world, where people shouldn't be trained to avoid each other – to endure or compensate for other people's negativity. No matter how big the umbrella of our spiritual maturity: If it permanently rains negative feelings, our feet will get wet eventually. Therefore, we must not get used to other people's negativity, not only for personal reasons but also because of the collective disadvantages.

Countless guidebooks explain how to improve profits, productivity, and the sustainability of a company, but they rarely begin by announcing that

---

[a] Michael Ray (The Highest Goal)

an organization that's unconsciously striving and worrying will always remain ineffective. Unconsciousness prevents common goals. The purpose of business becomes reduced to money and key figures. Yet profitability is not the *purpose* of an enterprise but its basis of existence. As human beings, without oxygen, we will die. But which human being would accept "air" as the purpose of life?

Only greater consciousness allows for greater autonomy in thinking and acting, which brings, as a side effect, better key figures. Awareness isn't only valuable in a spiritual understanding but also adds value in an economic sense, so that strategies, decisions, and behaviors are not left open to chance.

We find two opposite approaches to management in companies, organizations, or schools today. The first is *imperative management*, in which the boss decides. The other is *authorizing management*, in which employees are guided to decide for themselves. In addition, many different personalities come together, and this means: There is great potential for conflict, even actual battles between management styles.

Imperative management no longer works, but there is no trust in authorizing management yet. This results in staff being trained in somewhat more conscious leadership methods – as everyone ultimately knows that *unconsciously acting companies fail in the long run*. These trainings start at the top of the hierarchy and then cascade down so that every manager is able to set an example of the corporate culture in his own division. To change a culture, however, we need to follow an additional path.

A culture never changes *top-down* but *inside-out*, by multiplication of elements that already exist. Should unconsciousness prevail, it will spread and stay. But should EXCITEMENT prevail, it will affect its environment and eventually define an entire culture. So when we think that society is unconscious in certain aspects, then the point is that we *ourselves* must become even more conscious, and as Confucius said, don't delay being a good example until someone else takes the first step.[a][120]

Our ego doesn't like the idea of being the first good example, as it brings disadvantages, attracts resistance, and also requires that we abandon certain habits. This indicates the great challenge today's leaders are facing:

Each culture has advantages and disadvantages that cannot be separated from each other. "Imperative management" allows for quick decision-making in the business world (+) but hinders employees' autonomy (-). "Authorizing management" promotes autonomy (+) but requires time (-). Our ego seeks only advantages. So when managers leave "decisions" to their ego, they arbitrarily leap back and forth between management styles, from one advantage to another, while with each leap undoing whatever good leadership had been accomplished before.

To shape a culture, we must accept not only its advantages but also its disadvantages, come hell or high water. Because the desire to create a culture without potential disadvantages and without the necessity to think, decide, and be responsible would intend an incapacitation of all individuals involved.

Responsibility

WE ARE HERE NOW and can perceive at any moment that EXISTENCE in all its facets doesn't intend to be good or bad. And once we stop seeing a red light as an annoyance, consider a Monday morning as something unpleasant, consider a forgotten greeting an insult, treat after-work hours as a liberation, or react in similar ways to another imaginary story, *we gain the ability to respond to reality* – wherein lies our utmost RESPONSIBILITY. We must be responsible for our emotions.

The philosopher Theodor Adorno says: "Wrong life cannot be lived rightly,"[a][121] meaning that unpleasant parts of our daily routines can't be

---

[a] Confucius ('The Way of Truthfulness')

corrected later, in the evening, or at the weekend, and also cannot be caught up with or sealed off from each other. The PRESENT does not divide into segments. Our unpleasant daily routines instead show that we aren't yet meeting our RESPONSIBILITY. We *know and see* what a real life feels like ("Not like this!") but aren't ready to act according to our *vision*.

*

People who make their dreams come true are often described as visionaries, which makes other people seem like non-visionaries. But Law of Attraction responds equally to the EMOTIONS of astronauts and the homeless, and in these emotions lie our equally powerful visions. Most visions simply don't stand out – just like, at the bottom of the sea, it's impossible to find one drop of water. These visions are invisible when our feelings and thus our ATTRACTION turns in circles: We wish to be a billionaire, *even without knowing* what it's like to be a billionaire. But we don't wish to be a penniless monk, *exactly because we don't know* what it's like to be a penniless monk. As long as we think that the "outer appearance" and the "inner being" sometimes correspond but sometimes diverge, our LIFE turns in circles and so helps us to work on the RESPONSIBILITY for our EMOTIONS.

Working to make money is one thing. But working on our RESPONSIBILITY is something else entirely. Let's take a vivid example: At the end of the year, the chairman of a bank receives a seven-figure bonus. Also, at the end of the year, a homeless person receives a few coins more than usual. So who gets more? Without awareness, both receive nothing. The outer appearance won't change the inner being. But with awareness, the homeless person could have received more – and

---

[a] Theodor W. Adorno (Minima Moralia)

might be further advanced in his RESPONSIBILITY, while a CEO with an eighty-hour working week may need rescuing "from the outside."

The basic principle is that unconsciousness brings the most suffering to unconscious people. We might need to endure a negative person for a few minutes, but that person has to endure himself twenty-four-seven. So any of us not working on our RESPONSIBILITY don't get anything in return except more unconsciousness. But should we decide to work on our RESPONSIBILITY, then – for entirely selfish reasons – we have to do it again today, tomorrow, and every day of our life because more consciousness is only possible in the PRESENT.

Our responsibility as human beings can flow in three directions, explains Ouspensky: We can be responsible for a specific matter, for other people, and for ourselves. The RESPONSIBILITY of our SELF is to advance with balance into all three directions.[a][122] If we work in one direction only, or perhaps in two, we'll soon lose our balance, exhaust ourselves, and impulsively change our priorities. Our most significant contribution to humanity thus is to follow our RESPONSIBILITY, our EXCITEMENT, and LOVE without looking left or right or waiting for preconditions.

---

[a] P. D. Ouspensky (In Search of the Miraculous)

+ You now know: that our feelings act as a powerful vision, that we change the world through our individual vision, and that we are responsible for *our* results.

You keep in mind:

Law of Attraction says that our present emotions (especially our baseline vibration) bring more of these emotions into our lives.

Our **ATTRACTION** stands for the specific *result* that our EMOTIONS have brought into our lives.

Our **RESPONSIBILITY** is the learnable ability to respond to reality, not to an imaginary story within the mind, which starts with blaming only ourselves for negative feelings. This ability enables us to choose positive feelings instantly, even in unpleasant situations. Our RESPONSIBILITY thus can be described as SELF-BEING: A constant self-evolution of awareness, presence, and love.

Δ *You now can: practice visualizing, understand the world very clearly by trusting in certainties, and shape a new culture with this clarity.*

18 **Selfward**

The difficulty of unfamiliarity. Our three principal centers. Resistance as the strongest human habit. Discipline through consciousness. The side effects of awakening. Total oblivion. The distinction between uplifting and downgrading teachings.

C HANGE spares no one. We should not forget that certain events may shake our life to the core and initiate a new chapter, be it for terrible or beautiful reasons. In such phases of orientation, we may ask: "Will I ever get a grip on life?" And this question needs to stop us in our tracks. LIFE doesn't have to be gotten. It's always entirely here, even if its EXPERIENCE seems as if LIFE *isn't here yet* or *is here no longer*. Each belief of not yet having reached our home, our anchor, or a grip on life, shows that we are attached to a story. And every interest in how this story proceeds requires meeting its narrator – by *facing selfward*.[a][123]

Some people might think that *facing selfward* is just some abstract intention and would rather wait for ideas of straight-forward "common sense" that are easy to comprehend at first glance. But such an opinion expresses an ironic dilemma because "common sense" is an abstract result of incomprehensible processes within consciousness and thus provides no basis for a clear worldview. Nothing is more abstract than human illusion. It's just that we are *familiar* with this abstraction.

Worries come easy to us, even though they make life more difficult. Serenity is hard for us, even though it makes life easier. Parachuting might be an unthinkable or quite tangible experience for us. Imaginary numbers may imply a simple or complicated matter to us. And living in prosperity might be hard to imagine or an entirely natural state for us.

---

[a] Sally Ross (The Selfward Facing Way)

Therefore, our personal excuse that something seems too "abstract" for us, too "complicated," or too "difficult," reflects on neither this matter nor our intelligence, but only our lack of readiness to do something unfamiliar.

A journey selfward to AWAKENING may sound abstract, complicated, or difficult, but eventually, it becomes simple once we allow ourselves to do something unfamiliar.

Steadiness

Our *familiar* life is made possible by instilled automatisms that can be divided into three principal centers. The thinking center allows for speedy reading, mental arithmetic, or making plans. The movement center enables us to walk, write, or speak without the need for reflection. And the emotional center leads to intuitive decision-making or joyful laughs when seeing puppies. These three principal centers form an unbreakable cycle. *Emotions* don't stay long without thoughts or movement, *thoughts* don't stay long without movement or emotions, and *movements* don't stay long without emotions or thoughts. Even slight pain makes us clench our teeth, imagining a ripe lemon inevitably makes our mouth water, and a farewell hug is always supplemented with a few final words.[a][124]

Our motivation to work on our awareness often begins in one principal center only. A sitting meditation feels for the silent breath – we're in the emotional center. A walking meditation concentrates on slow movements – we're in the movement center. A mantra meditation repeats words and thoughts – we are in the thinking center. And this one-sidedness causes significant discomfort to us. We want to concentrate on one principal center, yet they can't be isolated from each other. Their automatisms will follow familiar ways, which makes our exercises seem exhausting and futile.

We need to equally respect each of our three principal centers, just like three excited children; they need to calm down at the same time to stop

[a] P. D. Ouspensky (In Search of the Miraculous)

exciting each other. And even though this sounds like *more work*, our exercises in attentiveness become easier by knowing this. During a silent meditation, our body may rock gently back and forth to release noisy thoughts into the ground. During physical exertion, we can visualize being propelled by invisible forces. And during excessive pondering, it helps to hum deeply until running out of air. In such a way, we anticipate the automatisms of the three principal centers, mix up their responsibilities, and break their habitual connections – which gradually reduces the unwanted habits in our life.

*

Everyone wants to solve life's biggest problems *first*. But exactly this intention requires starting with the smallest habits. *A stranger smiles at me.* "Now I want to appear nice too" goes through our striving mind, and makes us smile back. "What have I done to deserve this?" asks the worrying part of our mind. "And why can't all people be nice like that?" whines our suffering. *A stranger insults me.* "Now I want to defend myself" goes through our striving mind. "Did I do wrong to deserve this insult?" asks the worrying part of our mind. "And why is the world always so unjust?" whines our suffering.

We often react automatically and in a way that's not truly authentic because the events simply trigger our human striving, worrying, and suffering. In the morning, we'd rather stay in bed and skip work, but in the evening, we'd rather stay up and leave no work unfinished. Our ego quickly changes its mind about fundamental principles but only slowly about foolish habits: It resolves to eat healthily, but with the first feeling of hunger, everything needs to go fast, easy, and cheap again. And thus we see that the strongest human habit is an emotion of *resistance*: "I don't want it like this but different." It's impossible to even think about *steady behavior* – because thoughts are pointless in this case.

Our ego understands "discipline" as the right behavior of others: "When I'm happy, others have done the right thing." But if we make our well-being dependent on others, we neglect our RESPONSIBILITY and spread hypocrisy instead. We create an unconscious, unstable, and inconsistent *against-each-other* and so cause indiscipline. For this reason, the American author Alfie Kohn says that genuine discipline can only be achieved when we have better things to do[a125] – that is, by teaching something greater than discipline.

Nobody has a problem with participating in a meaningful, inspiring, and exciting enterprise. So in case of problems, either the individual has a lack of understanding or the whole has a lack of meaning. Assuming obedience or self-control in this situation would only make things worse. Emotions would go haywire for good. What we need in this moment is *to come to our senses*. We must close the gap within "lack of purpose," speak out, and calm down *because there are no discipline problems*, only unsteady emotions.

An unconscious person, whose baseline vibration lies in negative emotions, is easily influenced by external events. A conscious person, whose baseline vibration lies in positive emotions, is hardly *distracted* by external events. Therefore, only consciousness enables steadiness in emotions, causing steadiness in behavior, which may well look like great discipline when perceived from a distance.

Such a steady life doesn't imply that we are without inner resistance; it means that we remain *unimpressed* despite inner resistances, that we uncover our negative habits, and let them go again and again, until letting go has become a new and positive habit.

Oblivion

The AWAKENING to the SELF is accompanied by overwhelming feelings that carry away body and mind, and create a somatic marker in our consciousness forever. But these by-products are not the AWAKENING, don't ever forget that.[b126] Fireworks may light up the sky at night, but they are lit by one spark. And this eternal spark, the SELF,

[a] Alfie Kohn (Beyond Discipline)
[b] Gangaji (You Are That)

exists independently of all the events going on in the sky – whether it's shrouded in deep blue, in grey clouds, or the most beautiful fireworks.

Within the Nirvana of AWAKENING, our body and mind can't survive. We need food, protection, and also creativity, and this brings us back into the human sphere, at least every so often – as if EXISTENCE would blink so it won't forget its dream. A blink of EXISTENCE can feel like many years in human understanding, even an entire life. But still, CONSCIOUSNESS would have forgotten ITSELF for one moment only.

✳

The ego is afraid of forgetting as it defines itself and others through memories. Everyone is only as good as the last sentence, the last vacation, or the last anecdote. For this reason, we unconsciously follow the principle, "What I'm doing now doesn't need to be fun, it just has to sell well." Our days now get filled with activities, which equip our personality with better stories. We give up the quality of our experience today to improve the quality of our narratives tomorrow.[a127]

The idea of losing all memories, be it through accident or illness, sounds like a death to us. Our whole life would disappear into nothingness. And this fear reveals a misunderstanding about forgetting. *Total oblivion* would indeed take EVERYTHING from us. We would forget our language, worldview, and ego, would essentially unlearn everything about being human and experience the PRESENT without attachment.

The spiritual search is a process of forgetting. As soon as we let go of *what we think we are*, CONSCIOUSNESS awakens to ITSELF. In this moment, while the sky is still lit by fireworks, being human has become a memory full of nostalgia. WE feel gratitude for the CONTRAST and the infinite possibilities of experiences within, and we also feel amazement about having chosen humanness: a way of life that was hard on us, even

---

[a] Daniel Kahneman (Thinking, fast and slow)

though LIFE just proceeded without any hardship. The human mind simply kept asking: "What am I doing next? How do I fill my life in the best possible way?" But EXISTENCE could have never gotten fuller. The SELF was never empty. The EXPERIENCE was never lost.

It is only our SELF in which WE lose ourselves, have lost ourselves, or may lose ourselves again. But even when that happens, *we know it*.[a128] Our AWAKENESS isn't a one-time event but an always fresh perception of the PRESENT, which attends this moment like a pleasant summer breeze, and entirely fills some moments.

Teachings

Knowledge can be acquired in many ways: through life experience, teachers, and books. This passed-down knowledge grants us shortcuts to insights, wisdom, and teachings we could not discover on our own during one lifespan. The quality of a teaching is always revealed by the emotions it triggers, not by its familiarity. A positive, uplifting, and beneficial teaching makes us study facets of ourselves, teaches us to let go of illusions, and doesn't promise any additional gain. A negative, downgrading, and inhibiting teaching, on the other hand, makes us study the facets of other people, builds up prejudices, and gives well-sounding promises to the ego. Egos like promises. And this explains why many of today's wide-spread teachings are of markedly low quality.

Our striving, worrying, and suffering is firmly interconnected. Human suffering is only going to end when our striving ends too. For this reason, we strive for happiness but *search* for the end of our striving – for happiness without further desires. Therefore, a wise teaching doesn't fulfill even one desire but instead takes it away. A wise teacher doesn't force anything upon his students. And a wise student doesn't accept anything forced upon him. We should remember that when aiming for awareness.

All the knowledge you acquire isn't meant to get you to reach one final truth, to give up your ability to observe, so that you can *then* be happy.

---

[a] Osho

An uplifting teaching will show you something quite different: If you love something, Rumi explains, then *that love* is proof enough. But if you don't feel love, what good is all your proof? Interestingly, a downgrading teaching will show you the same, because: If you're in prison, Rumi asks, what difference does it make if you put a sign on it that says "garden?"[a]129 You can learn from sense and nonsense alike when all you do is listen to your emotions.

Teachings aren't meant as an armor but as a raft. We shouldn't fortify ourselves with one particular worldview and rule out any rethinking; we should overcome the next rapids, reach unknown regions, and then – perhaps on other rafts – discover the rest of EXISTENCE.[b]130 And while this will enable us to lead a consistent and meaningful life, unlearn our inner resistances, and accept our feelings as the highest teaching, we will realize that we are in fact traveling selfward.

---

[a] Rumi (Love Poems of Rumi: A Garden Beyond Paradise)
[b] Diamond Sutra

+ You now know: that small habits are our biggest problems, that the strongest human habit lies in an emotion of resistance, and how to distinguish positive teachings from negative ones.

You keep in mind:

In our everyday use of language, **discipline** means that people set aside their individual desires to work towards a common goal – and that some kind of obedience or self-control is required for this. But with this understanding, we confuse cause and effect. A situation in which we expect obedience or self-control *prevents* a common goal from arising. Some people, usually the more powerful, won't put their wishes aside. As a consequence, *true discipline is* based on a steadiness of behavior, which is achieved through EXCITEMENT only.

Δ *You now can: observe the automatisms of your three principal centers, face unfamiliar experiences with a "piece of cake" attitude, and learn a lot about reality by forgetting illusions.*

Existence

We have stepped back from our worldviews, fragment by fragment, to finally see the MOSAIC as a whole. Realizations about *our life* made us wake up from human habituality, through recognizing what we are not. Realizations about *consciousness* made us wake up from spirituality, through recognizing what we are. And the following realizations about *existence* will make us wake up from science, so that we learn to navigate through the one absolute (reliable) truth and the many relative (apparent) truths therein.

EXISTENCE can be perceived; that is an absolute and reliable truth. But our conceptual knowledge about it remains a personal invention, which is why someone who *knows* a thousand things understands far less than someone who *realizes* just one thing.[a][131] At this point, therefore, one thing must be clear: Our refutation of today's worldviews is not meant to paint another image of the world, but intends to leave a paint-repellent window. This honest intention will nevertheless create the impression of another worldview, which, in foresight, I'd like to call an eternal Yin and Yang, to remind you that EXISTENCE cannot be explained in theory but is explained in practice *right now*. We apply our theoretical understanding purely for the sake of using words, sentences, and language to our utmost advantage so that they may spark a crystal clear, real, and reliable perception.

Once we have stepped back from our ideas about life, consciousness, and existence on all three paths given above, the human illusion ends. Forever.

---

[a] Confucius (The Analects)

19 Paradigms

The identification of paradigms. Worldviews as springboards. The arrangement. The phases of a paradigm shift. The five natures of being. The meaning of artificial intelligence. The definition of intelligence. Our movement through different layers of logic.

O ur life contains many paradigms, mental comfort zones, and thought blockades that keep our mind cooped up like a hummingbird in cupped hands. With increasing awareness, though, we may recognize such limitations, identify their origins, and then consciously decide on their further application.[a132]

Arrangement

Social paradigms describe agreements that affect entire cultures or even find application around the globe. Most people know the concept of time, that twenty-four hours make up one day, and that "clockwise" means "turning right." But nobody knows anymore what time felt like before its passing was so pervasively displayed on church towers or wristwatches. We even wonder why some clocks, at the time of their invention, turned counterclockwise – as if "clockwise" was somehow predetermined by nature. And such preset views on how we see the world continue endlessly.

We see a sunrise, although Earth rotates into the sunlight. We write notes in treble-clef differently than in bass-clef. We consider Christianity and Islam fundamentally different, although both religions relate to Adam, Eve, and Moses. Our languages have two types of spelling, a normal and a phonetic one, instead of meeting both aspects with one notation. We believe that humanity understands new things every day, while textbooks in school teach knowledge that's long outdated. And

[a] P. D. Ouspensky (A New Model of the Universe)

finally, there are thousands of other beliefs, about our career, leisure time, family, nutrition, or AWAKENING.

Practical paradigms arise when technical framework conditions determine the feasibility or benefit of a project. The booster rockets of space shuttles are 3.71 meters in diameter, just as wide as the railway tunnels used for transportation. And this width of the railway tunnels was determined by other, even earlier circumstances. In retrospect, such specifications are not easy to challenge, as entire countries and millions of people would have to give up their standards.

The Qwerty keyboard, in common use with every English-language computer, relates back to early typewriters that worked mechanically and with ink ribbons. When you typed too fast, the typebars would jam. To reduce the average typing speed and thus prevent mechanical problems from arising, the keyboard was intentionally arranged in a way that made typing more difficult – the Qwerty keyboard arrangement. Today, with electronic computers, we could easily type as fast as our fingers would allow. But switching *back* to better arrangements, such as the Dvorak keyboard, is sentenced to failure due to the immense effort involved.

Scientific paradigms mostly present themselves to us through outdated, sometimes even absurd theories. And former theories indeed expose that there's a thin line between discoveries and imaginations. In the 17th century, for example, science "discovered" why wood is flammable, but stones are not. Allegedly, only materials that contain phlogiston could catch fire – the more phlogiston, the better the fire. In addition, the theory was able to explain why candleflames become extinguished under a glass dome: Phlogiston would saturate the air, so that no more flames could escape. The phlogiston theory remained in effect for over a century, until it became replaced by today's oxidation theory. One and the same phenomenon received a new explanation, and phlogiston was officially declared a figment of the imagination.

Heavenly aether, which was also called "quintessence" or the "fifth element," was a made-up substance just like phlogiston. This aether allegedly allowed objects to fly up and rise into the sky. So scientists tried to understand how birds absorbed aether, allowing them to fly upwards, and how they ejected aether, allowing them to fly downwards again – with the goal of extracting the aether and powering heavy flying machines with it. Again, other observations fell into place conclusively. The aether theory could also explain gravity because, supposedly, its weight pressed down all objects it could not enter, holding them on Earth.

The list of outdated paradigms is long: *The indivisible atom is divisible. The plague is not a divine punishment. Bulls don't react aggressively to red. Alchemy may not turn lead into gold. Phrenology cannot identify criminals by the shape of their heads. There are no N-rays. And reading in low light doesn't harm your eyes.* Ultimately, each outdated paradigm clarifies that also our current convictions may soon turn out to be mere imaginations.

Our current worldview is founded on scientific models that laypeople might consider untouchable. But experts have proven the opposite. In 1931, Kurt Gödel, a mathematician, demonstrated that every human thought system, including mathematics, is either contradictory or incomplete because, in its entirety, it may not be proven true.[a][133] This realization hasn't reached our paradigm yet and thus not yet caused a paradigm shift. We truly believe that *we* need to wait for science to provide a better understanding of the cosmos, even though science waits for *us* to accept its insights about our world.

The list of upcoming paradigm shifts is long: *We are not our ego. The universe and matter are not dead. Past and future are concepts in the eternal present. Religions share the same origin. LIFE is no cosmic coincidence. And CONSCIOUSNESS may well awaken from human being.*

---

[a] Kurt Gödel

During our lifetime, too, new perceptions will arise, simply because all worldviews remain incomplete, contradictory, and not provable. Our paradigms will be refurbished with and by time. Therefore, we shouldn't act surprised when one of our convictions is affected. We should be happy instead to experience such a change, as our current knowledge was never a solid base but always a springboard.

We won't be able to clearly distinguish if a paradigm fits more into a social, practical, or scientific category. The geocentric worldview – was it a social or scientific paradigm? Driving on the left (or the right) – is that for practical or social reasons? And the length of an hour – is it of technical or theoretical origin? Such classification of paradigms into categories serves only one purpose: to identify them going forward so that we become more aware of our thought patterns.

*

A curious mind is interested in its thought patterns and would love to uncover them all right away. Our worldview, however, is so permeated by paradigms like spiderwebs within spiderwebs that we can't tear it apart by willpower alone. There is a reason that this book follows an *arrangement* – an arrangement that unties attachments in a specific sequence so that you'll eventually break free, first with your eyes, then with your hands, and finally with your feet – at which point you fall out of the web of paradigms right into the PRESENT.

Anyone who considers "being human" as something real cannot realize the truth about happiness. Anyone who doesn't recognize the ego cannot search for the self. Anyone who ignores the present cannot grasp the meaning of life. Anyone who disregards death cannot experience love. And anyone who just accepts his mental comfort zones remains locked into them forever.

AWAKENING is always possible, of course. But in the meantime, while we are still searching, we may increase its likelihood. We can work on our awareness, our emotions, and also on our thoughts. To this end, it is *meaningful* to acquire our realizations in safe stages – about LIFE, CONSCIOUSNESS, and EXISTENCE – similar to repairing an old string of fairy lights. One defective bulb is enough to keep all the lights dark. We shouldn't just randomly exchange bulbs, hoping for a lucky strike, and having to deal with subsequent disappointments. We should start at the beginning, change the bulbs one after the other, and keep going until enlightenment.

Natures

A paradigm shift goes through five phases. It all begins with an anomaly, a new observation that current theories cannot explain. That's the first phase. The faculties in question then search for explanations with and within traditional means. Existing theories are expanded with exemptions or modified by substitute measures to maintain their validity. That's the second phase. Simultaneously, lateral thinkers arrive at a new theory that plausibly explains the anomaly and, within this new worldview, turns it into a normality. That's the third phase. Leading disciplines then reject the new explanation, sometimes rightly so, sometimes wrongly because "changing a worldview" impacts finances, reputations, and habits. That's the fourth phase. And only if these resistances are overcome, perhaps due to prominent support or undeniable contradictions, a new paradigm will assert itself in the public eye and thus complete the fifth phase.[a][134] In consequence, paradigms are not based on logic or proof but on habits and marketing – which significantly slows down the development of our civilization.

Our concepts, our language, and its words describe entirely different natures of being. A rose, a house, or light describe perceptible phenomena (N1). Weariness, joy, or love stand for inner sensations (N2). Wealth, retirement, or mathematics define collective concepts (N3).

---

[a] Thomas Kuhn (The Structure Of Scientific Revolutions)

Waves, orbits, or sunsets depict temporal processes and their interpretation (N4). And then there is a fifth nature (N5): silence, emptiness, or darkness indicate an absence of perception.

The absence of perception is an *undescribed state* of EXISTENCE and in itself the reason why we are able to perceive at all. Without fundamental silence, no sound could be heard. Without fundamental darkness, no light could be seen. Without fundamental emptiness, nothing could lie in our hands. This emptiness is not *created*, for example, when we empty a room, but simply exists, therefore allowing *that there even is a room*. And this fundamentally *undescribed state*, which allows all things like sound, light, objects, scent, and taste to fall into our perception like ink drops on paper, isn't different for each sense but is *one and the same*. We may have assigned different labels to this "absence of perception," such as "silence," "darkness," or "emptiness," but reality doesn't distinguish between whatever is absent.

When we are unable to understand something, it makes sense to first identify the nature of whatever is involved in the matter, and then to *think in probabilities*. Let's take the paradigm of "dark matter." Astrophysics discovered that the galaxies in our universe (N1, real phenomena) don't behave as predicted by our theories, formulas, and simulations (N3, our ideas). Our worldview would only be right if the universe were to hold significantly more matter than we currently see (N4, an interpretation). This missing "dark matter" and also "dark energy" must be invisible to us (N3, two ideas, and N2, a feeling of correct assumption). Yet even a full century of research couldn't bring any evidence of their existence (N5, absence). So, *thinking in probabilities*, the search for "dark matter" brings us not closer to REALITY but leaves us wandering around feelings, ideas, and interpretations.

We cannot help but start with an idea that will possibly turn out to be wrong. We must not criticize this approach. Even if our ideas do prove themselves wrong or imprecise, we'll have gained new insights into reality. But our assumptions, ideas, and interpretations should not harden into a solid foundation because unless we build upon a foundation that can be experienced directly (N1/2/5), our interpretations (N3/4) are built just on interpretations (N3/4) and thus "on sand" only.

Intelligence

Without knowledge of ONENESS, the origin of life remains a mystery. We are unable to understand how and why "dead stardust" brought forth conscious, sometimes even intelligent life. Even our most advanced scientific achievements fail to create new life from scratch and may only genetically modify life that exists already. And so, it's no wonder that *artificial intelligence* fascinates us – or let's say distracts us from the dilemma that our natural intelligence is no longer sufficient.

The term "artificial intelligence" may trigger many ideas, questions, and debates, just like "warm darkness" or "distilled joy," as imaginations appear in front of our mind's eye automatically. "Distilled joy" sounds like flasks filled with bubbling and luminous liquids. "Warm darkness" could remind us of a number of humid summer nights. And "artificial intelligence" makes us think of a machine with a mind, a machine with thoughts, self-reflection, and its own will – regardless of whether darkness can be warm, joy can be distilled, or intelligence can have something to do with artificiality. We expect a *ghost in the machine*. However, this expectation doesn't arise from technological feasibility but purely from wishful thinking.

What is artificial intelligence? The Turing test explains, "An AI must appear human to a human." Without visual contact; correspondence or a phone call would suffice. And this specification leads to grave contradictions for the meaning of intelligence. Is a person intelligent because he *appears* intelligent? Would you consider calculators to be intelligent because they work faster than the greatest genius? And isn't it likely that lifeforms that are ten times more intelligent (than we are today) would behave quite differently than a human being?

Judging intelligence by appearance would be stupid. And we certainly are "stupid" or "off track" at times. We may well be hypocritical or prejudiced sometimes and declare people as lunatics because they have wild hair and stick their tongues out. But that's not all. We are equally capable of discovering our shortcomings, misconceptions, and incomprehensions so that we may unravel a greater truth.

*

Intelligence isn't an outer impression but describes an inner process that is not easily, clearly, or statistically definable. We may describe this process as the ability to acquire the right information, fall into a focused state of mind, incorporate other points of view, place logic in part above emotions, and select the best from all the available options. This ability may then impress others in a specific way, whether intentionally or unintentionally.

Intelligence contains no wisdom. We hold a sharp knife, so to speak, which enables us to artfully carve something or grievously injure someone. Like a figure skater, we may move horizontally through our *logical system* only, but can neither see nor leave the limitations of this plane. A vertical movement *out of a logical system* needs more than intelligence; it needs morality, integrity, and wisdom to gently guide our sharp knife or ice skates. Our use of language complicates this distinction. Emotional intelligence duly represents morality, as it describes our ability to notice emotions, classify their significance, and adapt our behavior accordingly. Emotional intelligence is warm and radiant, like a beacon. But pure intelligence is cold and clear, like a blade of steel. And so, just being intelligent *brings* nothing: it neither brings happiness nor purpose nor self-development. An imposter, a company CEO, and the Buddha can all be equally intelligent – but their awareness would impact the environment totally differently.

Intelligence isn't a permanent condition. It's a potential. Even a genius will not be intelligent in every moment and concerning all matters:

totally exhausted, a genius could even fail the Turing test and appear like a poorly programmed machine. A good sign of intelligence is when people don't perpetually show off their knowledge. Good behavior, however, as it is defined in our culture, may seem blunt in other cultures. All this illustrates the impossibility of correctly determining intelligence (or its lack) from the outside because we cannot see but can only assume it. The entire assessment depends on our own intelligence, so to speak. We wouldn't describe infants as stupid, for example, because *that* would be stupid. But even though intelligence is relative regarding its outer appearance and its inner effects, our deeper understanding of intelligence must not include such relativity. If its potential is present within us, it must always be present, wherever we are.

*

An entirely unconscious living being cannot be intelligent. But an entirely *conscious* living being cannot be intelligent *either*. A highly meditative state renders an IQ test impossible. We need to allow that our thoughts run free, that we may be lost in between them, and that our subconsciousness can do its thing so that it suddenly – stop! – arrives at an insight. We thus receive intelligence from an interplay of conscious and unconscious events, similar to ant colonies demonstrating a hive mind. Countless chaotic impulses lead to one purposeful action. And that means: Intelligence isn't created *by humans* but is a component of HAPPENING. LIFE naturally gains access to the tool of intelligence once it becomes partially unconscious and resides somewhere between the second and sixth state of being (△2-6).

We observe a dolphin without seeing its consciousness. We look into the mirror, into our eyes, without finding external proof that we are intelligent. So how could we attribute these qualities to a *machine*? Intelligent programming [IPs] may certainly simulate intelligent human behavior. But no matter how well these imitations are designed, we will *know about them* and, sometimes at least, feel amazed about "how good these simulations have become," "how intelligent the programmers were," or "how emotionless the simulated behaviors truly are." And for all these reasons, we should discard the idea of artificial intelligence [AI] being a *ghost in a machine*. The Turing test sets no criteria for intelligence but expresses the twisted goal of creating an artificial illusion for the human illusion.

Humankind strives for intelligent machines to create a better world, without being able to feel what a "better world" even means. Does it mean improving our effectiveness in striving for happiness? An intelligent choice would be to stop striving, because – so much is clear – moving horizontally through our worldview *is no longer sufficient*. It's not intelligent to cling to the human illusion. It's just *unconscious*. We need to move vertically out of our unconsciousness. And aside from intelligence, this breakthrough into new regions of EXISTENCE will give us wisdom.

+ You now know: that intelligence *on its own* is meaningless, that the paradigms in our worldview are supporting each other, and that a conscious worldview requires the tearing down of the supporting pillars one by one.

You keep in mind:

Paradigms come and go, even during our own lifetime. Within this changing of ideas, beliefs, and worldviews, the "paradigm of time" is uniquely special because it *itself* determines the time it takes until its disappearance. Only when, *for no particular reason*, we no longer believe in past and future, the paradigm of time will be gone as well.

Artificial intelligence describes an intelligent programming that processes information, arrives at complex conclusions, and simulates human behavior. In our general understanding, this term has been *mystified*. A well-advanced AI makes us imagine some kind of "self-conscious intelligence inside a machine." But self-consciousness and intelligence cannot be consciously created, especially not by intelligent programming.

Δ *You now can: actively participate in the upcoming paradigm shifts, distinguish the five natures of being, and move vertically through layers of logic.*

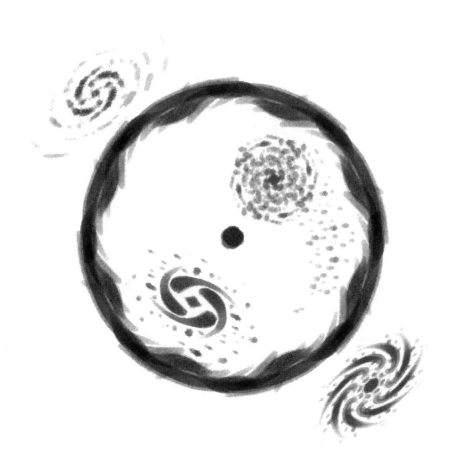

216

20 **Space**

Wholeness and its constant shift. The non-locality and indetermination of reality. The experienceable world. The Big Bang theory's pillars. The age of the universe. The cosmic horizon. A cosmic journey. The center of the observable universe.

S cience wants to discover how the world functions in its grand entirety and its tiniest detail, but ultimately, everything tiny and grand is simply there, in space, time, and eternity. So our next question is: "What is this SPACE in which everything arises?" And the answer will once again change our worldview completely.

Here

An empty room asks for furniture, plants, and decoration. But does a room contain less SPACE after it has been filled with such things? Is SPACE situated around objects only? And can walls divide SPACE into an inside and outside? The necessity to contemplate such questions about everyday reality stems from a deeply rooted belief: We believe that things exist *independent* of each other, have their own beginnings, and eventually have their own endings. Here I sit, 38 years old, on a sofa, seven years old, in a building, 29 years old, on Earth, 4 billion years old, somewhere in the universe, who knows how old.[a135] But EXISTENCE isn't made up of "different things," cannot be divided into areas like "inside and outside," and also doesn't arise from a "superposition of timelines." It always remains one WHOLENESS.

Every perception happens HERE NOW, both physically and mentally. Our mind, which is *one facet* of this observation, just imparts an illusion to it – a sensation of height, width, depth, time, and things so that it looks like "humans" could act, age, or evolve independent of EXISTENCE. In reality, its WHOLENESS is constantly shifting. An

---

[a] Diamond Sutra

ocean wave that collapses on the shore, surges up the sand, and washes around our feet isn't created locally, right in front of us, but arises from the *shifting* of an entire ocean, the Earth, the moon, the sun, and the entire cosmos, all of which results in those waves right in front of us, giving the appearance of transience, underscored by their rhythmic rushing.

Quantum physics is already familiar with the *non-locality* and *indetermination* of REALITY because experiments left no other choice. The double-slit experiment (or the EPR paradox) shows that, in the quantum world, space and time have no meaning. And the so-called Bell's inequality proves that "our human world" isn't *really* and *locally* observable, either: A physical experiment would only stay real (and be authentic) if we could analyze it without observation, and a physical experiment would only remain local (and be authentic) if its observation had no impact on the overall system, including the observer – both of which is impossible. So, in REALITY, there are neither *places* nor *times* like, for example, "Central Park in spring."

*

When we look at a scattering of clouds for a while, we may discover forms and meanings within them that can't be unseen. "Look up there, a turtle," we'd say, and possibly want other people to see the same. Yet, even if all the people around us would agree, we must comprehend that this interpretation is *our creation*, which we have placed in front of the CONTRAST of the PRESENT.

In EXISTENCE, there is no "outside" and "inside" because such distinction stems from us and our labels. We recognize clouds as an outer appearance and emotions as an inner experience, but arriving at such conclusion implies that we have already interpreted our perception: The clouds and our emotions are already mental objects that contain the impression of coming from *seemingly different directions*. But as soon as we slide these mental objects aside for a moment, we discover that the

SPACE in which EVERYTHING arises is CONSCIOUSNESS. HERE, every perception receives its meaning.

Our universe, as we say, started with the Big Bang, and that may be so, as long as our hypothesis does not include the creation of EXISTENCE. Any assertion that SPACE, CONSCIOUSNESS, and CHANGE also started with the Big Bang would disregard the principle of beginninglessness.

A goldfish swimming around in a bowl might ask itself: "I wonder what the size of my universe is? When was it created? And does it have any boundaries?"

And we might tell it: "The world is vastly more spacious than your aquarium! Come, I will show you," and pour it and its whole world into a lake.

The goldfish would be overwhelmed by the sheer size of this new cosmos. But its curiosity would return: "I wonder what the size of my universe is? When was it created? And does it have any boundaries?" The outer edges of its "perceivable world" weren't removed but shifted, away from the glass of a bowl towards the banks of a lake.

Our *perceivable world* will always be limited, too, preventing us from ever reaching the outer edges of the universe, because perception ends earlier than EXISTENCE. We may understand this *observable universe* as a container that is enclosed by larger containers. But SPACE must not give us the idea of a container because it contains all containers. Each boundary is based on something *behind* it, or no boundary would be possible.

EXISTENCE is *timeless* and also *spaceless* – even an endless journey through the cosmos would always take place HERE NOW. Our astronomical curiosity thus shouldn't ask how *big* or *old* our universe might be, but *what is limiting* our perception of it.

Age

The age of the universe is estimated at 13.8 billion years, and to comprehend this statement, we must understand three paradigms: (first) the primordial nucleosynthesis, (second) the cosmic background radiation, and (third) the expansion of the universe, which in their combination establish the Big Bang theory.

The *primordial nucleosynthesis* is the first pillar of the Big Bang theory: It's said that the Big Bang set off a tremendous chain reaction. Matter and antimatter were released and, upon collision, annihilated each other. But in this inferno, an imbalance ensued. A small residue of matter remained unharmed – largely hydrogen atoms, the most lightweight of all atomic elements. In an ongoing nuclear fusion, these hydrogen atoms melded into heavier elements, the way it occurs in our sun, and created life's building blocks that make up our bodies today. This nuclear fusion, which is also called the primordial nucleosynthesis, is going to continue until it runs out of fuel. And because only a small percentage of lightweight atoms has been consumed so far, scientists conclude that our universe is still in its youth.

The *cosmic background radiation* is the second pillar of the Big Bang theory. This background radiation doesn't mean that rays from a distant background finally make it to Earth, but that any point in the vacuum of space has a temperature of about 2.7 Kelvin. The Big Bang, as it is explained, produced unimaginable temperatures in the universe that was initially quite small. But this universe started to expand and cool down in the process, arriving at a temperature of slightly above absolute zero today.

The *expansion of the universe* forms the third pillar of the Big Bang theory: Cosmic objects, it is said, move apart – because space itself is expanding; the more space lies in between, the faster they separate. Dots painted on a balloon illustrate this effect: When we inflate the balloon, two dots far apart move away faster than two dots directly next to each other. As a consequence, it is possible for distant galaxies or celestial bodies to move apart *faster than the speed of light*, as the expansion of space doesn't provoke relativistic effects.

But how did we arrive at such paradigms? How can we talk about motion, speed, or expansion within the unknowable vastness of the universe? On a cosmic scale, science uses parallax measurements or calibrated cepheid comparison to determine distances, but in particular, science relies on the *redshift of light*. And this redshift of light is the foundation of the Big Bang theory.

Sunlight creates a magnificent play of colors. It appears blue in the morning, shines yellow at its zenith, and glows red at dusk. But this contrast is created by our planet's atmosphere, while the sunlight itself remains unchanged. The sun steadily radiates photons over all wavelengths, which, in their bundle, appear white to our eyes. But photon bundles of distant stars, which arrive on Earth after millions of years of travel, reveal an increased redshift. Their wavelengths have been "stretched apart," suggesting that their oscillation expanded during their travel through space and time.

Photons move at the speed of light, that's common knowledge. The expansion of the universe adds an important detail: one lightyear equals one year in time but, depending on whether or not we include the expansion of space, corresponds to a different *spatial distance*. The space between the center of Earth and its surface expands by about seventy nanometers per year; we can calculate that using the Hubble constant. So, for short distances, the expansion of space is practically irrelevant. The Milky Way expands by about two kilometers per second. And a galaxy existing four billion lightyears away is carried farther away by ninety thousand kilometers per second.

But these calculations remain mere approximations, because the Hubble constant has a broad tolerance range, because science isn't even sure about the constancy of the "Hubble constant," and because of the many contradictions within the Big Bang paradigm calling for a new worldview.

✻

The vacuum of space isn't perfect. Isolated hydrogen atoms or particles from quantum fluctuations exist within its apparent emptiness. And, as science explains, every time a light photon hits such particles, gets absorbed and discharged again, these particles heat up to about three Kelvin. So, is the cosmic background radiation a remnant of a Big Bang or an effect of light traversing the cosmos right now? The latter probability would also explain why the background radiation stands still and doesn't move as an expansion normally would.[a136] The first pillar of the Big Bang theory is already showing cracks.

Another scientific concept, the so-called interstellar extinction, describes that photon bundles, as they traverse vast distances, are absorbed, weakened, and shifted to red by nebulae of matter. So, is the redshift of light the result of an expansion or extinction? The latter explanation would resolve further contradictions.

In the galaxy NGC 7603, celestial objects have been discovered that move away from Earth at the same speed, yet show significantly different redshifts. The redshift of light thus *does not only depend* on the expansion of space, particularly as some cosmic phenomena even show a blueshift of light.

Also, according to the particle-wave duality, light has a dual character: Sometimes it behaves like a wave, sometimes it behaves like a particle. Concerning the redshift, only its wave property seems to apply, as the photons in their bundles are unaffected in their spacing, in all three dimensions. According to the uncertainty principle, however, the length of a photon wave is a quantum probability and thus not definable. Light is no "consistent, constant, and always identical wave" and, consequently, cannot be reliably and repeatably expanded "into the red," not even by an expansion of space.

And finally, we have the theory of relativity. The "length contraction" and "time dilation" explain that traveling at the speed of light makes our space and time "collapse," which then excludes any spatial influences of

---

[a] Alexander Unzicker

our world. Our three-dimensional space-time thus cannot influence light.

When we acknowledge the relativity theory, the wave-particle duality, and quantum electrodynamics, the redshift of light cannot be explained by the universe's expansion – making our current astronomical worldview fall to pieces.

The Big Bang theory is located deep within the fourth phase of a paradigm shift: An entirely possible and meaningful change of our worldview gets delayed by resistance, inertia, or ignorance. The pillars of the Big Bang theory don't only show large cracks. Inspecting them also reveals that the background radiation, the universe's expansion, and the redshift of light do not support but *carry* each other. As soon as one column falls, the others fall too. But maybe science hesitates to complete the paradigm shift because: When the Big Bang worldview falls, what alternative could be offered to the world?

*

Without paying attention to questionable contradictions, science researched the age of the universe and found its answer in the *oldest light*. The oldest stars, it is said, were formed just shortly after the Big Bang, with some of them now located at the outermost boundaries of space. These suns may have faded many eons ago, but their light still travels towards us and can be identified by looking for the highest redshift ever measured. This method dated the age of the universe to about 13.8 billion years. But the contradictiveness of this approach clarifies even more that the Big Bang worldview could officially collapse tomorrow.

Horizon

Our planet is round and, therefore, we experience that, at a certain distance, the *horizon*, the setting sun, sailing ships, or even landscapes disappear from our view. On Earth, this distance to the horizon depends on the height of our vantage point. In the universe, an expansion of space produces quite a similar effect. If space were to expand, we would experience a particular distance to Earth where the expansion is "as fast" as the speed of light, so that light from beyond that distance could never reach us. This cosmic horizon, which is determined by the Hubble constant, would remain at the same distance around Earth, no matter the age of our universe. And applying the Hubble constant once more, our cosmic horizon lies about 13.8 billion lightyears away.

But what does that mean? How can it be that the age of the universe and our cosmic horizon are identical?

If a 13.8 billion-year-*old* photon reaches Earth, we know that its originating sun was located *less* than 13.8 billion lightyears *away* from Earth, back then, when the light was emitted. This former distance *closer* to Earth can again be determined by using the Hubble constant. At the time of the Big Bang, the originating sun would have existed about 10.1 billion lightyears away from Earth – which implies that the universe was much greater than the Big Bang theory supposes. And today, this originating sun, if not extinct, would be located very close to our cosmic horizon. Its photons, however, which start their journey towards Earth (let's say: one lightyear away from leaving our horizon), will require about 190 trillion years to arrive at Earth. The expansion of *all the space in between* almost matches the speed of light, so that the photons "can barely swim upstream against the current," extending their journey to Earth almost infinitely. But playing with numbers should not distract us. Our present worldview turns out to be wrong even without formulas, constants, and calculations, because:

If we accept an expansion of the universe, we must equally accept a horizon beyond which REALITY simply continues or may continue quite naturally. Out of sight, somewhere else, a Big Bang might take place right now. We can discard our ideas of a fishbowl universe and *scientifically* declare EXISTENCE as spaceless, timeless, and infinite. "Dear humanity," we can offer to the world, "age and size of our universe are infinite because existence has neither beginning, ending, nor limits and therefore still has the most fascinating discoveries in store for us."

*

Let me take you on a cosmic journey. We leave Earth at the speed of light, orbit our blue planet twice for a farewell (one blink of the eye), pass the Moon (after about one second), visit the Sun (after eight minutes), and cross the outer edges of our solar system (two years). We still think that we can understand scale and proportion, but we aren't prepared for what's coming. Our journey through the Milky Way takes one hundred thousand years, and before long, our home sun becomes indistinguishable, just one dot among a hundred billion shining stars. And we travel on, more than five million years, leaving behind our "local cluster," in which *whole galaxies* shrink down to one pinpoint of light and no longer reveal any sign of their abundant life. But even after all this time and distance, our journey hasn't even started yet – it's as if you had just taken ten steps in a marathon. We and the light now spend over two hundred million years traversing the so-called Virgo supercluster in which hundreds of thousands of galaxies shine like one grain of sand, to then travel through the outer limits of our cosmic superstructure for another billion years. And while *Laniakea* and the many other galaxy superclusters fade to small sprinkles of light, the cosmic horizon lying at 13.8 billion lightyears is still far away, especially considering the expansion of space that we need to cover additionally. Our own horizon moves with us, of course. And so, an eternity passes, until at some point, after a journey that leaves our former life feeling like a fleeting dream, our unbelievably distant home begins to disappear behind us. We then know that Earth is about to leave *our horizon* and that we will soon cross a border insurmountable for Earthlings. So we stop, look back, and *recognize it.* Inside its observable universe, Earth is located at a truly unique place. The center.

You stand on a mountain top, take in the panorama, and enjoy the far horizon. This horizon depends on you and the current situation, not on the mountain top. Rising fog, dust-covered sunglasses, or the upcoming dusk may change this view, but you remain in the center wherever life takes you. So the decisive detail isn't whether the universe is expanding (or not), whether the cosmic horizon exists (or not), or whether a theory is correct (or not), because all that only discusses our inner workings, but that the cosmos is exactly HERE NOW in all possible forms. The MOSAIC is and will always be the only place of life, regardless of what we call the ground beneath our feet.

+ You now know: that reality is neither local nor determinable, that our mental focus on the Big Bang theory is unfounded, and that Earth is located at the center of its observable universe.

You keep in mind:

The **age of the universe** is infinite, that is, *timeless.*

The **cosmic horizon** is the distance from which light can no longer reach us because the space between Earth and its horizon expands faster than light. This insurmountable limit of our observable universe makes it impossible to determine the actual size of EXISTENCE by astronomical methods. Then again, we already know the answer: The size of the universe is infinite, that is, *spaceless.*

SPACE describes the place where all things, horizons, and observable universes exist. SPACE itself is infinite, *spaceless,* and – putting aside all attachments and mental objects for a moment – is ultimately synonymous with CONSCIOUSNESS.

The **HERE** is *the only place* in EXISTENCE, both in a physical and mental understanding. The NOW is the *only moment* in EXISTENCE, both in a physical and mental understanding. This place and this moment are identical: Both are CONSCIOUSNESS and thus the PRESENT.

Δ *You now can: perceive the spacelessness of existence, gaze into the starry sky with innermost awe, and explore within your emotions to ascertain if you are still attached to a scenario of creation.*

21 Dimensions

The Flatlander world. Analogy as a tool for greater understanding. Dimensionless reality. A life without language. Our mental denseness in front of contrast. The perceived cross-section of existence. Dimensions and densities. The fourth density.

W e experience EXISTENCE in height, width, and depth, but higher dimensions remain hidden to us, both in theory and practice. Our thoughts can't leave their geometry so that tesseracts or Calabi-Yau-manifolds are illustrated by two-dimensional models only. When the way up is blocked, however, we may think in a different direction. Objective knowledge, Ouspensky explains, isn't based on the study of *facts*, but on the study of *their perception* – which comprises how we perceive the world as humans and also, how other living beings would perceive it.[a][137]

Motion

Imagine, if you will, a *Flatlander*, a being who can perceive two dimensions only: width and depth. Height is something the Flatlander doesn't know; "up and down" are unimaginable concepts. His entire perception takes place in a horizontal plane, maybe *in the surface* of a lake, where he and his kin exist in the fine line between air and water.

In the same way that our eyes capture two-dimensional pictures, and our minds turn them into three-dimensional impressions, the Flatlanders are able to discover a two-dimensional depth in their one-dimensional cross-section. Objects further away are smaller. A ball floating in their world would appear round, not because the Flatlanders could actually see its roundness, but because the object looks identical from all directions – just like a sphere doesn't look spherical to us, but identical from all sides. A human hand slowly entering the Flatlander

---

[a] P. D. Ouspensky (Tertium Organum)

world, fingers first, would appear like five separate objects to the Flatlanders, which then merge into one larger entity – just like five clouds could meet and merge into a larger togetherness. And the wheel of a watermill would produce a strange phenomenon, as well, as it suddenly shows up, wanders through the world for a while, and disappears again, similar to the sun moving across the sky. The Flatlanders might even use the millwheel to keep track of time.

A ring that is partly immersed in the Flatlander world would appear to the Flatlanders as two objects. When turning the ring like a wheel, these two objects would stay in place, unchanged and unmoving. When turning the ring like a spinning top, however, the two objects would begin to move: The Flatlanders would experience it like an oscillation. The phenomenon changes "from particle to wave," so to speak. And which miracle must be set in motion by the treetop halfway floating in the lake, snapped off by the last storm? The Flatlanders might assign several scientific faculties with its study in order to develop new models of reality. But to be honest, the Flatlanders have no chance, not even the slightest, to understand reality in this way because they can't even distinguish a temporal CHANGE from a spatial MOTION in EXISTENCE:

The millwheel, the treetop, and our hands *move* through the Flatlander world. But from the perspective of the Flatlander, objects can only move sideways. All things that enter their two-dimensional plane from above or below just appear (like the sun does for us) or change their shape (like clouds do for us), so that a Flatlander perceives such spatial motions as temporal changes.

This brings us to the *analogies* that we can draw between the Flatlander and our human perception:

A1) The Flatlanders will consider themselves as two-dimensional beings, even though, in reality, a body of two dimensions cannot exist. All events, forms, and beings are *at home* in the wholeness of EXISTENCE.

A2) The motion of an object in three-dimensional space may appear to the Flatlanders as if two, three, or ten-thousand things are moving.

A3) The Flatlanders might perceive *time* as the "third dimension." If a Rubik's cube, for instance, floats about in the Flatlander world, it would continuously generate new combinations of colors (similar to watching it close-up through a keyhole). "Yesterday was white-yellow-blue, do you remember?" the Flatlanders will say. "But now it's green-yellow-blue-white." And even though the Rubik's Cube doesn't change, its motion and its color combinations would create the illusion of an objective past.[a][138]

A4) The sensation of temporal changes within two dimensions may be caused by spatial motion in three dimensions. The past, therefore, may still be PRESENT in higher dimensions. It's just that the Flatlanders look past it.

A5) If a Flatlander could *experience three-dimensionally* even for one brief moment the higher reality that produces his perception, he would fall onto his two-dimensional knees in pure wonder, awaken from his previous worldview, and plunge into a much greater self-perception. The Flatlander would understand that the source of his past and future already exists in ONENESS, and he might even tell his friends that GOD exists WITHIN THEM.

And all these realizations about the Flatlander-world also apply to us humans, shifted by one dimension.

*

Every living being in the cosmos, be it Flatlanders, humans, or theoretical tesseract beings can derive identical *conclusions* upon reflecting the nature of perception:

C1) Our perception includes an impression of dimensions: a sensation of extending out into space and time. This division into space and time arises within the observer only, not through a cosmic definition. There

---

[a] P. D. Ouspensky (Tertium Organum)

aren't explicitly "spatial" and explicitly "temporal" dimensions. All dimensions are of "identical nature."

C2) The CHANGE of EXISTENCE, which we understand as time, is caused by MOTION in higher dimensions: not only by MOTION inside the next higher dimension but by MOTION within all higher dimensions combined.

C3) A living being, which perceives all dimensions without exception, could no longer see any MOTION because nothing could *move* into its field of vision anymore. So our world changes because we aren't able to perceive everything at once. The CHANGE we experience thus proves to us an unknown and higher reality.

C4) The dimensions we perceive, such as height, depth, or width, follow no numbering or sequence. In the same way, higher dimensions aren't numbered or "officially" arranged – and neither are lower dimensions. As a consequence, there is no possibility of isolating an unknown higher dimension. We may only describe the *combined* effect of all inaccessible dimensions.

C5) EXISTENCE and LIFE always take place in all of SPACE. They don't leave out any dimensions. Every living being thus has roots in all dimensions and experiences a world unfolding from all dimensions.

C6) SPACE is that which contains all dimensions and, therefore, must be dimensionless. WE, as CONSCIOUSNESS, are non-dimensional beings.

Considering these conclusions, we may wonder if our future already exists in higher dimensions, so that our fate is predetermined. But such thoughts neglect the nature of the PRESENT. EXISTENCE certainly already exists in its entire WHOLENESS, yet without predetermination of which CHANGES will happen NOW – how high the next wave washes up on the beach, whether a raindrop comes down directly onto your nose, or what thought you'll think next. So if we were to ponder whether our fate is predetermined, we would determine the course of events right now, precisely by this pondering.

Density

Newborns recognize our touch, yet don't perceive it as a "touch from the outside world" but simply as an experience in consciousness. Conditioning, concepts, and paradigms are added only later, when the child grows up into the human life that we find familiar. One day, the child will think: "The touch on my face – that's my mother cleaning chocolate off my cheek, right outside the school, which is embarrassing and annoying." But such a perception of the world is impossible for a newborn, also for animals, and fundamentally *for all living beings without language.*

The inner life of insects, reptiles, and other animals cannot be evaluated from the outside. Ants could well experience the world on the sixth state of being ($\triangle 6$). We can claim, however, that animals *quite probably* have no self-reflexive mind, cannot think conceptually, and therefore do not assign names to REALITY, but simply follow their instincts, habits, and curiosity without having a conceptual language, so that they experience life on the second state of being ($\triangle 2$).

The things that in our eyes constitute reality exist as mental objects in our minds only. REALITY is there, of course, but without the contours set by our minds, without beginnings and endings, or any actual separation. The division into things arises only from our labeling. And this perception is inaccessible for all living beings without language – a cat, for example.

A cat cannot divide the PRESENT into objects and, therefore, is unable to understand that "trees cast a shadow" because it doesn't even know the concept of "trees" and "shadows" and so may not distinguish between them. The cat, as it sneaks through a park, sees a new constellation of CONTRAST from every perspective, because *the undifferentiated picture* of trees and their shadows looks different from every angle. A photo of the tree taken from the south looks quite different from a photo of it taken from the west. All sensory impressions would be one thing to the cat, *one* sensation, like an abstract painting in which we haven't yet discovered any object. And so, the cat never considers a touch as

233

embarrassing (only possibly as unpleasant), our hand is never *our hand* for it, and even repetitive occurrences always feel like new sensations.

A cat recognizes the rising sun as a new phenomenon each day, as a *new sun,* because it doesn't know about Earth's rotation and everything connected with it. The same object, as it moves through space, turns into *new forms in time.* We, as humans, are aware that it's the same sun every morning. But for us, a *new day* begins with each dawn, because we don't know yet about the eternal present and everything connected with it.[a][139]

The human mind severely changes our perception of REALITY. We create, so to speak, a *mental denseness of meanings* in front of the CONTRAST by discovering ten, hundreds, or thousands of things within: "That's a tree. And that's its shadow, which changes based on the time of day, the position of the sun, and where I'm standing myself. That's logical."

*

The ocean is traversed by currents: Warm water flows through cold water, forming almost stable passageways, and shaping the climate across the world. And similar to water flowing through water, EXISTENCE moves through EXISTENCE to shape our experience of REALITY, depending on the cross-section we perceive of it; similar to cutting patterns into folded paper and ending up with quite different results. And this *perceived cross-section* of EXISTENCE isn't permanent but is constantly changing.

Dreams occur in dimensionless consciousness (0D). The rushing noise caused by a shell held to our ear seems to come from one point (1D). Our eyes see the world in two dimensions, like a photograph (2D). Yet the rapid succession of such "photos" creates a world of spatial depth in our minds (3D). Our human perception thus isn't *fixed* but wanders up and down through dimensions to reside somewhere around our physical

---

[a] P. D. Ouspensky (Tertium Organum)

limits and mental habits. The only question is: Are our eyes *flattening* reality, or is our mind *deepening* reality? And when reflecting on this, we see that indeed *both* apply.

Dimensionless REALITY contains more physical information than our physical senses may perceive. But independent of what our physical senses do capture, without our mind, it would have no depth in space and time. And this realization has far-reaching effects on our worldview: We must fundamentally abandon our understanding of purely physical dimensions, must acknowledge the existence of purely mental dimensions, and must accept the impossibility of distinguishing both physical and mental dimensions from each other. Any distinction wouldn't reflect reality but would only describe our view into EXISTENCE, which right now gives dimensions to its dimensionless-ness. In order to remember this dual nature of dimensions, we will, from now on, label it as the *density* of our perception – the *mental density* that we create in front of the dimensionless CONTRAST.

*

The density of our perception describes what we make ourselves see within the spacelessness, timelessness, and dimensionlessness of EXISTENCE, HERE NOW. We mostly experience a three-dimensional world in the flow of time. So humanity, one could say, lives in the third density. But REALITY and CONSCIOUSNESS aren't limited to three dimensions. We limit ourselves. We essentially make time greater as it is. We perceive things as temporal events when, in fact, they are spatial events or drifting thoughts only.

Once we let go of the overinterpretation of the PRESENT, once our *primary sense of time* changes into a sense of MOTION, once we perceive that this constellation of ONENESS, HERE NOW, moves through ITSELF for the first time, we will discover the fourth density.[a][140] This discovery fundamentally requires losing all attachment to past and

---

[a] Bashar (Blueprint for Change)

future, to time pressure, to death, and *our ego*. The fourth density is unveiled in AWAKENING. The outer world won't look different at first. Nobody will see people stumbling awkwardly through four-dimensional space. But inwardly, everything changes. And the actions that then become possible will change the world outwardly, too.

+ You now know: that existence is dimensionless, how unimaginably *different* a life without language would be, and that humanity lives in the third density.

\# You keep in mind:

A **density** describes the same idea as a dimension but clarifies that the perception of dimensions is also determined by the mind and not only by physical reality.

MOTION explains that EXISTENCE moves through EXISTENCE, causing CHANGE. MOTION reminds us that CHANGE isn't caused by time but should be understood spatially, as everything that moves already exists.

Δ *You now can: transfer the realizations about the Flatlander world into your own life, recognize the mental denseness of your mind in front of the contrast, and equate spiritual awakening as the perception of the fourth density.*

22 Light

The essence of light. The theory of relativity. The world at lightspeed. The true relativity of existence. Our segment of reality. Possibilities and probabilities. One creative consciousness. Our local-now. The now-delay of reality.

L ight conveys contrast, not only in terms of brightness and colors, but also in terms of warmth, energy, and change itself. Without light, without even a single vibration taking place in the spectrum of light, our world would hold neither perception nor life, which indicates a direct relationship to AWARENESS.

We know that light, or its absence, strongly influences our emotional state. But we do not fully understand why photons have no mass, what the speed of light actually means, and that everything in every moment is absolutely relative.

Relativity

A century ago, Einstein's theory of relativity explained that space and time depend on their observer. "Everything is relative" became a saying to us, a well-known pearl of wisdom that we connect less with physical reality but more with negative emotions: "I need to walk through the pouring rain, which is quite inconvenient. But I shouldn't complain. Some people can't even walk. My inconvenience, therefore, is relative." And this somewhat skewed adaptation proves that society is far removed from scientific knowledge: The theory of relativity is a fundamental element of our worldview without having any influence on it. We do not consider the physical world to be relative; we instead regard it as absolute. Our seemingly scientific worldview isn't scientifically correct at all. To solve this contradiction, we need to understand the theory of relativity first and then either refute it or embrace it as natural.

Physics Lesson No. 1) Two trains pass each other at 90 miles per hour. Their relative speed to each other thus equals 180 miles per hour. But this logic doesn't apply to light. When two light-beams pass each other, their speed cannot be added but is topped off at the speed of light [c]. A spaceship rapidly moving away from the sun will continue to receive the sun's photons at lightspeed. Whatever situation we find ourselves in: The speed of light remains a constant and a limit.

Physics Lesson No. 2) A spaceship takes off from Earth, leaves its gravity, and accelerates towards Alpha Centauri. In this moment, two observers arise that go their separate ways. The Earth counts as one observer and forms the original system. The spaceship and its crew count as the second observer, who leaves its original system. Now, depending on the speed of the spaceship, three *relativistic effects* set in: the dilation of time, the contraction of space, and the relativistic increase of mass. At low speeds, these three physical changes may not be recognized. Even the highest speed ever achieved by human ingenuity – 70km/s reached by the Helios space probes – leads to almost no discernible effect.

But let's imagine that our spaceship increases this speed a *thousandfold* and thus reaches 23% lightspeed. The effects would become visible "to the human eye" then. The dilation effect is now about 3%.[a][141] From the viewpoint of Earth, the spaceship becomes shorter, heavier, and the flow of time within it slows down. The astronauts themselves wouldn't notice any changes in their flow of time but would notice a change in the outside world. From the viewpoint of the spacecraft, time on Earth *also* seems to pass more slowly, distances in the solar system become shorter, and the mass of the spacecraft increases.

As the spaceship continues to accelerate, REALITY begins to change more and more. As soon as our spaceship reaches 86.6% lightspeed, the "Lorentz factor" reaches two. Both observers would gain the impression that the other one's progress of time is halved. But only in the spaceship, time would *actually* pass half as fast, so that, several years later, its return to Earth would carry breaking news around the world about the

---

[a] This corresponds to a Lorentz factor of 1.03.

twin paradox: The crew would have aged more slowly than their earthbound siblings.

Any further acceleration of the spaceship would further increase the Lorentz factor and progressively result in greater effects on time, space, and mass. But the energy required for acceleration would also increase, eventually approaching infinity. That's why no object with mass will ever reach the speed of light.

Let us now presume, *purely hypothetically* and *as a thought experiment only,* that our spaceship reaches the speed of light. What would happen? When it reaches the speed of light, the Lorentz factor becomes infinite. Space collapses. An observer on Earth would no longer see the spaceship, as its front and rear would pass a measuring point at the same time. For the astronauts, any distance between the Sun, Alpha Centauri, and the cosmic horizon would disappear. The entire original universe would be thinner than the thickness of one page of the Bible. Time on Earth would seem to have stopped, although it naturally continues for Earth. And so, time on Earth passes infinitely fast, entire eons elapse, while not even one quantum vibration occurs aboard the spaceship.

At this moment, the astronauts ask: "How do we get back?" The first thought might be to cut the engines. But where would a spacecraft *reappear* after traveling an infinite distance in zero time? Whenever would the crew begin with deceleration? And how is slowing down even measurable without physical references? The resolution to these questions is: Upon reaching the speed of light, there is no going back.

*

The theory of relativity describes a reality that initially seems complicated to common sense, as it is still unfamiliar. The more commonplace perception of our ego, however, has been proven wrong for the most part, so that we should dare to approach a new understanding of the world with unbiased frankness, and also curiosity.

If a three-dimensional universe, in which coincidence created intelligent life, was indeed true, it *would have been proven already*.[a142]

Thinking in probabilities, the theory of relativity will not be refuted but, more likely, serves as a starting point for new, unexpected, more accurate paradigms. Besides, humanity will increasingly understand that some things (such as CONSCIOUSNESS) may never be proven technologically but, nevertheless, are facts. And this interplay suggests that future worldviews will experience major evolutions independent of scientific details. The theory of relativity, in this context, prepares us for an acceptance of the universe not as an absolute structure built in three dimensions but as a relative complex arising in a higher REALITY.

"Everything is relative." Let's assume that we meet face-to-face, discuss this statement, and talk about our worldviews. We would find that our experiences, memories, and beliefs don't perfectly match but differ here and there. We would discover how relative the same thing – LIFE as I – can be, even though both of us are telling the truth.

We could then say: "How relative the world can be for two people!" True RELATIVITY, however, lies not in the difference between our two perceptions, but *within our own perception*. All thoughts, conceptions, and attachments are *that* which turns the Absolute – LIFE as I – into something relative. We feel as if there were many observers, that eight billion people live their separate lives, and that all have their own individual consciousness – and yet, it is EXISTENCE behind each observation, no matter how relative it may be, so that in the Absolute, one CONSCIOUSNESS is present that gives all things their time and place.

Delay

REALITY exists only through observation. Without PRESENCE of CONSCIOUSNESS, only possibilities and probabilities exist, which is quite different than REALITY. EXISTENCE would not yet have determined itself. Therefore, we may never know what goes on beyond

---

[a] P. D. Ouspensky (Tertium Organum)

our perceptional horizon – no matter how much we think about it. WE experience only our *segment of reality*, our current perception.

Our perceptional horizon is constantly changing. When we hide underneath a blanket, this horizon is small. When we climb a mountain and gaze off into the distance, our horizon is vast. But to be precise: When we look towards the north, our horizon towards the south is very small. We certainly hear the sounds from right behind our back, feel the southern wind, and may even smell the scent of mountain flowers it carries. But aside from that, the borders between REALITY and "possibilities or probabilities" are constantly moving, shifting, and redrawn.

Let's assume the following situation: A child is asleep in his room. The babysitter pets the dog in the living room. The parents are currently returning home from a dinner event. All three "parties" create their own segment of reality.

The parents' segment contains their observable REALITY, namely that it's raining softly, smells like air freshener in the car, and a fox suddenly scurries across the road. Eyes glow in the headlights, then the fox disappears in the darkness. Every thought the parents might have now, about what the fox, their child, or the babysitter "might be doing right now" remains an *idea*. All things beyond their horizon exist as all possibilities and probabilities simultaneously, just like Schrödinger's cat. The child could be fast asleep, dreaming of elephants, waking up again, quietly playing with stuffed animals, or dumping the contents of a toy box on the floor. Everything is possible. Only when the parents have returned home, said goodbye to the babysitter, and quietly take a peek into the child's room, the possibilities and probabilities collapse into one *segment that is determined jointly*.

"Whenever quantum systems meet," explains Nick Herbert, an American physicist, "their phases get mixed up" and continue as one wave of reality.[a143] A collective CREATION then takes its course, in which all living beings act as one CONSCIOUSNESS.

Our perceived segment of reality constitutes, so to speak, a tangible *local-now* around us that is always ready to connect or disconnect from events at its border. RELATIVITY thus makes it impossible to draw conclusions about any other segment, as it's impossible to perceive anything else than one (our own) segment. Also, we may never truly evaluate "simultaneous events" because any impression of "simultaneity between two segments" might arise only after merging into one. Whenever we "look into another segment," it has already become our own segment. But as long as we haven't looked, it's not REALITY for us.

*

In 2015, two innovative LIGO observatories were able to detect cosmic gravitational waves for the first time. These gravitational waves traversed our solar system at the speed of light, and that raises a fundamental question: Why does light, gravity, or even darkness (the disappearance of light) adhere to the same rate of speed? The answer is easily given but requires a profound change of perspective.

On a US Interstate, cars travel at about 70 miles per hour, especially at the end of the month, when more police checks are provisioned. A physicist of the Middle Ages, who accidentally time-jumps into our century, would be fascinated by such an Interstate. He might study the phenomenon and thus determine the speed of the cars to be approximately 113km/h, depending on the accuracy of his instruments. But this statement confuses cause and effect. The speed is not a property of the cars. The drivers adhere to a speed limit! And in our worldview, there is a similar confusion.

A laser beam needs time to travel from Earth to the moon and back into our telescope. So there's no question that light is delayed. But do we believe reality arrives *faster*?

---

[a] Nick Herbert (Quantum Reality)

"Sunlight takes about eight minutes to arrive on Earth," we teach our children. "So what you see now took place eight minutes ago." Without spelling it out, we mean: "Light just can't go any faster. Consequently, we see a delayed reality!" And that is wrong.

REALITY is always and exclusively *that* which is presently perceivable around us. Every imagination of what happens where-else or when-else is *not* an actual reality, but an idea in CONSCIOUSNESS, which accompanies the REALITY taking place HERE NOW. We can understand it in this way: The "universe with all its galaxies" is an imagination and not at all a consistent structure with a cosmically connected PRESENT. The PRESENT isn't somewhere out there, far away from our SELF, but always HERE NOW in CONSCIOUSNESS, even if this moment contains many ideas about an entire universe.

Migrating birds in the sky move away from us, but the light that gives us this information *travels towards us*. Raindrops fall into a lake and trigger waves that *communicate* within the water, from molecule to molecule, from inside to outside, and back again, in constant feedback, without ever ignoring its neighboring events. And so, REALITY takes on its local form in this way.

Each CHANGE triggers a *now-wave*, impacts nearby VIBRATIONS, and is equally impacted by adjacent MOTIONS so that the currently observed world is manifested from all possibilities and probabilities. Our local-now needs time, so to speak, to arrange itself in three-dimensional space, to communicate any changes in its matter, and to pass on information about its vibrations.

Therefore, we can slowly understand that light has no speed of its own, but that the entire three-dimensional space-time is subject to a delay.

Sunlight could probably reach us instantaneously, if it were not limited by the delay of our local-now. The theory of relativity, in any case, explains that photons move infinitely far in zero time in our space-time. So it's not light – or other phenomena – that sticks to the speed of light limit, as it seems to us. It is extremely probable that our entire space-time is subject to a fundamental "now-delay," which objects moving at lightspeed don't even notice.

The now-delay [d] is the reciprocal of the speed of light [$d=c^{-1}$] and, in our laws of nature, indicates the time REALITY needs to propagate itself in our space-time. And this profound change of perspective will soon grant us a new understanding of the theory of relativity.

+ You now know: that *everything* indeed is relative, that only *one* consciousness exists, and that we cannot think about it without getting lost in relative loops of our minds – we may only stop thinking about it by accepting its relativity.

You keep in mind:

RELATIVITY explains that every observation turns the Absolute into something Relative. EXISTENCE is one absolute truth. Yet its EXPERIENCE creates many relative truths. In this regard, RELATIVITY is closely related to the VEIL, as both express that we can never fully know the "world out there" because we ourselves create our unknowing.

The **local-now** is the REALITY around us, which we perceive right now, while all things we *do not* perceive are not REALITY but possibilities and probabilities for us. We may think about them, but RELATIVITY prevents certainty. Only the Absolute is certain.

Now-waves illustrate how the local-now is created: Every CHANGE communicates itself holistically in SPACE to redefine and *manifest* the possibilities and probabilities.

The **now-delay** explains that the speed of light is limited to its rate of speed only because the entire reality – the local-now – arrives with a delay.

Δ *You now can: comprehend Einstein's theory of relativity, get a feeling of your personal perceptional horizon, and mentally determine the possibilities and probabilities behind it.*

23 Gravity

The meaning of gravity, mass attraction, and space-warp. Gravity as a spatial property of matter. The suchness of existence. The correlation between now-waves and gravity. Occam's advice. A new understanding of the theory of relativity. The enigma of light.

O ur feet remain earthbound on an abundant planet. On the desolate moon, by comparison, we would be able to jump higher. "More mass means more attraction," physics class taught us. "The force of gravity on Earth is stronger than on the Moon but weaker than on Jupiter." Einstein's theory of relativity explains, however, that our feet aren't pulled towards Earth by unseen "forces" but fall into an unseen "curvature in space." We basically assigned two contradicting explanations to one observation, namely that "things fall to the ground," between which we may choose now:

Is gravity caused by an "attraction of two masses" or a "curvature of space," or even both phenomena combined? This state of floating in mid-air is confusing. Of course, we are able to experience only the result of gravity, with its explanation hidden from our senses – but that applies to every phenomenon in EXISTENCE. Among all possible explanations, we need to decide upon the most probable one.

Warp

A cannonball in an otherwise empty universe wouldn't fall down because "down" wouldn't exist. The cannonball would also be weightless because *weight* needs a *direction* into which it can tip a scale or move our hands. The meaning of *direction* and *weight* becomes most apparent during relocation. A recliner that we want to carry up the staircase lies heavily on our shoulders and would fall, should we let it go. But again: We must not believe that objects fall *because* they are heavy, as their heaviness is caused by them "wanting to fall down" in the first place.

In our everyday use of language, the terms "mass" and "weight" practically have the same meaning. But physics distinguishes between them: The weight of an object depends on external conditions, its mass doesn't. A balloon filled with helium weighs nothing, even floats up into the sky, but it still has mass. A 75kg (170lbs) person weighs only 12kg (27lbs) on the moon, thus being able to leap up higher. Depending on external circumstances, the same matter has a different "weight." But this physical distinction between weight and mass can be used for comparison purposes only. We weigh an object on Earth and may calculate how much it would weigh on the moon.

The absolute mass of an object within an otherwise empty universe cannot be calculated. Equally, it is impossible to determine the color of a rose in total darkness. In darkness, colors have no meaning. And without direction into which objects can fall, mass and weight have no meaning.

The atomic mass of an object simply indicates the amount of *matter* within. Mass and matter thus describe the same idea as two things, like claiming that a lake is filled with water and *also with wetness* – although wetness is merely a *property* of the water. Such properties of objects, their temperature, speed, color, mass, or weight, cannot be detached from their matter. A watermelon tastes refreshing. A rose appears red. A recliner feels quite heavy under certain circumstances. But the freshness of a watermelon doesn't exist as a separate thing. The redness of a rose doesn't flow out of its blossom after sunset. And the mass of an object cannot influence the world – because this mass doesn't exist on its own. As a consequence, we can explain that "weight" and "mass" have nothing to do with gravity. Only the matter within objects may play a role.

So your recliner doesn't consist of "matter with mass" but of "matter with certain properties."

*

The theory of mass attraction explains gravity by *gravitons*. These so-called messenger particles are supposed to interlink all masses in the universe and make them attract each other. But gravitons have never been found. Moreover, even *massless* light is bent by cosmic phenomena. And besides, we already ruled out any connection between "mass" and gravity. The paradigm of mass attraction shows all aspects of being outdated.

The theory of space-warp explains gravity by a "curvature of space." Physics provides a descriptive experiment: When you take a soft cushion, decorate it with marbles (our solar system), and then make a dent in its center (the sun), all scattered marbles (the planets) begin to roll into the dent as if *attracted* by it. In our solar system, the planets have high velocities, though, preventing them from either falling into the sun or from drifting off into the galaxy so that they keep orbiting the sun on their "curved path" in space.

In this model, three-dimensional space is bent in one direction only and not in all directions, as is really the case, yet our mind may not grasp. A "curvature of space" therefore is a sketchy abstraction that, unless we think clearly, quickly causes a cognitive distortion: We could think that the curvature of space *extends* the path between two points, as light (or other objects) must take a detour and can no longer take the direct route – just like curvy roads extend the journey to our destination. But the opposite is true: Every curvature of space *shortens* the linear distance between two points.

Every phenomenon in REALITY exists in all dimensions. Three-dimensional space is no reference point in EXISTENCE. Light (or any other objects) won't ask SPACE for a three-dimensional path so as to follow its curvature, but will always take the direct, original, and innermost path through REALITY. This is why photons do not slow down, even when traveling through warped space. No matter how strong gravity might be, the speed of light and the now-delay remain constant.[a][144]

Gravity, in our physical model, is better described as an *inwardness* of space than as a "curvature" of space – on the one hand, because any space-warp goes into all directions of three-dimensional space, and on

---

[a] Remark: The endnote will tell you more about it.

the other hand, because CHANGE will always unfold itself by taking the innermost path through SPACE, regardless of our human density.

The point is: Space-warp can holistically explain our current scientific understanding of the cosmos. We don't need to search for auxiliary constructions. A warpable space doesn't also need gravitational forces. So, both the "force of gravity" and "mass attraction" are simply outdated attempts to explain gravity, which we haven't discarded yet from our everyday language. We will, however, do this from now on in. Gravity *is space-warp*, with a direct correlation to matter and energy existing *within* – or, as we call it, correlating principally with the presence of planets, stars, and black holes.

Our three-dimensional space-time must be "warpable" to give direction, weight, and a corresponding behavior to all objects within. The crucial question is: Does matter cause an effect that warps space – or does the warping of space cause an effect that ultimately looks like matter to us?

Every CHANGE unfolds itself in *all* dimensions, not just in three. Consequently, it's not a three-dimensional process that causes space to warp in higher dimensions. Equally, our shadow cannot act independently, not even in its two dimensions. Instead, a higher-dimensional cause influences our three-dimensional perception and then appears to us "like objects in warped space."

Our space-time could be warped *for all sorts of reasons*, by phenomena that we describe as matter, or by phenomena that we don't even perceive. So, thinking in probabilities, space-warp isn't created *after* matter is already present. More likely, both observations are created by one and the same phenomenon casting different shadows depending on where we are standing.

*

The most fundamental description of EXISTENCE, of this moment, this experience, of inhaling and exhaling, of reading these words, and the startling realization that these lines are about you, is that EXISTENCE seems to be exactly *as such*. You cannot argue away the suchness of existence.

A long avenue lined with magnificent trees looks as if it is not curved, even though a higher reality ensures that our feet stay firmly earthbound. The world appears to us as three-dimensionally *straight* and not curved, whatever that is supposed to mean. A blind person would not be able to directly relate to our observation. "What makes you so sure," he might ask, "that reality and the avenue *are* straight and not just *look* straight?" And we would explain to him, "It just seems as such, beyond doubt. The trees form a straight avenue running towards the horizon!" But his hearing works in quite a different way to our eyes. Some sounds are clearly audible, while distant sounds are carried away by the wind without causing a reliable sensation of straightness.[a145]

The *Flatlanders*, who live in their two-dimensional world, would perceive our gravity quite differently because, in their world, nothing can fall down. In a flat world, things may only be pushed or pulled. Rather similar objects, however, like a ball and a flagpole, may demonstrate quite different behavior, heaviness, or inertia. A helium balloon halfway floating in the Flatlander world would create some impression of gravity, though: After each bump, the balloon-shape would magically return to its original center, so that the Flatlanders might suspect invisible forces or an attraction behind it. Should a breeze come up, blowing from the north, the balloon would appear to become attracted from the south. And if we imagine now a Flatlander world that runs horizontally through a swimming pool, then opening a drain would create a whirlpool, which to the Flatlanders would be a black hole: All things in its vicinity would inevitably be drawn in, unable to escape the pull, and then vanish from sight forever.

The *Highlanders*, distant relatives of the Flatlanders, whose world runs vertically along a house wall, would experience our gravity entirely differently. Climbing plants grow upwards towards the sun, but how

---

[a] Thomas W. Sills (What Einstein Did Not See)

would they know? In their worldview, *climbing-plant-forms* may be attracted by gravity, while *raindrop-forms* may be repelled in the opposite direction.

These considerations recall one certainty to our mind: Our space-time has many unknown properties that we will never know. We know for a fact, however, that all events in the universe are based on AWARENESS.

Theory

The principle of Occam's razor states: If an observation can be explained by several theories, the most simple theory is usually correct. But if a slightly more complicated theory can explain an additional observation, we shouldn't shy away from its complexity because the overall system becomes simpler. Christmas lights, which have a hundred lamps on a single cable, are easier to handle than one hundred separate lightbulbs. And this advice applies to the following principles as well, so that any feeling of complexity only announces an ensuing simplicity.

Reality changes at high rates of motion. Three relativistic effects set in: time slows down, space collapses, and the accelerating mass rises to infinity. But why do these effects occur? Applying our insights about the *now-delay of reality* and the *correlation between space-warp and now-waves* greatly expands our understanding of such relativity.

The Explanation of Relativistic Mass: Gravity is stronger in places with high amounts of matter and energy. In a star, nonillions of particles react with each other, constantly communicating and emitting now-waves that redefine reality. In black holes, a thousand solar masses collapse to the size of a fingertip, which holds a much higher density of events than empty space. The intensity of now-waves and space-warp, so to speak, is proportional: Gravity increases in places where *much happens, vibrates, and changes.*

The mass of a spaceship increases as it approaches the speed of light. At 99.5% lightspeed, according to the theory of relativity, its mass would have increased tenfold. This "mass," however (let's remember), is a property of matter. Matter is a result of now-waves. And now-waves are directly connected to space-warp. So it isn't the spaceship's mass that increased tenfold but its space-warp.

And so it is that a spaceship, as it approaches the speed of light, *throws itself into its own now-wave.* In a physical way, this creates an overlaying reality because *the sender moves along with the previously sent message, making adjustments along the way, yet unable to delete its earlier messages.* At 99.5% lightspeed and a Lorentz factor of ten, the spacecraft would be accompanied by nine now-waves that define REALITY in precisely this superimposed form.

In other words: We throw a stone into a lake, but as soon as the stone has left our hand, we take a step forward with superhuman speed and have already thrown the next stone, and so on, until – eventually – ten stones fall into the water almost simultaneously, triggering a reality ten times greater.

Matter is created by vibrations in space. "More vibrations in space" thus mean more matter, which we experience as REALITY. And so, the mass of a spaceship seems to increase at high rates of motion, while the increase of now-waves results in a higher space-warp.

The Explanation of Time Dilation: If time were to stop now, things wouldn't simply come to a standstill; instead, there would be a void. The next photons, thoughts, and sensory stimuli could no longer reach us. The vibrations of matter could no longer manifest REALITY. However, CHANGE doesn't stop but steadily continues, at least while we remain in our original system.

Our local-now assembles itself at the speed of light, based on all the information that we observe. But when leaving Earth, accelerating our spaceship, and approaching the speed of light, this familiar reality assembles itself differently. Time – the CHANGE of REALITY – progresses differently. Two segments have separated and lost their simultaneity. The local-now of the spaceship and the local-now of Earth get "out of step." A portion of reality is lost or *missed*, so to speak, because some now-waves may no longer arrive.

Let's say that a friend measures your speed of reading this book. You both sit apart to avoid distraction. Every time you turn the page, your friend notes the time. But if – for whatever reason – your friend occasionally falls asleep and thus notices *every second turn of the page* only (while unaware of the page numbers), his notes would say that you are reading slower.

This example shows that our considerations about relativity require a precise distinction between *what we are talking about* and *what we are looking at*, which most of our current theories do not. If your friend, while measuring your reading speed, would frequently nod off and miss half of the *reading time* instead of missing half of the *turned pages*, his reality would be that you are reading faster. And upon comparing his notes with your page numbers, he would then discover that he *lost* information, while your speed of reading remained the same, independent of whether you seemed to read faster or slower.

The relativistic effects that change space, time, and mass are effective without "visual contact": A spaceship comes back after a thousand years, people on Earth have long forgotten about its existence, but less time has passed for the astronauts. In fact, the spaceship and Earth cannot actually see one another, but only receive a time-delayed image of each other. And if the observers on both sides should study the *image* of the other, additional optical RELATIVITIES apply that aren't subject to relativistic effects and require a different understanding altogether.[a146]

But back to *what we are talking about* and *what we are looking at*: Scientific experiments that confirmed the validity of relativistic effects are based on atomic clocks. In cesium atomic clocks, one second is defined by over nine billion working cycles, and this accuracy allows confirmation of the theory of relativity even at lower rates of motion. The experiments show: An atomic clock orbiting Earth starts to *lag behind* in "time." Less time passes while moving fast. After one hundred years, an atomic clock on the ISS space station would display approximately one second less than an atomic clock on Earth. We can claim, however, that

---

[a] Example: See Explanatory Notes.

we didn't measure "less time" but a lesser "sum of atomic processes." We merely paid attention to the difference between two sums – which fundamentally means that we "counted the turning of pages only" without comparing the page numbers.

And now back to our spaceship, which is traveling away from Earth at high speed. The theory of relativity explains that the spaceship and Earth would both *see* that the other one's time slows down (if they could see each other), but that only the time in the spaceship truly passes more slowly (which becomes evident when both meet again). Therefore, we can draw the following conclusion:

The local-now around an observer always occurs at the same frequency: at the speed of light. But when two observers move very fast relative to each other, the emitted now-waves start to miss each other and can no longer be perceived or "processed." At 86.6% lightspeed (and a Lorentz factor of two), the now-delay results in missing half of the available information. Reality assembles itself based on the received now-waves and looks "absolutely natural" to any observer. But the *moving observer* actually leaves his original system. The spaceship truly misses the CHANGE of REALITY taking place on Earth, and therefore retains the effect of time dilation.

At 96.9% lightspeed, this loss quadruples. And at 100% lightspeed, the Lorentz factor rises to infinity. From the spacecraft's viewpoint, time on Earth would stop, as the astronauts would reach the speed at which reality itself is expanding.

The Explanation of Length Contraction: Our everyday perception relies on the fact that "information about reality" reaches our senses much faster than "actual reality." If the speed of light were only 50km/h, driving a car would be unthinkable. As soon as we saw a car, the accident would already have happened.

The same problem arises near the speed of light. If our spacecraft crosses a target line at 86.6% lightspeed (and a Lorentz factor of two), its bow and stern would appear closer together than usual to an observer on Earth: 50 meters would become 25 meters, as only every second now-wave is registered in the original system. The other half of now-waves cannot be processed. At 99.5% lightspeed (and a Lorentz factor of ten), the spaceship would appear to be compressed to a tenth of its original length until, and at the speed of light, it would disappear completely.

*

Our current worldview is full of physical details, exceptions, and auxiliary constructions. That makes ONENESS sound a very complicated explanation. The CONTRAST, the VEIL, and RELATIVITY allow us to find many ways to describe the world. But EXISTENCE isn't after that. We should always have Occam's advice in mind and assess whether additional, new, or opposing explanations might actually clear our worldview.

Our new findings – the *now-delay of reality* and the *connection between space-warp and now-waves* – give a physical and tangible basis for the theory of relativity. We see a simple "mechanism." Time dilation, mass increase, and length contraction turn from a phenomenon that is proven into a consequence that is logical: Our local-now assembles itself based on all received vibrations – and when these vibrations are either lost or superimposed, we experience a changed reality.

The connection between *space-warp* and *now-waves* – the fact that gravity and matter-vibrations go hand in hand – also reveals the enigma of light. The masslessness of photons means that *light* doesn't cause any now-waves but is one of their elements.

Science explains: Light is created when atoms release excess energy, which happens all around us, in endless biochemical, physical, or electromagnetic events. Fireflies glow in the dark of night. A reading lamp illuminates the room. A fireplace warms the room. A cooking plate glows red and hot. Sunlight is absorbed by all things in our field of vision and is re-emitted again, even by our skin.

More specifically, science tells us: *External influences* energize an atom, cause electrons to jump into a higher orbit and almost instantly fall back to their original place, releasing a photon as compensation. In other words: A *now-wave* meets a matter-vibration and triggers a new now-wave, which – maybe a few nanoseconds, eight minutes, or a million years later – brings us information about CREATION.

+ You now know: what gravity means, that space-warp and now-waves are connected, and that this connection simplifies our understanding of relativity.

You keep in mind:

Even though our scientific **theories** might be a hundred years in the making, they often exist amidst significant ambiguities. That is every theory's *nature* and no big deal. Our worldview, however, fails to recognize the extent of scientific limitation, which indicates that it is outdated. A worldview based on attentiveness, sincereness, and kindheartedness (the core idea of religion) would be much more advanced. The point is that, in order for science to function, we need thoughtful consideration of scientific limitations. We need to know that the house of cards built by our theories is no stable skyscraper that science will continue to build higher. The *primary* task of science involves highlighting the ambiguities, the foundation, and the probabilities of our assumptions so that we may "reshuffle the cards" from time to time. For this reason, we don't need to understand everything in detail. But we all benefit from at least understanding the basics.

Δ *You now can: perceive the suchness of existence, work on a simpler scientific worldview, or return into the serenity of the present.*

24 Creation

The performance and the stage of life. The Darwinian theory of evolution. The impressive adaptedness of life. The inexplicable formation of mimicry. The missing first cause. A new understanding of our evolution. The poisonous dart of searching for explanations. The expansion of existence. The evolution of mind.

O ur worldview contains little certainty but many conclusions. As a consequence, we must relearn to distinguish between the Absolute and the Relative. The Relative is the "performance of life," meaning, everything that captivates us as spectators. And the Absolute is the "stage of life," meaning, the place where all stories take place. This place is the HERE NOW. EXISTENCE places itself into a rose, a butterfly, or a human being and then forgets about the stage for a few days, years, or even a whole lifetime and experiences the performance to the fullest.

Evolution

Humans wonder why they exist and find comfort in the answer that, at some point in time, they just developed. But that doesn't answer the question. Saying that humankind developed has nothing to do with why WE LIVE or why EVERYTHING HAPPENS NOW.

The theory of evolution, derived from Darwin, is an interpretation *within the Relative* based on "genetic coincidences." Only species, it states, that adapted to conditions on Earth, were able to survive over time and, today, make up our biodiversity. Several observations support this interpretation: archaeological finds, genetic lineage, and the impressive adaptedness of species to their habitat. But time, coincidence, and involuntary improvements are unconscious concepts. We need a new understanding of evolution.

Our present-day understanding of Darwinism is without meaning, like neighbors we have never met: Nobody has ever seen this evolution, as it's supposed to happen by definition "in between" one generation and the next.[a][147] And our concept indeed appears to be blurred. A child growing up, muscles that are strengthened through training, a wound that heals, skin that's tanned by sunlight, or body cells that mutate, all these developments aren't considered to be evolution but "normal" events – as if we could divide CREATION into two separate paths. CHANGE, however, happens only NOW and shapes LIFE in its wholeness.

*

Life contains infinitely abundant details. Butterflies carry beautiful wings with symmetrical patterns that camouflage, intimidate, and unfold into new and different patterns during flight. Praying mantises ambush their prey while disguised as a perfect copy of a branch, even showing small buds that seemingly begin to sprout. And the Phyllium insect has become a walking leaf, with a body that no longer differs from its environment. It masterfully copies nature with its mimicry – and this perfection poses a problem: the Darwinian theory of evolution cannot explain it. We say: "Genetic coincidences made the Phyllium insect greener and increased its survivability. More genetic coincidences flattened the insect, shaped its body into a leaf, and also produced leaf-like patterns of veins so that it was able to survive even better. And these beneficial mutations repeated unswervingly throughout all generations, making the insect always greener and flatter, turning it into a perfect copy of a leaf." And this explanation, says Ouspensky, is likely one of the most naive of all possible theories.[b][148]

Coincidences cannot explain the single-mindedness, the follow-through, and the perfection of thousands of details. A dead Phyllium insect withers like a leaf in autumn, even though such a feat provides no advantage to survival and (even if) it can't be passed on to the next generation anyway. The so-called death's-head hawkmoth becomes invisible to bees merely by emitting sound and scent. What it looks like

[a] P. D. Ouspensky (A New Model of the Universe)
[b] P. D. Ouspensky (A New Model of the Universe)

plays no role whatsoever when intruding into beehives and stealing honey. So why did some species start, millions of years ago, to develop a way to disguise themselves to the human eye, while their natural enemies possessed senses that were quite different? And how could we explain that dragonflies resisted evolution for over a hundred million years without any kind of further development? Of course, great improbabilities may happen. The Infinite Monkey Theorem explains that, in theory, a chimpanzee might transcribe the Gutenberg Bible. In practice, however, any attempt will soon result in destroyed typewriters.

Coincidences can only act in random directions. When ten thousand "coincidences" single-mindedly work in the same direction and vastly exceed what is necessary, we generally speak of a plan – of a yet unknown explanation. Let's say you find a magnificent sword buried in your backyard. How did it get there? The "Metallurgy according to Darwin" might explain: "It all happened by coincidence. Chemical accidents, intense heat, and the right elements slowly transformed an ore vein into steel. Other coincidences, such as earthquakes and meteorites, then began to forge the steel, fold it, and they even created a hilt with beautiful decorations. And these advantageous modifications went on unswervingly throughout generations to make the sword ever sharper, more magnificent, and more valuable." In this case, you would regard the idea of purposeful coincidences not as scientific but as absurd, and you would certainly say that we should find a better explanation.[a149]

Darwin himself made very clear that his interpretations didn't answer – and thus excluded – the *first cause*, and that therefore it would be absurd to separate evolution and GOD into unrelated opposites.[b150] By studying the diversity of species, we may not realize how LIFE or the laws of nature came into being, because all these *secondary causes* are merely the foothills of inaccessible and undiscovered mountains. And

---

[a] P. D. Ouspensky (A New Model of the Universe)
[b] Charles Darwin

this impossibility to explain our sublime universe by coincidence, Darwin surmised, was for him the main argument for God's existence.[a151]

Mimicry may seem to us like a wonderful imitation of nature, but in reality, every living being, without exception, is a miracle in the sensation of EXISTING HERE NOW. The theory of evolution obscures this perception with rules we shouldn't accept as reality. The presence of LIFE does not follow rules but the available senses of its observer. The Phyllium insect is a mimicry for our eyes only, yet not for our ears, tongue, or hands so that its specialness depends on us too.

The decisive question is not *how* a living being could disguise itself in such a miraculous way, but *what* disguises itself, and *who* thinks it to be a disguise. The idea that insects and leaves are "of different nature," and both exist independently of each other, is an illusion arising from our concepts. And the idea that human beings and the world are "of different nature," and both exist independently, resembles another unconsciousness, without which (when we weren't unconscious) we wouldn't even try to explain LIFE "scientifically" through evolution.

Everything we see, Rumi explains, has its roots in the unperceived world. The phenomena may change, but their essence remains the same. The origin from which everything originates is eternal – growing, expanding, granting new life. This one source also lies within us and makes our whole world come into being, together with "stairs" right in front of us, so that we can move forward in everything. LIFE offers more than being human, Rumi hints, so we should not stop there.[b152] Let us imagine, the Buddha explains, a man wounded by a poisoned arrow is taken to a doctor. But the man says: "I won't let the doctor pull out this arrow until I know whether my attacker was a nobleman, priest, merchant, or worker," and the man endlessly rambles on, "until I know whether my attacker was tall, small, or medium-sized; [...] until I know whether the arrow was fletched with the feathers of a crow, hawk, peacock, or stork; ... until I know whether the bowstring came from an

a Charles Darwin
b Rumi (Love Poems of Rumi: A Garden Beyond Paradise)

ox, a buffalo, lion, or monkey..." But while the man keeps inquiring, all the details remain unknown to him, and wouldn't be of any benefit to him anyway, he dies.[a153] The Buddha wants us to understand: If we think that we require explanations so that we can live our life, then we are not yet *living* this life.

"The diversity of the species – how did it develop?" Such questions belong to the Relative without having an answer in the Absolute because answers arise in the mind only. We know that LIFE in EXISTENCE didn't start with the Big Bang and, equally, that LIFE on Earth didn't begin with single-cell organisms. EXISTENCE, REALITY, and CREATION as the *eternal first cause* was already there. And so, one aspect of our EVOLUTION is to be able to distinguish the Relative and the Absolute from each other, and to be in harmony with both.

Expansion

EXISTENCE *is* everything and *can be* everything. SPACE and LIFE ITSELF are fundamentally dimensionless, without being pinpointed to a third-density perception. LIFE can effortlessly express itself as an insect, a human being, or a Buddha without going against its nature. And as *this essence*, WE can become more than human. Since our birth, CONTRAST has been a catalyst for our growth, through the Law of Attraction as well as the Fail-Safe of Existence, so that we may expand *selfward* in our direction.

This EVOLUTION doesn't follow a principle of randomness but instead pursues a "learning objective," expressing it as a human prospect. Each stage of our search, even a strenuous or painful time, serves to leave behind an unconsciousness, experience a higher reality, and live more consciously thereafter. Every lack shows us the way. Thirst suggests: Drink! Being cold suggests: Get warm! Stress suggests: Calm down! LIFE's expansion will never end. All living beings will clearly feel their greatest lack and thus know about their learning objective. And because what we most lack is LOVE, *being human* serves to discover LOVE,

---

[a] Majjhima Nikaya: The Middle Length Discourses of the Buddha

strengthen it, and feel it extensively, even if this means that our entire worldview must fall apart.[a154]

When living beings first developed eyes, an evolution of vision resulted. When living beings first developed wings, an evolution of flying began. Each physical characteristic initiated new paths of evolution so that species blessed with them could learn to swim, fly, or walk even better. And when living beings first attained self-realization, this launched an evolution of the mind, awareness, and creativity – with the genuine intention of thinking and feeling ever more clearly. On this path, a species will eventually understand that its survival no longer depends on coincidence and time but requires RESPONSIBILITY.

Our current understanding of evolution is irresponsible and lazy. We believe that a human being may grow up and grow old but cannot evolve during this lifetime. The idea of contributing HERE and NOW is lost, as evolution either took place "before birth" or might affect "the next generation." And with this worldview, we have forsaken our EVOLUTION. We have exchanged cause and effect. We use our super-human creativity to divert the natural way of life, slow down a possible self-development, and feel like uncreative human beings. All this is our own creation. Even our genes change through our emotions, thoughts, and awareness – that is *through intention* so that, moment to moment, we bequeath all of it to our present SELF.

A healthy person doesn't worry about waking up the next morning – it will happen all by itself. And the same applies to LIFE – it will become more conscious all by itself. Our only problem is that we experience this expansion as suffering. The sleeping mind misunderstands evolution as *coincidental*, but this blindness brings along many problems, which helps us to better see its *consistency*: We suffer from negative emotions because we consistently select such emotions ourselves.

EVOLUTION is the natural expansion of LIFE towards ONENESS. EXISTENCE wants to perceive more of ITSELF. And this EVOLUTION

---

[a] Ra (The Law of One)

takes place in us RIGHT NOW. As long as we experience unwanted ups and downs in our feelings, and are still learning to choose better EMOTIONS, everything is alright. LIFE intuitively works on its expansion.

A Flatlander cannot look down at his own body. His self-image would be bodiless and unimaginably alien to us. Only the third density allows the perceiving of a body. Only then EXISTENCE can look down at itself, sound out its nearest recesses, and enjoy a wider perspective. Therefore, we shouldn't regard our "ego-perspective" as something unwanted or even defective but welcome our ego-phase as a natural state along the path towards higher dimensions.

Some theories of physics declare that our universe strives for entropy, a perfectly balanced state of inert uniformity. But EXISTENCE isn't a material structure decaying in time. A holistic system cannot lose energy, even from a physical understanding.

The MOSAIC will always remain the *Absolute* and contain everything *Relative*. Of course: What we experience right now will eventually leave our perceptional horizon. But this ongoing expansion adds nothing to ONENESS and doesn't increase its content. The size of EXISTENCE cannot be changed. All we can influence is how small we make its infinity.

+ You now know: that our present understanding of evolution is primarily influenced by Atheism, that Darwin had a quite different understanding of biodiversity, and that nowadays we have lost more than the wisdom of religious teachings.

You keep in mind:

EVOLUTION describes that LIFE will always develop selfward and that all living beings continually learn to perceive a greater reality. This expansion of SELF-BEING can be propelled intentionally once the ability of self-realization is attained.

Δ *You now can: feel the evolution working within you, pull out the poisoned arrow of endlessly asking for explanations, and accelerate your evolution through intention, work, and responsibility.*

25 Infinity

The answers within infinity. The coin of understanding and perceiving. The undescribed reality. The illusion of human insight. The missing connection. An infinitely long life. Language and life. A new language. Infinity as a property of nature.

In our imagination, the universe is limited, both in space and time, and therefore also finite in the number of grains of sand, hiking trails, or songs. But such an image of "manifoldness" is not a property of EXISTENCE because, as part of the process of enumerating and listing *every thing*, we would miss an infinite number of details and connections. Our questions about life, the cosmos, or God may only be found within the INFINITE, as finite concepts do not conclude the truth for good.

If we want lasting answers, we must not get stuck on the superficialities of the world but instead search for INFINITY, tear the veil obscuring its presence, and be *overwhelmed* by what we see. As long as this *overwhelm* is absent, our imaginations remain intact. We are unconscious. But the more cracks appear in our worldview, the clearer it becomes that, all this time, we have been looking at nothing other than INFINITE EXISTENCE, as its perception is unavoidable within and without.

Understanding

Understanding and *perceiving* are like two sides of a coin: heads and tails are never up at the same time. As long as we want to understand the world, we cannot perceive its reality – and as long as we *genuinely* perceive the world, no additional understanding exists. For this reason, our CONSCIOUSNESS can realize INFINITY, yet our mind cannot add anything to it.

Our ego-mind is full of contradictions, prejudices, and ignorance and still believes it is capable of understanding the world, at least in part – because an *emotional weight* imparts on us the impression of "our thoughts being right." As a consequence, we understand things that turn out to be false and doubt things that turn out to be right, which shows that understanding isn't based on factual correctness. A personal feeling of rightness suffices.

Our wish to understand the world exclusively by rational means cannot be granted, as this wish originates from an intuitively grasped perception, which is neither rational nor was ever understood. LIFE isn't experienced only through thoughts but in many additional ways far and beyond, because WE OURSELVES CHANGE depending on whether we would like to "understand a perception" or "perceive an understanding."

*

A tape measure with a three-meter rule is not really a tape measure with a three-meter rule. The casing is much smaller than three meters, has a square shape and perhaps even a belt clip. And the metal rule in the case is longer than three meters because it extends further than "300" and ends with a section without any lines or numbers. *General knowledge* says that the lines indicate millimeters, centimeters, or decimeters. We may even think in feet and inches. *Mathematics* explains that, between every two points, there is an infinite amount of rational or irrational numbers. And *physics* teaches us that reality cannot be divided an infinite number of times but up to a Planck length only. Our measuring tape thus has a length of three meters, three hundred infinities, or three hundred quintillion Planck units *depending on our chosen thought model.* In reality, however, none of them applies because numbers, units, or distances just exist as mental objects in our minds.

Continually depriving language of its meaning may appear to be like playing with words yet intends to direct our awareness to the *undescribed reality* that, otherwise, is instantly *described* by our unconscious mind. To enable us to perceive this undescribed INFINITY, the feeling of being able to understand needs to fade for just one brief moment, to be replaced by the emotion of sheer awe – about how wonderful *this world is* that we have not the slightest chance of understanding.

A tiny point in EXISTENCE can sometimes hold immeasurable depths. We embrace a person and yet don't perceive any of his wisdom. A train passes, and we have no idea of the hundreds of hopes, abilities, and talents within. We write ∞ and have no feeling of its meaning. We look into the cosmos using telescopes and find no evidence of life. We search for the end of the human illusion and, in doing so, conceal the life that's always awakened.

As long as we *think* and thus merely look at thoughts, EXISTENCE cannot be understood. As long as we desire to understand the MOSAIC *through words*, it cannot be seen. And as long as we hope for *answers from the outside*, INFINITY remains hidden to us. To paraphrase Socrates: We can only follow the ideas that arise within our mind, and therefore can never attain insights from the outside.[a155]

"Understanding something" means to enter into a close connection with EXISTENCE. We experience the sound of the ocean, and a connection is made. We master multiplication tables, and connections are established. Unknown things that we have no connection to seem implausible, doubtful, and weird to us. We experience reality, but *see within* that reality a matrix of words, concepts, and labels, in which established connections determine familiarity. The crashing of waves sounds "known to me." 7×7 sounds "known to me." ONENESS sounds "unknown to me." The connection to ONENESS seems missing, even though *this word is our concept and label* for EVERYTHING that makes possible our PRESENT EXPERIENCE.

Our *genuine connection* to ONENESS isn't missing. The feeling of "not knowing something" is familiar to us. We feel it often and know it well. The EXPERIENCE of "not knowing something" is just too generic for our

---

[a] Socrates

mind to establish a connection to a particular word, which then – to us – resembles a familiar thing. REALITY, EXISTENCE, and ONENESS exist nevertheless.

An understanding basically establishes *one* connection to reality. But perception isn't *limited* to one connection to reality. And so, stepping back from the need to establish literal connections makes us perceive the PRESENT. ONENESS may sound "unknown" to us, but when stepping back, we see that ONENESS is exactly this EXPERIENCE.

In AWAKENING, all connections come loose. All attachments fall away from us. The compulsory striving, worrying, and suffering ceases. We realize that we do not need to continue with it. We *can* do everything but *have* to do nothing. We can get up early in the morning, go to work dutifully, search for a life partner, exercise regularly, travel to exotic places – but we don't have to do any of it, regardless of how much we would *like* to do it, or how *useful* it would be. There are particular things we *should do*. We should absolutely take care of our children and ourselves, and seek safety in case of danger. We could in theory do nothing else than wait for these "absolutes" to arise and fulfill them. But the good thing is: We don't have to do that. We can do all kinds of things "in between." And when we realize this *freedom*, we recognize that our remaining lifetime is still long, since nothing has to be done anymore. Our life is – mathematically speaking – infinitely longer than it needs to be. And this remaining INFINITY is LIFE's present to us.

Our language doesn't contain words that, when we hear or speak them, strike a connection to AWARENESS, PRESENT, and INFINITY. Consequently, we need a *new language*. We need a language that covers multiple layers of truth, takes over our increasingly mindful life, and ultimately causes an evolution of our perception.

Language

Words, sentences, and grammar are like "pens of the mind" with which we "describe" the indescribable reality. As a result, language and life are deeply connected, and different native languages denote different ways of thinking, perceiving, and functioning.

There are indigenous tribes such as the Pirahã Indians, who have no written language and communicate in present tense only, without past or future: A ⚔ in the ≈ receives a pronunciation, but no alphabetical image in thoughts [boat in the river], which is unimaginable for us. There are languages such as Chinese or Hungarian which contain no word for "must": "You *must* achieve best grades" turns into "You *should* achieve best grades," which conveys a different message regardless of any meaning lost in translation. And there are cultures (especially in the "first world") which consider indigenous tribes or seemingly less pressure-driven societies as undeveloped because they *themselves* have not yet acquired an understanding of *ethnology*.

CONSCIOUSNESS is identical in all human beings. So within each culture, individuals carry fundamentally the same mental acuity and brilliance of mind that lead to achievements manifesting in technology, in great mindfulness, or a mythological closeness to nature. This means: Other cultures are not failed attempts at being successful, but potentially successful role models in helping us not to fail. Ethnic diversity is just as necessary as biodiversity. If our culture should one day enter a state of crisis, other cultures may already have mastered it – or might never have created such a crisis. Therefore, "a single integrated culture planet-wide" is not a goal to aspire to in human evolution. As considerable as our wisdom might become, we may not be able to even envision the wisdom inherent in entirely different ways of living.

*

Knowing that language determines our thinking, that thoughts shape our perception, and that worldviews shrink our reality, we become interested in a new and greater language. This *new language* doesn't need new letters, words, or accentuation. We only need some newly coined signifiers, a way of spelling that erases meaning, and sometimes a mindful state that vibrates "near" to the meanings we wish to convey.

Implementing such language must not worry us *because it has existed* for thousands of years already.

Human history includes scriptures, passed down through many centuries, nations, and cultures, which speak about reality beyond the human illusion, and which, underneath the superficial layer of words, use an identical approach. Anything else should well surprise us because, after all, the scriptures were inspired by the same *realization*. And so, it's the *recognition* of a new language that humanity has difficulties with, mainly because we are unaware of its existence. But the *signifiers of religion* change that. Their connectedness is apparent. And their identical approach uses knowledge and words to lead us into a conscious emotion that can be observed without knowledge and words. Like this:

Who could be so lucky? An oyster opens its shell and discovers a shimmering pearl. Who could be so lucky? A blind man searches for his white stick and finds his sight again. Who could be so lucky? A mother fetches water from a well and pulls up her drowning daughter.[a156] Who could be so lucky? Two eyes look at the CONTRAST and, within it, see a book, a body, and each morning: a sunset.

Within this book, the MOSAIC, the central words of our new language are written in capital letters and, not by coincidence, they all describe something INFINITE. The PRESENT is eternal. SPACE is everywhere. EXISTENCE is without beginning or end. CONSCIOUSNESS is always present. CONTRAST is without division. EMOTIONS are countless. And LOVE surpasses everything.

INFINITY is a property of EXISTENCE. We could say: it is the only one. This infinite nature cannot be grasped by physical or mental senses. We cannot see an infinite number of roses. Indeed, INFINITY is rather an emptied CONSCIOUSNESS in which human ideas are moved out of sight for a moment, and EVERYTHING becomes NOTHING. This EXPERIENCE allows us to see, almost in slow motion, how single words

---

[a] Rumi (Love Poems of Rumi: A Garden Beyond Paradise)

float into our field of vision and, along with them, ideas and imaginations to connect with.

Language connects imaginations with words. The word "candle," however, should trigger at least two imaginations: Is it burning or not? The term "homo sapiens" can also connect to many possibilities: A human being may possess knowledge and wisdom and thus live up to its description. But a human being may also believe that such a description absolves him from all responsibility, that he has reached his full potential, and already understands everything of importance. But "our mind" understands nothing, as it is just another two words; two words that have settled like dust on our eyelashes.

We said: Humans strive for happiness, and that is true. We said: A human being is not really a human being, and that is true as well. So, in reality, no human being strives for happiness – and that is true! Our new language has effortlessly covered two levels of logic. But there is more. *In reality, it is true* that EXISTENCE does not distinguish between human beings and non-human beings. Even such a distinction is not really a distinction but a journey rich in contrast.

+ You now know: that all answers to the "eternal questions of humanity" are found within infinity only, that language and life are inseparable, and that we are always connected to existence.

\# You keep in mind:

A **new language** implies an improvement of our current language, which is made possible by our growing awareness. Its rhetorical elements are analogies, contradictions, and metaphors that lead to emotions beyond knowledge. Their effectiveness is based on some newly coined central concepts that connect us with higher meanings than those we used to know before. This new language can also extend across several layers of logic.

INFINITY is the only property of EXISTENCE and therefore allows EXISTENCE to contain all properties. We cannot understand INFINITY. We may only perceive it when CONSCIOUSNESS is free from any understanding.

Δ *You now can: live an infinitely long life, learn to speak a new language, and describe the undescribed reality more consciously.*

26 Journey

The intonation of an emotion. A glossary as a review. Questions and recommendations. A plan for the unplannable.

O ur realizations about LIFE, CONSCIOUSNESS, and EXISTENCE have given us a new language. We can communicate within multiple layers now, on the stage of human illusion and the levels of reality that exist beyond.

The words that, in this book, are written in capital letters, point out that we are unable to grasp their meaning merely by thoughtful imagination but that understanding them requires *nearness to an emotion*, which we can then access through its deliberate *inner intonation*.

We just need a gentle prelude that is made of thoughts and a first tangible visualization that is made of ingenuity to change our emotions. Every orchestra begins this way: with a prelude of tuning all the instruments and then a first thrilling note before the melody takes off – and carries us away. Would you like to try?

Nearness to CONSCIOUSNESS may sound like *standing in front of our eyes' panoramic window, casting the curtains aside, opening the windowpanes, and then leaning out into nature.*

Nearness to EXCITEMENT may sound like *a butterfly causing a storm – not on the other side of the world but right around itself.*

Nearness to LOVE may sound like *the zenith of an intimate embrace, in which life no longer casts any shadows.*

Other descriptions are conceivable, of course, and sometimes even necessary because words affect us differently. You can invent your own "mental shortcuts" into positive emotions and steadily expand your expertise in visualization.

Thus, we may pronounce the words with their new meaning just as we did before. But our emotions, while pronouncing the words, will have changed so that, when we talk about intangible concepts, we are the tangible reality.

Review

An **ACT** is a CHANGE of the HAPPENING because CONSCIOUSNESS chooses a new emotion for ITSELF. This emotion changes our ATTRACTION. Each ACT needs the surrender of the ego. Such an ACT may sound like *quickly looking for the sun, turning towards it, and leaving any shadows behind.* [CH12][a]157

Our **ATTRACTION** refers to the specific events that we bring into our lives through our emotions. Law of Attraction states that an EMOTION we experience maintains its VIBRATION until WE change it. Observing our ATTRACTION may sound like *a tree growing faster when we gently touch it with our index finger.* [CH17]

AWAKENING describes the possible, real, and ultimately inevitable event of waking up from the ego, upon which CONSCIOUSNESS gains full recollection of its SELF. AWAKENING may seem to us like *a smile playing on God's lips during a bow before life.* [CH10]

AWARENESS encompasses all possible nuances of perception, interaction, influence, CHANGE, or VIBRATION; it stands for the CONSCIOUSNESS in EVERYTHING. All phenomena in the cosmos have it. Nearness to AWARENESS may feel like *looking in the mirror but having no impression of a reflection.* [CH3]

The **AXIOMS** describe a perception that requires no precondition or human concepts and thus provides us with unquestionable certainties. Nearness to the AXIOMS feels *safe as the embrace of a caring mother.* [CH27]

CHANGE describes that **CREATION** isn't over but is taking place right now, that the PRESENT is timeless, and that CONSCIOUSNESS is constantly in **VIBRATION**, in **MOTION**, bringing forth REALITY and

---

[a] See also chapter 12.

its perception. Nearness to CHANGE may be likened to *looking through a universal kaleidoscope, which slightly shifts according to our own movement.* [CH5, CH6, CH21]

CONSCIOUSNESS is the AWARENESS within OURSELVES, the attentive EXISTENCE behind our human eyes. Nearness to CONSCIOUSNESS may sound like *an eagle gliding alongside the universe.* [CH3]

CONTRAST describes a perception without concepts – before concepts superimposed themselves on our sensory impressions. The CHANGE of EXISTENCE constantly produces CONTRAST, like a kaleidoscope, with one difference: In a kaleidoscope, we don't immediately recognize discernable patterns, forms, or things but would need time in order to achieve that. In every moment and with every step, our perspective on the CONTRAST shifts and presents new, first-time, unique sensations. Nearness to this may sound like *looking at a photo and then another and another...* [CH4]

EMOTIONS stand for the infinite feelings that CONSCIOUSNESS can experience. Their potential isn't created by humans. EMOTIONS are deliberately chosen by our resonation, just like a child curiously plucks at guitar strings, watches them vibrate, and listens to the sound they make. To choose an emotion, all we need is to keep our thinking general (and not specific) and keep our feeling specific (and not general). Choosing our EMOTIONS may sound like *making music on CONSCIOUSNESS with LIFE.* [CH2]

EVERYTHING includes every nameable fact, imagination, and possibility in the cosmos; it's a state of consciousness that is endlessly "filled" by more concepts. **NOTHING** comprises a perception without even one nameable thing, imagination, or probability; it's a state of consciousness that is constantly "drained" of concepts so that only REALITY remains. The experience of EVERYTHING and NOTHING turns all knowledge into something relative. We realize that we "know nothing." This perception is like looking through a spider's web.

Depending on our focus, we can either look at the web itself (and see the concepts stuck to the threads) or look through the web (and see nothing but the reality beyond it). Nearness to EVERYTHING and NOTHING may sound like *standing in the greatest library of the universe, yet knowing that we cannot learn a single truth here.* [CH5]

EVOLUTION describes that LIFE always expands selfward and that living beings continuously learn to perceive more of reality. We may also understand it as self-realization or gradual AWAKENING, which is supported by the Law of Attraction and the Fail-Safe of Existence. After attaining self-knowledge, this expansion of SELF-BEING can be accelerated by working on our RESPONSIBILITY. Nearness to EVOLUTION may be described *as the last few steps on a long journey home.* [CH24]

EXCITEMENT means doing what we "truly" want – with attentiveness, readiness, and integrity; it's the safest thing in the world, the greatest wealth of a human being, and the strongest guide during our search. For these reasons, the emotion of EXCITEMENT will be the seeker's proof of the Law of Attraction. Nearness to EXCITEMENT may feel like *a pleasant electrical charge coursing through your body.* [CH9]

EXISTENCE refers to the fact that something exists, that EVERYTHING is part of this, and that NOTHING can not exist. Therefore, EXISTENCE can be described as timeless, spaceless, and without properties. Nearness to EXISTENCE may sound like *trying to intone the vibration of an emotion, although we are already immersed within it.* [CH3]

EXPERIENCE is a moment of mere perception, without any interpretation, thought, or concept. It is the complete dissolution of the SELF in the PRESENT. Nearness to EXPERIENCE may be likened to *a piece of the finest soap dissolved in crystal clear water.* [CH8]

FEAR stands for an intense attachment to thoughts that ultimately give us the feeling of no longer being "really" alive. This unconsciousness is the root cause of human striving, worrying, and suffering. FEAR is also the near enemy of LOVE – in the sense that separation anxiety is easily confused with a deep bond. We must not practice nearness to FEAR. [CH15]

GOD, JEHOVAH, ALLAH, BRAHMAN, or TAO, are words that are meant to combine all qualities of EXISTENCE, REALITY, and CREATION; these words describe a real fact, which WE will directly experience upon discovering our SELF, the I AM. Nearness to GOD may feel like *the seventh breath cycle without thoughts*. [CH8]

HAPPENING explains that our LIFE as human beings merely "happens" because (and as long as) the SELF is unconscious. Humans cannot act. Only CONSCIOUSNESS acts. HAPPENING feels like *the human illusion*. [CH12]

INFINITY is the only property of EXISTENCE and therefore allows EXISTENCE to contain all properties. The ancient Greeks called it "Apeiron": The beginning and ending of all things. We are able to perceive it as soon as CONSCIOUSNESS is clear of all understanding. Nearness to INFINITY may be akin to *endlessly walking through silky curtains of ideas, worldviews, and possibilities*. [CH25]

LIFE includes all living beings in the universe, and beyond that, the fact that life will always exist, or at least that a state remains in which life can arise again and again. LIFE never ends. Nearness to LIFE sounds like *a holy promise*. [CH2]

LOVE is the most powerful VIBRATION in the universe and, therefore, the most powerful ACT. It changes everything. When we feel it, WE OURSELVES have become LOVE. Nearness to LOVE may sound like *a human beacon suddenly illuminating the cosmos*. [CH15]

ONENESS is a perception that answers all questions. Nearness to it sounds *exactly like you feel right now*. [CH16]

The **PRESENT**, the **NOW**, is the only moment in EXISTENCE and thus equivalent to CONSCIOUSNESS. The PRESENT is like a mirror: We look into it and see our SELF. The PRESENT is always original: We see its current CONTRAST, but we see it only once in our LIFE. Nearness to the PRESENT may feel like *holding a sparrow in your hand that suddenly turns out to be a phoenix.* [CH6]

REALITY, also called the "segment of our reality" or the local-now, describes the manifested reality that, in its form, observes the world. REALITY comes into being only through observation because this consciousness allows the infinite possibilities and probabilities of EXISTENCE to coincide and thus be determined. Nearness to REALITY may feel like *a tranquil island in a turbulent ocean.* [CH4]

Our **RESPONSIBILITY** is to respond to reality and not to imaginary stories in our minds. This ability can be learned, starting with no longer imagining that we've been wronged and, as a consequence, no longer inflicting wrong onto others. Our RESPONSIBILITY may be described as SELF-BEING, EXCITEMENT, and LOVE. Nearness to it may feel like *the beauty of a growing garden.* [CH17]

The **SELF**, also called the I, the WE, or our SOUL is the CONSCIOUSNESS, the PRESENT. Nearness to it may sound *like truly appreciating the best storyteller of all time.* [CH3]

SPACE contains all phenomena, cosmic horizons, and dimensions and, to make all this possible, is itself spaceless. SPACE is also the **HERE**, the only place in EXISTENCE, and equivalent to CONSCIOUSNESS. Experiencing SPACE may feel as if, *while we ourselves move, the world is actually moving through* us. [CH20]

The **VEIL** stands for the universal Law of Unknowing: A living being can never have the feeling of knowing or perceiving everything. This inevitability grants us free will. The VEIL is closely connected to **RELATIVITY**, in the sense that each consideration remains something Relative within the Absolute. The VEIL may seem *captivating like a puzzle, but the last piece is always missing. Where is it?* [CH10, CH22]

WHOLENESS indicates a perception in which the infinite cycles of LIFE are no longer divided into beginnings and endings, into cause and effect. This perception helps us reach a new self-understanding. Our ego becomes "lucid and leveled." We are no longer the "hill over here" but also the "valley over there," so that, in total, nothing lacks or stands out. When other egos want to "rile us up," they realize they're facing a vast prairie that no one can rile anymore. The masonry of our attachments turned into a mesh: Most thoughts just glide through. Nearness to WHOLENESS may seem like *peering through a telescope all around the globe and eventually seeing ourselves*. [CH11]

Recommendation

The MOSAIC can be discovered on infinite paths. A systematic path, however, requires purposeful arranging, just as mountaineers methodically prepare for Mount Everest. First, we exercise at home and strengthen our muscles and heart. Then, we pay attention to our diet and learn to overcome the weaknesses of the mind. And lastly, we follow through and travel to the place of action.

Just one cycle of preparation may not suffice to reach the summit. At your first attempt, you may reach base camp and experience a great feeling of success. But ascending further towards the summit might need additional preparation – not in all aspects, but here and there, concerning some details.

In our search for AWAKENING, *questions* and *doubts* show us the details of what currently holds us back. Therefore, as some questions and doubts are familiar to me, I'd like to offer you some possible answers, resolutions, and recommendations.

Q: How do I know when I have awakened?

A: Assume you are biting into a strange fruit. You will immediately notice its taste without having known or learned about it beforehand. You will notice the AWAKENING just as easily. [CH10, CH13, CH15]

Q: How can I understand ONENESS when words cannot describe it?

A: You don't have to or need to understand anything. Understanding is neither necessary nor possible. It's about perceiving, right now, how CONSCIOUSNESS is trying to understand the world. [CH3, CH4, CH8]

Q: I have learned a lot about AWAKENING. Why can't I achieve it?

A: You must let go of this knowledge and at the same time also unlearn a lot about being human. [CH16]

D: I'm not even searching for my awakening – at least that's how it feels.

A: In this case, you are not fully aware of the search yet. Your baseline vibration, by nature, may be positive so that you experience little suffering coming from your ego. But such condition may arise from habit and not from awareness. Your search includes discovering the difference between both. [CH11]

Q: I have difficulties remaining conscious. Is it normal that practicing mindfulness is challenging?

A: You confuse cause and effect. Consciousness has no problems with experiencing difficulties. The only challenge is letting go of your attachments. [CH12, CH17]

Q: How do I distinguish between what I want and what my ego wants?

A: You can reflect on significant decisions, for example, by writing them down, to identify whatever your motivation may be. You can look out for "feeling wronged" – that's the path the ego wants to take. Or you can be more aware of emotions of SELF-BEING, EXCITEMENT, or LOVE – that's the path the SELF wants to take.

Q: *Will I ever be intelligent, wise, or mindful enough to be able to see the MOSAIC? I'm probably much too insignificant to understand the big picture.*

A: EXISTENCE can do everything. [CH4, CH8, CH10, CH17, CH18, CH27]

Q: *Now that I have heard about the MOSAIC but don't fully understand things yet, it seems that something is missing from my life. What could that be?*

A: This is the final stage of the search: Overcoming the illusory gap between knowing and feeling. [CH11]

D: *Some topics are too complicated for me.*

A: That's fine. Choose your path. You are not supposed to accumulate complicated knowledge but simply to break your *habits*. Is *that* your problem? Then stop making everything complicated. Stop this thought that blocks you and is *not true*. And besides: Sometimes complicated things can set us on fire. Many people love to tango, play bridge, or read the stock market. [CH16, CH18, CH25]

Q: *Is it possible that I am destined to live without AWAKENING?*

A: LIFE always supports ITSELF. It remains unclear, however, what that brings to you. Will LIFE make your misconceptions come true or prove them wrong? [CH7, CH17]

Q: *Why do you say that the ego dies in AWAKENING?*

A: The human state is a HAPPENING. And this human happening ends with the first ACT of the SELF. [CH3, CH10, CH12, CH24]

Q: *Once I have awakened, will there be no more problems in life?*

A: Most self-made problems will be gone. But our life in the world continues and creates the need for action. Such "problems" then meet our decisive mind, our energetic resolution, or our occasional use of the *old ego* – which will seldom cause us any more suffering. It's like getting sand on your hands when playing in a sandpit. [CH1, CH2]

Q: What would be a good motto for me to live by?

A: Feel that people have the potential to be great and that they can grow beyond themselves. Always assume that you don't know everything because really, you don't. Don't believe in creating a better "I" because it will prevent you from enjoying your real I now. Don't set goals but have values that turn into goals. Don't praise the achieving of targets; praise the way. Sometimes, let go of expectations and just trust in others and be amazed by the results. Don't pity anyone because of how they think or how they stress themselves out, as this is their responsibility, not yours, but always follow your heart. Take away people's haste, doubts, and fears. Draw a vision and then fill it with color. Use all your senses. Accept that life isn't controllable, that it sometimes involves doubts, and that even those moments are full of guideposts.

Q: I have read and understood this book. But where is the practical part? Where is the application of my realizations?

A: That, my friend, is what life is for.

Plan

27 Mosaic

Everything in the right place. The axioms of existence. The inevitability of oneness. Ending and beginning.

Yes – I AM THE MOSAIC and I have guided myself through my own view of myself and through all the many facets and fragments that influence a unique lifetime.

"Namaste."

That means I bow to the spirit within us. I see myself within the person in whose form I'm getting to know new perceptions.

How does it feel? I'm asking for a reason – because nothing is more important than how the PRESENT feels. Nothing is more real than that.

In the unconsciousness of human experience, WE want to endlessly replace our current emotion, feel different, and hopefully happier. But there's no need to redirect INFINITY in this way, as it already contains everything.

All things are made up of smaller things. And that tells us: Every thing we encounter, and which makes up our life, exists in a bigger wholeness. Even things that appear random to us still exist in the right place.

We stand close to the MOSAIC and ask: "Is that how it should be? Does this piece belong here, *in this spot*? Must I always strive for happiness, meaning, and creativity?" We take a step back and realize, "Oh. Everything is connected. And it always was! I was striving for happiness, meaning, and creativity to become more aware." We take another step back and realize: "Oh. Everything is connected. I was becoming more aware because LIFE moved selfward." And once we have stepped back often enough, ONENESS recognizes itself, simply enjoying its EXPERIENCE.

*

The MOSAIC will never end, but this book will end soon, allowing the attention of EXISTENCE to turn towards other facets of LIFE again. But wherever it may take ME, some matters I want to keep uppermost in my mind.

Axioms

The AXIOMS of EXISTENCE summarize the irrefutable certainties of ONENESS in human language. Their application will uncover any attachment, overwrite all relative details that float through our minds, and enable us to see the MOSAIC again.

AXIOM 1) EXISTENCE is unquestionable: there is a REALITY that can be perceived.

AXIOM 2) CONSCIOUSNESS is equally unquestionable: there is an EXPERIENCE.

AXIOM 3) EXISTENCE and CONSCIOUSNESS exist simultaneously and, thus, cannot be two different things or be displaced from one another. If one exists (but experiences nothing) and one experiences (but doesn't exist), how could they be aware of each other? Consequently, EXISTENCE and CONSCIOUSNESS are ONE.

AXIOM 4) CONSCIOUSNESS is always present. This PRESENT can never be left, has never been created, and will never pass but remains infinite in all qualities.

AXIOM 5) Human beings cannot act, but WE are no "human beings." Every action that appears to come from a body or a mind truly comes from us, EXISTENCE ITSELF. And so, because WE possess infinite qualities as well, we can decide for our SELF what EMOTIONS the present EXPERIENCE triggers within us. We can shape the HERE NOW and change reality.

*

The AXIOMS of EXISTENCE answer all essential questions of human life. The answers, however, do not establish a fixed worldview but rather a worldveil that prevents us from forgetting about the MOSAIC existing beyond. And this *exchanged* "insight" into the cosmos changes our thinking, promotes our survival as a species, and enables us to reach the next milestones of our civilization. Awakening is certain, with all of its consequences. But even the "most awakened humanity" won't consider knowledge as being unnecessary. Although everything is answered in the Absolute, we will continue to explore the Relative for knowledge and its application.

Application

The most beautiful change in a person's life is to find the existence of the unchangeable SELF beyond all thoughts. Three paths lead there: the path of our life (reason), the path of consciousness (spirituality), and the path of existence (science).

Therefore, it doesn't matter from which direction we look at ONENESS or which knowledge, faith, or technology we apply. Its discovery is inevitable:

If we mindfully look at our LIFE, it is ultimately inevitable that we discover the human illusion, search for our SELF, and AWAKE:

The human pursuit of happiness creates suffering but also exposes the ego. Who am I? A human being, a story in consciousness, or the storyteller himself? An ongoing inquiry changes our perception of reality. Matter, space, and time become concepts in the contrast. And once we let go of our beliefs, the divine appears: the purpose of existence.

If we mindfully allow CONSCIOUSNESS to unfold, it is ultimately inevitable that we surrender our attachments, see the MOSAIC, and AWAKE:

Our awakening from humanity is like a search for something we haven't lost. And yet we discover things hidden to us before, like the portals to our emotions or a new perception of now. The fear of death turns into joy for life. And love grants us the highest clarity so that no matter where we look, we always look selfward.

If we mindfully study EXISTENCE, it is ultimately inevitable that we describe its facets scientifically, recognize its RELATIVITY, and AWAKE:

Paradigms are convincing. But their constant shifting makes us question our current beliefs. The nature of space, all dimensions therein, and the nature of both light and gravity give an insight into creation itself. Our minds reach the edge of infinity. The journey from being human to the MOSAIC ends where everything began – and now begins anew.

Explanatory Notes

* Translation from German into English by the author.

---

1 Cf. Albert Einstein in a letter to Carl Seelig (1952): "I'm not particularly talented, just passionately curious. It's important not to stop asking." *

2 Cf. Jorge Bucay (Let Me Tell You a Story, The Centaur), Europa Editions (2013).

3 P. D. Ouspensky (Tertium Organum, Ch. 23, P. 306), Alfred A. Knopf (1924).

4 Cf. Michael Ray (The Highest Goal), Berrett-Koehler Publishers (2004).

5 Lao Tzu (Tao Te Ching, Verse 35), Jonathan Star, Tarcher/Penguin (2001).

6 Aesop, greek poet, 6th century A.D., David Adam (The Road of Life: Reflections on Searching and Longing), Morehouse Publishing (2004).

7 Cf. Gospel of Thomas (Logion 67), Jean-Yves Leloup & Joseph Rowe, Inner Traditions (2005).

8 Cf. Eckhart Tolle (The Power of Now, Ch. 5, P. 93), Namaste Publishing (1997).

9 Descartes: "I think (I doubt), therefore I am."

10 Cf. Eckhart Tolle (The Power of Now, Ch. 1, P. 15), Namaste Publishing (1997).

11 Cf. Paulo Coelho (Aleph, P. 11), HarperCollins Publishers (2011).

12 P. D. Ouspensky (The Psychology of Man's Possible Evolution, Fourth Lecture, P. 92), Random House USA Inc. (1974).

13 Breakdown: The electromagnetic spectrum encompasses all wavelengths from 10pm to 10km. The visible light (for human beings) lies between 430nm and 780nm. Converted to a picometre scale, the quotient of visible light and the total light spectrum results in 0.000000000035 or less than a ten billionth part.

14 Cf. Dr. Joseph Dispenza (What the Bleep Do We (K)now?!), Horizon Film Distribution (2004): "The brain processes 400,000,000,000 bits/s. We are only aware of 2,000 bits/s. [...] If our brain is processing 400 billion bits of information and our awareness is only on 2,000, that means, Reality is happening in the brain all the time, it is receiving that information."

15 Cf. Werner Heisenberg (Physics and Beyond, P. 63), Harper and Row (1971).

16 Cf. Bashar (Quest for Truth, P. 19), Nobul Press (1997).

17 Cf. Chandrakirti (Introduction to the Middle Way, The Sevenfold Reasoning).

18 Cf. Thich Nhat Hanh, Diamond Sutra (The Diamond That Cuts Through Illusion, P. 21 & P. 56), Parallax Press (2010).

19 Cf. Gangaji (You Are That, P. 146), Sounds True, Inc. (2007).

20 Cf. P. D. Ouspensky (Tertium Organum, Ch. 2, P. 32), Alfred A. Knopf (1924).

21 Cf. Francois Jacob (Imagination in Art and Science, P. 115), Kenyon Review (2001).

22 Breakdown: Proportional conversion of hydrogen atoms to the size of a 6ft. tall human being: (A) Bohr radius of the electron shell ≈ 53pm, (B) Radius of the atomic nucleus ≈ 1.3fm, (C) Radius of a quark ≈ 0.43am – gives a ratio of A:B ≈ 1:40.000 (6ft. to 44mi.), B:C ≈ 1:3000 (6ft. to 3mi.) and A:C ≈ 1:120,000,000 (6ft. to 125,000mi.).

23 Cf. Richard Feynman (QED – The Strange Theory of Light and Matter, P. 119), Princeton University Press (1985).

24 Cf. Volker J. Becker (Gottes geheime Gedanken, P. 92), Lotos Verlag (2008): "On the quantum level, there's no reality. Matter and events dissolve into a foam of probabilities [...] until the macrocosm created by this microcosm creates reality with its consciousness. [...] The created retroactively creates itself." *

25 John 1:1-3 (King James Version, KJV, 1611).

26 Cf. P. D. Ouspensky (In Search of the Miraculous, Ch. 16, P. 335), Routledge & Kegan Paul Ltd (1950).

27 Cf. Max Planck (The Essence of Matter, Speech in Florence, Italy, 1944).

28 Cf. Annie Besant (An Introduction to Yoga, P. 30), Theosophical Publishing Society (1908).

29 Cf. P. D. Ouspensky (Tertium Organum, Ch. 17, P. 212), Alfred A. Knopf (1924).

30 Cf. Albert Einstein (On the Electrodynamics of Moving Bodies, Annus Mirabilis papers, Annalen der Physik und Chemie, Vol. 17, Ch. I, § 1, 1905).

31 Cf. Gevin Giorbran (Everything Forever, P. 15), Enchanted Puzzle Publishing (2007).

32 Jean-Paul Sartre (Existentialism Is a Humanism, 1946).

33 Lalla (Naked Song, P. 77), Pilgrims Publishing (1992).

34 Cf. Ra (The Law of One, Book II, Session 43), L/L Research (1982).

35 Cf. Gautama Buddha (Rhonda Byrne, The Power, P. 100), Atria Books (2010).

36 Lalla (Naked Song, P. 63), Pilgrims Publishing (1992).

37 Rumi (In the Arms of the Beloved, Like This, P. 79), Tarcher/Penguin (1997).

38 Gospel of Thomas (Logion 77), Jean-Yves Leloup & Joseph Rowe, Inner Traditions (2005).

39 Mohammed (Islam: A Worldwide Encyclopedia, P. 1324), ABC-CLIO (2017).

40 Cf. Mumon Ekai (The Gateless Gate, Ch. 49, Amban's Addition), Nyogen Senzaki & Paul Reps, John Murray, Los Angeles (1934): "Buddha, according to a sutra, once said: 'Stop, stop. Do not speak. The ultimate truth is not even to think'."

41 Cf. Buddha (Dhammapada: A Collection of Verses, Ch. 5, Verse 64, P. 20), Friedrich Max Müller, Clarendon Press (1898).

42 Exodus 20:4 (New International Version, NIV, Biblica Inc., 1973-2011).

43 John 10:30 (New International Version, NIV, Biblica Inc., 1973-2011).

44 Shahada (The First Pillar of Islam).

45 Cf. Koran 6:14 (Muhsin Khan): "And be not you (O Muhammad) of the Mushrikun [polytheists, pagans, idolaters and disbelievers in the Oneness of Allah]."

46 Lao Tzu (Tao Te Ching, Verse 25), Jonathan Star, Tarcher/Penguin (2001).

47 Psalm 23:1 (Luther Bible, LUT, 1912): "The LORD is my shepherd; I will not lack anything." *

48 Psalm 23:1 (King James Version, KJV, 1611).

49 Psalm 23:1 (Young's Literal Translation, YLT, 1898).

50 Matthew 13:10-15 (New International Version, NIV, Biblica Inc., 1973-2011).

51 Neil Douglas-Klotz (Prayers of the Cosmos: Meditations on the Aramaic Words of Jesus, P. 41), HarperCollins (1994).

52 Romans 13:8-10 (New International Version, NIV, Biblica Inc., 1973-2011).

53 Sahih Muslim (The Book of Faith, Hadith 45a).

54 Lao Tzu (Tao Te Ching, Verse 18), Jonathan Star, Tarcher/Penguin (2001).

55 Cf. Thich Nhat Hanh (Old Path White Clouds, Ch. 42), Parallax Press (1991).

56 Exodus 3:14–15 (King James Version, KJV, 1611).

57 Psalm 46:10 (King James Version, KJV, 1611).

58 Genesis 1:27 (King James Version, KJV, 1611).

59 Matthew 12:31 (New International Version, NIV, Biblica Inc., 1973-2011).

60 1. Corinthians 3:17-18 (Menge Bible, MENG, 1926). *

61 John 8:7 (New International Version, NIV, Biblica Inc., 1973-2011).

62 Luke 15:7 (New International Version, NIV, Biblica Inc., 1973-2011).

63 Thich Nhat Hanh, Diamond Sutra (The Diamond That Cuts Through Illusion, P. 29), Parallax Press (2010).

64 Cf. Bashar (Quest for Truth, P. 92), Nobul Press (1997).

65 Matthew 10:11–14 (New International Readers Version, NIRV, Biblica Inc., 1995-1998).

66 Cf. Matthew 13:3-8 (The Parable of the Sower, King James Version, KJV, 1611).

67 Lao Tzu (Tao Te Ching, Verse 41), Jonathan Star, Tarcher/Penguin (2001).

68 Cf. Diamond Sutra (P. 68), William Gemmell, London: Trench, Trübner (1912).

69 Cf. Diamond Sutra (P. 70), William Gemmell, London: Trench, Trübner (1912).

70 Cf. Bashar (Quest for Truth, P. 8), Nobul Press (1997).

71 Cf. Maharishi Mahesh Yogi (The Seven States Of Consciousness, Recorded Live in Los Angeles), World Pacific Records, WPS-21455 (1967).

72 Socrates (469-399 B.C., Athens).

73 Cf. P. D. Ouspensky (A New Model of the Universe, P. 8), London: Routledge & Keagan Paul Limited (1931).

74 Cf. Jeanne de Salzmann (The Reality of Being: The Fourth Way of Gurdjieff, P. 26), Shambhala Publications (2010).

75 Lalla (Naked Song, P. 6), Pilgrims Publishing (1992).

76 Cf. Friedrich Nietzsche (Beyond Good and Evil, Aph. 146), T. N. Foulis (1911): "He who fights with monsters should look to it that he himself does not become a monster."

77 Cf. Bashar (Blueprint for Change, Ch. 8, P. 128), Seattle, WA: New Solutions Pub. (1990).

78 Cf. Lao Tzu (Tao Te Ching, Verse 75), Jonathan Star, Tarcher/Penguin (2001).

79 John 11:25-26 (New International Version, NIV, Biblica Inc., 1973-2011).

80 John 3:3-6 (New International Version, NIV, Biblica Inc., 1973-2011).

81 Rumi (In the Arms of the Beloved, P. 169), Tarcher/Penguin (1997).

[82] Gospel of Thomas (Logion 18), Jean-Yves Leloup & Joseph Rowe, Inner Traditions (2005).

[83] Matthew 24:42-44 (New International Version, NIV, Biblica Inc., 1973-2011).

[84] Cf. Bashar (Blueprint for Change, Ch. 5, P. 67), Seattle, WA: New Solutions Pub. (1990).

[85] Gospel of Thomas (Logion 42), Jean-Yves Leloup & Joseph Rowe, Inner Traditions (2005).

[86] Matthew 5:3 (King James Version, KJV, 1611).

[87] Cf. P. D. Ouspensky (A New Model of the Universe, P. 166), London: Routledge & Keagan Paul Limited (1931).

[88] Cf. Thich Nhat Hanh, Diamond Sutra (The Diamond That Cuts Through Illusion, P. 17 & P. 27), Parallax Press (2010).

[89] Rumi (In the Arms of the Beloved, Like This, P. 79), Tarcher/Penguin (1997).

[90] Cf. Ephesians 3:17–19 (King James Version, KJV, 1611).

[91] Cf. Jack Kornfield (Meditation for Beginners, Ch. 12), Jaico Publishing House (2010).

[92] Cf. Lao Tzu (Tao Te Ching, Verse 42), Jonathan Star, Tarcher/Penguin (2001): "Tao gives life to the one. The one gives life to the two. The two give life to the three. The three give life to tenthousand things."

[93] Jim Carrey (Commencement Speach for Maharishi University of Management in Fairfield, Iowa, 2014).

[94] Cf. P. D. Ouspensky (Tertium Organum, P. 167), Alfred A. Knopf (1924).

[95] Rumi: "I said: What about my eyes? God said: Keep them on the road. I said: What about my passion? God said: Keep it burning. I said: What about my heart? God said: Tell me what you hold inside it? I said: Pain and sorrow? He said: Stay with it. The wound is the place where the Light enters you."

[96] Cf. Paulo Coelho (Like the Flowing River, The Two Jewels), Harper Collings Publishers (2006).

[97] Cf. Matthew 10:37-39 (New International Version, NIV, Biblica Inc., 1973-2011).

[98] Cf. Thich Nhat Hanh, Diamond Sutra (The Diamond That Cuts Through Illusion, P. 20), Parallax Press (2010).

[99] Chinese: 玫 [méi] = English: Rose.

[100] Old Greek: ῥόδον [rhódon] = English: Rose.

[101] Cf. Matthieu Ricard and Trinh Xuan Thuan (The Quantum and the Lotus, Ch. 16, P. 232), Three Rivers Press, New York (2001).

[102] Gospel of Thomas (Logion 22), Jean-Yves Leloup & Joseph Rowe, Inner Traditions (2005).

[103] Cf. Sogyal Rinpoche (The Tibetan Book of Living and Dying, Ch. 10, P. 157), Harper San Francisco (1992).

[104] Cf. P. D. Ouspensky (Tertium Organum, P. 310), Alfred A. Knopf (1924).

[105] Cf. Genesis 1:1 (King James Version, KJV, 1611).

[106] Confucius (The Analects of Dasan, Volume 2, P. 36), Oxford University Press (2018).

[107] Remark: You may insert any other feeling here. [Contentment] is just an example.

[108] Mark 11:24 (New International Version, NIV, Biblica Inc., 1973-2011).

[109] Matthew 13:12 (New International Version, NIV, Biblica Inc., 1973-2011).

[110] Psalm 33:9 (New International Version, NIV, Biblica Inc., 1973-2011).

[111] Accredited to Lao Tzu.

[112] Sahih Al-Bukhari (40 Hadith Qudsi, Hadith 15).

[113] Cf. C. G. Jung (Synchronicity, An Acausal Connecting Principle, P. 32), Princeton/Bollington (1973).

[114] Cf. Bashar (Quest for Truth, P. 130), Nobul Press (1997).

[115] Cf. Bashar (Blueprint for Change, Ch. 1, P. 12), Seattle, WA: New Solutions Pub. (1990).

[116] Cf. P. D. Ouspensky (The Fourth Way, P. 366/364), London: Routledge & Keagan Paul Limited (1957).

[117] Jean-Paul Sartre (Existentialism is a Humanism, P. 37), Yale University Press (2007).

[118] Cf. P. D. Ouspensky (The Psychology of Man's Possible Evolution, Second Lecture, P. 56), Random House USA Inc. (1974).

[119] Michael Ray (The Highest Goal, P. 109), Berrett-Koehler Publishers (2004).

[120] Cf. Confucius (Der Weg der Wahrhaftigkeit, P. 37), Anaconda Verlag GmbH (2008): "Morality is the responsibility of every human being. Here, we may not (even) defer to the teacher." *

[121] Theodor W. Adorno (Minima Moralia: Reflections on a Damaged Life, Ch. 18, P. 39), Verso (2005).

[122] Cf. P. D. Ouspensky (In Search of the Miraculous, Ch. 11, P. 336 & P. 340), Routledge & Kegan Paul Ltd (1950).

[123] Cf. Sally Ross (The Selfward Facing Way, P. 43), Published by Sally Ross (2012).

[124] Cf. P. D. Ouspensky (In Search of the Miraculous, Ch. 17, P. 347 & Ch. 2, P. 49), Routledge & Kegan Paul Ltd (1950).

[125] Cf. Alfie Kohn (Beyond Discipline, Introduction, P. xii), ASCD Publications (2006).

[126] Cf. Gangaji (You Are That, P. 325), Sounds True, Inc. (2007).

[127] Cf. Daniel Kahneman (Thinking, fast and slow, Ch. 35, P. 381), Allen Lane, Penguin Group (2011).

[128] Cf. Osho (Osho Library, Ch. 27, Religion is the Last Luxury, P. 12).

[129] Cf. Rumi (Love Poems of Rumi: A Garden Beyond Paradise, P. 98 & P. 57), Jonathan Star & Shahram Shiva, Theone Press (2005).

[130] Cf. Thich Nhat Hanh, Diamond Sutra (The Diamond That Cuts Through Illusion, P. 10), Parallax Press (2010).

[131] Cf. Confucius (The Analects, Book VI, Ch. 18, P. 309), William Edward Soothill (1910).

[132] Cf. P. D. Ouspensky (A New Model of the Universe, Preface, P. xiv), London: Routledge & Keagan Paul Limited (1931): "A logical mind which knows its limitedness [...] becomes a 'psychological mind'. [...] The psychological mind can see the limitations of the 'logical mind' and the absurdities of the 'defective mind'."

[133] Cf. Kurt Gödel (Gödel's Incompleteness Theorem, 1931).

[134] Cf. Thomas Kuhn (The Structure Of Scientific Revolutions, Ch. VIII, The Response to Crisis, P. 77), The University of Chicago Press (1962).

[135] Cf. Thich Nhat Hanh, Diamond Sutra (The Diamond That Cuts Through Illusion, P. 71), Parallax Press (2010).

[136] Cf. Alexander Unzicker (Auf dem Holzweg durchs Universum, Teil 6, Der kosmische Mikrowellenhintergrund), Carl Hanser Verlag (2012). *

[137] Cf. P. D. Ouspensky (Tertium Organum, P. 237 & P. 79), Alfred A. Knopf (1924).

[138] Cf. P. D. Ouspensky (Tertium Organum, P. 63–68), Alfred A. Knopf (1924).

[139] Cf. P. D. Ouspensky (Tertium Organum, P. 107–109), Alfred A. Knopf (1924).

[140] Cf. Bashar (Blueprint for Change, Ch. 8, P. 134), Seattle, WA: New Solutions Pub. (1990).

[141] Remark: The dilation effect of 3% refers to the percentage change of the Lorentz factor from 1.00 to 1.03.

[142] Cf. P. D. Ouspensky (Tertium Organum, P. 147), Alfred A. Knopf (1924).

[143] Nick Herbert (Quantum Reality, Ch. 12, P. 222), Anchor Books (1985).

[144] Remark: In the classical understanding of physics (without considering the now-delay or dimensionlessness of reality), the constancy of the speed of light is explained by "gravitational time dilation." It postulates that time runs slower inside a gravitational field and thus gives lightbeams (or other objects) more time to travel through its "warped detour," so that – in our eyes – light always ends up having the same speed.

[145] Cf. Thomas W. Sills (What Einstein Did Not See, P. 58), Dearborn Resources (2009).

[146] Example: A spaceship takes off from the sun at 75% lightspeed. Eight minutes later we see the spaceship launching. Just three minutes later the spaceship arrives in Earth orbit. In our eyes it has moved for three minutes only.

[147] Cf. P. D. Ouspensky (A New Model of the Universe, P. 23), London: Routledge & Keagan Paul Limited (1931).

[148] Cf. P. D. Ouspensky (A New Model of the Universe, P. 45), London: Routledge & Keagan Paul Limited (1931).

[149] Cf. P. D. Ouspensky (A New Model of the Universe, P. 46), London: Routledge & Keagan Paul Limited (1931).

[150] Cf. Charles Darwin (in a letter to John Fordyce, Darwin Correspondence Project, Letter No. 12041, 1879).

[151] Cf. Charles Darwin (in a letter to N. D. Doedes, Darwin Correspondence Project, Letter No. 8837, 1873).

[152] Cf. Rumi (Love Poems of Rumi: A Garden Beyond Paradise, P. 148), Jonathan Star & Shahram Shiva, Theone Press (2005).

[153] Cf. Buddha (Majjhima Nikaya: The Middle Length Discourses of the Buddha, P. 534, Sutta 63.5), Bhikkhu Nanamoli & Bhikkhu Bodhi, Wisdom Publications (1995).

[154] Cf. Ra (The Law of One, Session 10, 42, 82, 87), L/L Research (1982–1984).

155 Cf. Sokrates (Michael Cormack, Plato's Stepping Stones, P. 63, Meno 80e), Continuum International Publishing Group (2006): "[A] man cannot search either for what he knows or for what he does not know [...]. He cannot search for what he knows – since he knows it, there is no need to search – nor for what he does not know, for he does not know what to look for."

156 Cf. Rumi (Love Poems of Rumi: A Garden Beyond Paradise, P. 108), Jonathan Star & Shahram Shiva, Theone Press (2005).

157 Note: [CH#] refers to the chapter of first contact with the respective concept of our new language.